Georg Eduard von Rindfleisch, William H Mercur

The Elements of Pathology

Georg Eduard von Rindfleisch, William H Mercur

The Elements of Pathology

ISBN/EAN: 9783743343344

Manufactured in Europe, USA, Canada, Australia, Japa

Cover: Foto ©ninafisch / pixelio.de

Manufactured and distributed by brebook publishing software (www.brebook.com)

Georg Eduard von Rindfleisch, William H Mercur

The Elements of Pathology

ELEMENTS OF PATHOLOGY.

RINDFLEISCH.

PRACTICAL HANDBOOKS AND MANUALS.
FOR PHYSICIANS AND STUDENTS.

Biddle's Materia Medica. 9th Ed.   Cl., $4.00; Lea., $4.75
Bruen's Physical Diagnosis. Illus. 2d Ed.   Cl., $1.50
Byford's Diseases of Women. Illus. 3d Ed. Cl., $5.00; Lea., $6.00
Gilliam's Essentials of Pathology. Illus.   Cl., $2.00
Heath's Minor Surgery and Bandaging. 115 Illus. 6th Ed. Cl., $2.00
Holden's Anat. and Manual of Dissections. 200 Illus. 5th Ed. *In Press.*
Kirke's Physiology. Illus. 11th Ed.   Cl., $5.00
Marshall and Smith, Chemical Analysis of Urine.   Cl., $1.00
Meigs and Pepper, Dis. of Children. 7th Ed. Cl., $6.00; Lea., $7.00
? Quiz-Compends ? 10 Students' Aids.   Each, Cl., $1.00
Reese, Medical Jurisprudence.   Cl., $4.00; Lea., $5.00
Richter's Inorganic Chemistry. 3d Ed. 90 Illus.   Cl., $2.00
Richter's Organic Chemistry. 4th Ed. Illus.   *In Press.*
Rindfleisch, Elements of Pathology. Ed. by Prof. Tyson. Cl., $2.00
Roberts' Practice of Medicine. Illus. 5th Ed. Cl., $5.00; Lea., $6.00
Roberts' Compend of Materia Medica and Pharmacy.   *In Press.*
Tanner's Index of Diseases and Their Treatment.   Cl., $3.00
Tyson's Examination of the Urine. Illus. 4th Ed.   Cl., $1.50
Van Harlingen, Skin Dis. and Their Treatment. Illus.   Cl., $1.75
Yeo's Physiology. 300 Illus. and a Glossary. Cl., $4.00; Sheep, $5.00

P. BLÁKISTON, SON & CO.,
No. 1012 WALNUT STREET, PHILADELPHIA.

THE ELEMENTS OF PATHOLOGY.

BY

EDWARD RINDFLEISCH, M.D.,

Professor of Pathological Anatomy in the University of Würzburg.

TRANSLATED FROM THE FIRST GERMAN EDITION,

BY

WM. H. MERCUR, M.D. (Univ. of Penn'a).

REVISED

BY

JAMES TYSON, M.D.,

Professor of General Pathology and Morbid Anatomy in the University of Pennsylvania; One of the Physicians to the Philadelphia Hospital, etc.

PHILADELPHIA:
P. BLAKISTON, SON & CO.,
No. 1012 Walnut Street.
1884.

Entered according to Act of Congress, in the year 1884, by
P. BLAKISTON, SON & CO.,
In the Office of the Librarian of Congress at Washington, D.C.

IN HONOR OF

THE FIFTIETH ANNUAL ANNIVERSARY OF THE

ZÜRICH HIGH SCHOOL,

HELD

AUGUST 2D, 1883,

THIS WORK IS RESPECTFULLY INSCRIBED,

IN GRATEFUL REMEMBRANCE OF THE YEARS

1861-1865,

DURING WHICH I WAS A

MEMBER OF THE INSTITUTION.

LONG MAY IT FLOURISH, AND CONTINUE TO INSPIRE THE

MINDS COMMITTED TO ITS CHARGE.

PREFACE

TO

THE FIRST GERMAN EDITION.

This little work does not pretend to be a text-book. The author expects, rather, that the majority of his readers are already conversant with the subjects herein treated. Nor is it desired to compete with any of the excellent treatises on this branch of medicine which have appeared in such gratifying numbers during the last few years. His aim has been simply to establish the natural groundwork which must exist in this, as well as in every natural science, and to place it in as clear a light as possible. These efforts have, in the course of several years, culminated in this little book, which is now issued with the hope of eliciting the opinions of his confrères.

EDWARD RINDFLEISCH.

REVISER'S PREFACE

TO AMERICAN EDITION.

A high appreciation of Prof. Rindfleisch's work on Pathological Histology, caused me to make careful examination of these "Elements" immediately after their publication in the original. From such an examination I became satisfied that the book would fill a niche in the wants of the student, as well as of others who may desire to familiarize themselves with general pathological processes, viewed from the most modern standpoint.

I believe Dr. Mercur has surmounted most of the well-recognized difficulties of translation. When we remember that it is not always possible to render into any language the precise meaning of another, and that even the most careful writers sometimes fail to make themselves clear in the original, it can hardly be expected that a translation shall be elegant and perspicuous throughout. Defects of this kind I have sought to remove by carefully reading every line of proof, unhampered by the work of translating, while I have also compared all doubtful passages with the original. But, for the above reasons, it is not unlikely that defects may have escaped attention, for which we crave indulgence.

Acknowledgment is due to Mr. A. J. Plumer for making the index.

JAMES TYSON.

1506 Spruce Street,
Oct. 1st, 1884.

CONTENTS.

INTRODUCTION AND CLASSIFICATION............................ PAGE 9

GENERAL PART.
I. THE LOCAL OUTBREAK OF DISEASE.
(Protopathic groups of symptoms)................................. 18
GENERAL CONSIDERATIONS.. 14
  a. Acute hyperæmia 18
  b. Congestive hyperæmia.. 19
INFLAMMATION... 20
  a. Inflammatory irritation 20
  b. Inflammatory hyperæmia...................................... 21
  c. Inflammatory exudation 22
  d. Resolution. 1. Arterial hyperæmia........................... 27
              2. Granulation and cicatrization............... 29
Varieties and Termination of Inflammation 30
  a. Parenchymatous; b. Diphtheritic; c. Catarrhal; d. Croupous; e. Ulceration; f. Inflammatory connective-tissue hyperplasia; g. Inflammatory hypertrophy; h. Specific Inflammation.. 30 to 38
FORMATION OF TUMORS... 39
  a. In general.. 39
  b. General ætiology of tumors 40
  c. General anatomy and nomenclature of tumors 42
  d. Pathological division of tumors............................. 46
  e. Benign and malignant tumors 54

II. ANATOMICAL EXTENSION OF DISEASE.
(Deuteropathic groups of symptoms)................................. 57
METASTASIS 58
  a. Metastasis through the lymphatics 59
  b. Metastasis through the blood................................ 60
    Coagulation of the blood; thrombosis in the veins; thrombi of the heart and arteries; embolism................ 60 to 72
FEVER 73
  Cause of fever; fever heat; disturbances in the heat-regulating apparatus; febrile disturbances in the circulation; febrile disturbances in the organs which form and purify the blood; febrile disturbances in the nervous system... 73 to 81
Cachexia and Amyloid Degeneration 82

B. ANIMAL DISTURBANCES.. 152
 I. Hyperæsthesia, neuralgia 157
 II. Anæsthesia... 159
 III. Hypercinesia, Convulsions 161
  Motor neuroses; epilepsy; catalepsy and hypnotism; chorea.. 164 to 167
 IV. Hypocinesia, Paralysis.. 168
  a. Peripheral paralysis... 169
  b. Spinal paralysis... 172
  c. Cerebral paralysis.. 174
 V. Psychical Irritation and Paralysis............................ 175
  Moderate psychical irritation; insanity; increased psychical irritation; melancholia; psychical neuroses; delusions; idiocy................................. 176 to 178
 VI. Neuro-Vegetal Disturbances..................................... 179
  a. Angio-neuroses.. 179
  b. Tropho-neuroses... 181

SPECIAL PART.

I. Traumatic Diseases 187
 a. Mechanical trauma.. 187
 b. Chemical trauma... 189
 c. Thermic trauma. 1. Increase of temperature............. 192
        2. Decrease of temperature............ 193
        3. Diseases of exposure................. 196
 d. Electrical trauma 201

II. Parasitic and Infectious Diseases............................... 201
 A. *Animal Parasites*... 206
  Arthropoda; nematodes; trematodes; cestodes; infusoria .... 206 to 215
 B. *Vegetable Parasites* 215
  Mould fungi; yeast fungi; cleft fungi............ 215 to 217

III. Defective Development and Growth............................ 236
 (Preliminary remarks) 236
 1. Defective arrangement of blastoderm (Monstrosities?)... 288
 2. Defective intrauterine development........................ 241
 3. Defective extrauterine development........................ 245

IV. Diseases due to Overwork 247

V. Diseases of Involution 250
 Conclusion 255

GENERAL PATHOLOGY.

INTRODUCTION AND CLASSIFICATION.

Disease is an abnormal condition of our life and body, which becomes apparent to the patient himself and to those about him by variously striking phenomena—the so-called symptoms of disease.

If we observe these symptoms attentively, noticing how they arise, develop and again disappear, we soon see that they seldom appear singly, but that a number of them are generally united, either at a certain spot in the body, or around a strongly-marked, so-called cardinal symptom. We distinguish *groups of symptoms*, viz.: those of Inflammation, of Fever, and many others.

In inflammation, we see in the inflamed part redness, pain, swelling, and increased warmth; in fever, the rise of bodily temperature is the cardinal symptom, which is accompanied by the minor symptoms of accelerated pulse and respiration, chills, loss of appetite, delirium and increase of uric acid and urates in the urine.

The number and variety of such groups of symptoms appear at first sight very great, but after a time we notice that the same ones reappear in the most dissimilar diseases; that, in short, typical groups of symptoms exist which are fundamentally connected.

The ordinary course of diseases is also somewhat typical. For almost all begin with a local affection, or produce one after a short time; inflammation sets in or a tumor forms. From this point local irritation spreads in two ways:—

First. The *anatomical changes* take place, either by means of a certain continuous process, or by a more interrupted advance. Abnormal products are likely to form at the seat of disease, spread to the surrounding parts, be taken up by the lymph and blood vessels, and thus enter into the entire circulation of the body. These products occasion new groups of symptoms, such as fever or metastases of disease to other parts of the body. The nerves of the diseased part also become irritated, and not only is the patient made painfully aware of their existence, but, through the agency of the central nervous system, all kinds of new symptomatic sensations are produced. Such are sympathetic affections and cramps, which at first glance seem to have little to do with the primary affection.

Second. The *disturbance of the function* of the diseased part must be considered as a means of spreading the local irritation. One for all, all for one—such is the great law of the division of labor, which governs the bodily organism as absolutely as it does, or should, the organism of the State. If now one part stops work, the whole body suffers in consequence. The importance of the work of the diseased part may be questioned, but all work has a certain value, and every cessation of it entails suffering upon at least a small number of adjacent parts. What happens then when the larger vital organs, the lungs, kidneys, heart and liver, partially interrupt, or imperfectly perform their work? The blood current moves more slowly, the blood loses its oxygen and becomes overloaded with carbonic oxide, uric acid and biliary products. New groups of typical symptoms then arise, such as cyanosis, dropsy, uræmia, jaundice and many others.

Thus every disease spreads. Even new local affections may in this way be generated. But if this is not the case, and no vital disturbance of function has taken place, the eventual disappearance of the primary local affection also obliterates its train of effects, and the body reverts gradually to its normal condition.

The question now arises: what is the cause of this typical uniformity, which shows itself as well in the combination of individual symptoms into groups, as in the succession of the latter in the ordinary course of disease? This might readily be answered by saying that these things exist in the nature of disease, and that minute investigation shows everywhere the workings of cause and effect, and renders all such questioning superfluous. Notwithstanding, I must confess that it now seems to me especially opportune to study the nature of disease in itself, and thereby to separate that which pertains to the cause of disease from that which is due to peculiarities of the diseased organism.

The present tendency is to refer all that is typical and

cyclical, all peculiar local and actual appearances, to the presence of lower organisms, and thus to inaugurate a new ontological era in Pathology. I desire to hold myself towards this movement, not in an antagonistic, but in a conservative attitude, while endeavoring to separate from disease as a whole that typical element which pertains not to the cause of disease, but to the diseased organism itself.

In general terms, the blood and nerves are the inner link, uniting the symptoms into typical groups. The uniform and general presence of these, and the similarity of anatomical and physiological structure, secure the unity of our body and the relationship of its parts; they determine the distribution of bodily diseases.

The foregoing conclusions may be summed up as follows:—

A certain number of groups of symptoms reappear, with typical uniformity, in the most dissimilar diseases, because they depend upon the constant factor of disease *in toto*, and the human body with its anatomico-physiological structure. This same factor also determines the general course of disease. This latter we may use as a framework in which to place the typical groups of symptoms. In this way we gain a comprehension of all that the most diverse diseases possess in common, as well as a view of certain matters usually considered under the head of General Pathology, which I purposely avoid designating as General Pathology, since it has been customary to include much under this head that belongs exclusively to Special Pathology, viz.: the study of parasites, anomalies, etc.

On careful examination, then, we discover that most diseases do not start spontaneously, but are the result of certain causes, and it is the diversity of these causes which determines the different varieties of disease. On this depends the changeful collectiveness and consecutiveness of symptoms, by which the practiced physician distinguishes individual disease.

Every cause of disease is an encroachment upon the normal course of life. Generally it is associated with a violent and forced change in the physico-chemical composition of a given part of the body. The disease, as a whole, represents the effect of this encroachment, proceeding partly from the nature of the cause of disease, and partly from that of the diseased body. The uniformity of these results springs, as we saw, from the nature of the diseased body; the absence of uniformity, from the diversity in the cause of disease. The cause of disease determines, above all, the seat of the disease, its duration and the succession and combination of the typical groups of symptoms. Those symptoms alone which are very unlike can be used for the purpose of diagnosis. I maintain, therefore, that there is only one true, natural principle of classification of disease, one single point of observation upon which a natural system of Special Pathology may be built—namely, the etiological principle of classification and the etiological system.

With this principle in mind, I shall endeavor in the second or Special Part of my work to group all diseases according to their mode of origin. We must then use the utmost care to search out the cause of each individual group, and each individual disease, and describe it—I might almost say —as in natural history; after this, to learn how and where it operates on the organism, in order finally to ascertain, from this action upon the organism and the resulting reaction, how to explain the special picture and the special process peculiar to each group of diseases or to any individual disease.

It is assuredly not my intention to furnish in this short work any comprehensive description of all these things. I beg my readers to bear constantly in mind, that my only aim is to find the natural foundation of our common science, and to give to Topographical Pathology—which now, on account of its immense bulk, denies to individuals a comprehensive view of the whole—a somewhat higher standpoint.

This Topographical Pathology has been erroneously called "Special Pathology," whereas the "species" of disease is alone determined by the cause. It would be more correct to designate it "Specialistic Pathology," and to treat it as a stepping-stone to "Casuistic or Practical Pathology."

1. THE LOCAL OUTBREAK OF DISEASE.

PROTOPATHIC GROUPS OF SYMPTOMS.

GENERAL CONSIDERATIONS.

Under the head of diseased states presenting protopathic groups of symptoms we may consider inflammation and tumor formation. Both can, at least, represent the initial step of a process of disease. Both are essentially local disturbances. By a local disturbance we understand a group of disease-phenomena which have a certain part of the body for a common centre, a diseased part. The "*typical*" feature of local disturbances arises from the uniform characters of the locality where they occur. While it might appear almost presumptuous, in view of the great diversity of our organs, to speak of a comprehensive uniformity between them, yet we may, on closer examination, readily separate the varying from the permanent, and with the aid of the latter construct a general plan of our bodily organs; in other words, describe the ground upon which every local disturbance takes place. In this plan the chief place is occupied by the "parenchyma," which is composed of or derived from homogeneous cells, and is intimately connected with the function of the organ. Side by side with the parenchyma stand the capillary vessels and nerve fibres, which connect the former with the system at large.

It was a bold and practical idea of Virchow to trace local disturbances back to the individual cell, hereby freeing pathology from the vagueness of one sided humoral and neurotic conceptions. But in attempting to specialize the field, he went a step too far. While we willingly acknowledge the individuality of a cell, we must not overlook those conditions which restrict its autonomy in its functional and nutritive capacity. True, the cells of the parenchyma are sensitive and active, but in this respect they depend partly upon the nervous system; they also nourish themselves and grow, but here again are partly dependent upon the blood vessel system.

The nervous system controls the sensibility of the body in general. The non-nervous elements of the organs have, for this reason, by no means forfeited their sensibility, but only yielded a large share of the same to the central system, upon which they, therefore, in a measure depend. If they are passively excited, a proportionate share of their excitement is immediately communicated through the sensitive nerves to the spinal cord and brain, and their contractions, if any such are perceptible, are reinforced by the central nervous system.

Still more clear is the dependence of the cellular nourishment upon the blood supply, so that any explanation of this point is needless.

I repeat, therefore: The territory of the local disturbances is made up of the three essential elements named—parenchyma, capillaries, and terminal nerves; but it is necessary to add another, which occupies a prominent place—connective tissue. Connective tissue, derived originally from the mesoblast not used in the development of the blood vessels, follows the course of the latter, and surrounds them in their principal distribution. Moreover, it accommodates itself, in its histological changes, to the peculiar needs of each in a wonderful and perfect manner. In order to sustain the connection between different parts, it produces filaments which are yet so soft and flexible as not to impede the mobility which the function demands. Still more to facilitate this mobility, there are formed, by fusion of the basement membrane, interstices, which are lined with a smooth, delicate membrane, composed of flattened endothelial cells. To give solid form to an enclosed part, or a solid foundation to superimposed epithelium, the basement membrane hardens into hyaline membrane. In like manner, after a little study, we may explain the origin of all other connective tissue substances.

For our present purpose we need only consider the position occupied by the connective tissue as an intervening substance between the parenchyma on one side and its blood and nerve supply on the other. Physiology, we know, tells us little

GENERAL CONSIDERATIONS.

about this intercommunicative office of the connective tissue. Pathology, however, is forced to call attention to a number of apparently subordinate points, the cognizance of which is of great weight in the comprehension of tissue changes in disease.

In regard to nourishment by means of the blood, it is important that the pathologist should recognize the capillary membrane as an endothelial boundary of the connective tissue. Let him not imagine the maintenance of the parenchyma by nutritive material simply as a process of soaking and rinsing, but rather as a flow of sap which escapes from the blood through that cement-substance which unites the rhomboid endothelial cells into closed membranes. Outside of the capillaries the nutrient fluid runs through a network of juice canals, which is more or less sharply limited by the contiguous basement membrane of the connective tissue, and contains in its nodal points nuclei with protoplasmic threads, called connective tissue corpuscles. Thus the nutritive fluid penetrates to the enveloping membrane of the functional parenchyma cells, and remains at the disposal of the latter. Then, loaded with the products of the retrograde metamorphosis of the parenchyma cells, it is taken up by the lymphatics, which are in intimate union with the enveloping membrane, and are also found in abundance in the connective tissue. In short, everything that comes from the blood passes by a somewhat devious course through the connective tissue, to the parenchyma cells, and from thence into the lymphatic system. When I reflect how many times I shall be forced to lead my readers over this road, and how the comprehension of localized disease is bound up in its different stages, I am tempted to call it the highway of knowledge of pathological histology.

As regards the nerve supply, it is a well-known fact that those nerve fibres whose office it is either to excite directly, or to reinforce the action of the parenchyma, are in immediate contact with the parenchyma cells, and form with them an inseparable whole. The same process takes place with the perceptive terminal filaments of the nerves of special sense. The connective tissue, of course, only invests and supports these nerve fibres.

It is quite different, however, with those sensitive nerve fibres which transmit general sensibility. For these there are no terminal organs with whose specific energies they might be closely connected. In consequence they are found only in the connective tissue, where they divide and form networks, which probably finally unite, without being sharply defined, with the network of the connective tissue corpuscles. Being thus merged into the connective tissue, these nerves relinquish their functional uses and become pre-eminently qualified to participate in the general physico-chemical changes of the organs, and thus by corresponding irritability communicate these changes to the central nervous system. For, together with the connective tissue, these nerves come in contact with the innermost structure of the organs; with it they are elongated and compressed, and are subject to the same chemical irritations, caused, it may be, by a greater accumulation of excretory products.

Such irritations are compatible, up to a certain point, with perfect health, and run their course without our consciousness. Beyond this point they cause a vague feeling of oppression, which is capable of a large number of peculiar variations, increasing perhaps to very severe boring or lancinating pain.* These feelings, conscious as well as unconscious, are not without their effect. The former, we know, lead not only to discomfort and distress, but also to all sorts of expedients intended to remedy the evil. But the unconscious movements are likewise transmitted through centrifugal paths, and thus occasion processes which tend to allay the local distress.

What, then, are these processes? First of all, undoubtedly, the wise regulation of the blood supply through the central nervous system, which must command the admiration of every thinking man. For by this the blood always flows in increased quantity to those parts where the metamorphosis is heightened by increased activity (active hyperæmia), while the inactive organs receive, for the time, a smaller supply of blood.

In what manner this peculiar reflex is accomplished is not yet fully explained. We know, from a number of established experiments, that there are centripetal nerve fibres, which, when irritated, check the action of the vasomotor centre

* Such variations are: The feeling of weariness, which is often rather pleasurable, as in yawning and stretching; or of heaviness, weight, fullness, tension, etc.

and its branches, depressing, by this means, the arterial tonus, and dilating the arterial lumen (depressor nerves). In certain vascular localities, whose functions demand an exceptionally high degree of hyperæmia, these fibres are collected into individual bundles (nervi erigentes). Still we may assume that the sensitive nerve fibres depress the vasomotor system, and are, therefore, liable to cause local hyperæmia.

If such be the case, we have before us one of the most ingenious contrivances of the animal body. For, taking, first of all, active hyperæmia into consideration, there can be nothing better adapted to overcome the pernicious effects of suddenly increased activity upon the general condition of an organ than arterial hyperæmia. The chief evil resulting from an increased activity of the organs is generally considered to be the accumulation of the so-called products of tissue metamorphosis, that is to say, retrograde chemical products which reduce the excitability of the parenchyma cells. With the relaxation of arterial tonus, the blood pours, as through an open floodgate, into the dilated capillaries, passing so swiftly through them that it has no time to give up its oxygen, and is still scarlet-red on reaching the veins. The products of tissue change are, on the one hand, more highly oxygenized, on the other more speedily driven out of the parenchyma, so that the exhausted and hungry cells can thus supply themselves with everything needful for the restoration of their normal shape and excitability.

In order to appreciate the full import of this reflex action, we must turn our attention once more to the general structure of our bodily organs. We now first perceive that active hyperæmia includes a series of changes whose beginning and end are in the parenchyma cells. These cells are active and need nourishment. In plants and unicellular animals, activity and assimilation are as yet inseparable phases of the same process. In animals, both are associated with the main organs of the body, and are, therefore, capable of great increase of activity. During a less active period the parenchyma cells of higher animals may lead a sort of plant life, but at a season of heightened activity it is possible for them, by invoking the aid of all the bodily resources (which, we believe, is effected by the connective tissue nerves), to increase their working capacity more and more until a point is reached where assimilation fails to keep pace with consumption. Thus originates a group of diseases, which our system will treat as diseases of over-exertion.

Upon this series of changes some of the most important principles of local nutrition may be based.

1. A moderate demand on the physiological activity of an organ, together with an abundant supply of blood, produces a well fed condition, which we will call *Eutrophia*.

2. Unusual, but gradually heightened activity, and a corresponding blood supply increases the volume of the cells, and also their number, still preserving their typical arrangement. The result is a surfeited condition, a *Hypertrophy*, which appears to the naked eye as an increase of bulk in the part.

3. Over-exertion, even in active hyperæmia, is, as already mentioned, injurious. It leads, among other things, to insufficient nutrition with a decrease in bulk of the parenchyma cells and the entire part, called *Atrophy of Fatigue*. In all these things we see the dependence of the assimilating power upon the work which has preceded it. Assimilation requires vigorous work, though in moderation.

4. An insufficient demand upon the physiological activity leads to insufficient assimilation, and at the same time to that form of atrophy called *Atrophy of Inaction*.

We will also state here that assimilation is an elementary, if not the most elementary property of the cells, which, under conditions hereafter described, may completely free themselves from the fetters of the main organism, by which they here seem bound. This by no means exhausts the important subject of the regulation of the blood distribution through an excited condition of the connective tissue nerves. According to recognized physiological laws it is of no consequence how a nerve fibre becomes excited; the effect upon the terminal organ involved is governed entirely by the intensity of the excitation. Consequently, we may look for arterial hyperæmia, even when the excitation of the connective tissue nerves is not caused by nutritive needs of the peripheral territory, but by entirely heterogeneous conditions, such as wounds, luxations, or chemical irritations of the centripetal nerves. Moreover, this same arterial hyperæmia, which, in one instance, is produced by centripetal irritation, may in another be the result of an equivalent action upon the vasomotor centre, which action is derived from other sources, or may also be caused by a corresponding disturbance of the centrifugal vasomotor nerve trunks, or by direct paralysis of the arterial tonus. It is only necessary for one member of this chain of originally united conditions to become prominent,—though it may be in an unusual manner,—in order to bring about the pre-established physiological end and aim—arterial hyperæmia. This abnormally produced hyperæmia often occurs in pathology, as fluxion, arterial hyperæmia or congestive hyperæmia, though its appearance only differs in degree from that of physiological hyperæmia.

The eventual elevation of the temperature of the hyperæmic part deserves to be especially mentioned among the phenomena of congestive hyperæmia, apart from the redness and swelling already mentioned. This symptom, naturally, is only observable in organs whose normal temperature is less than that of the blood, because they are continually yielding up large quantities of heat to the skin and contiguous organs. Even here the increase of heat may reach 3° C. (5.4 F). This must be attributed to the more abundant influx of blood, or rather to the increased and accelerated blood changes in the hyperæmic part.

This excess of blood, inasmuch as it runs in the supplying arteries, is also responsible for the increased tension of the arterial walls. This causes the pulse wave, unchecked by the almost exhausted elasticity of the blood-vessel wall, to communicate brisk pulsations to the finger, and also to pass with such unusual rapidity through the artery that it may even penetrate to the capillaries and veins. The pulsation of the arteries, having been incorrectly thought to denote their active participation in the hyperæmic condition, has given rise to the name of active hyperæmia. The microscopical appearances of congestive hyperæmia may be easily studied. They consist of dilatation of the capillaries to almost twice their normal size, and a rapid flow of red blood corpuscles.

Abundant transudation does not occur in pure congestive hyperæmia. Pre-existing exudates are diminished rather than increased by the development of a congestive hyperæmia.

INFLAMMATION.

In all cases where a certain part of the body is attacked by a cause of disease in such a manner as to produce marked alteration in the blood-vessel walls, the first and usual result is redness and painful swelling; but as the surrounding parts, which are generally cool, suffer under these circumstances a marked rise of temperature, it has long been customary to call the whole group of symptoms INFLAMMATION (Phlogosis, Inflammatio).

(*a*) INFLAMMATORY IRRITATION.—However great the number and diversity of the causes of inflammation, one feature is common to all, viz.: the body itself is in full sympathy with them. An attack is made—either extraneously, or by a poison circulating in the blood—upon the tissues of the spot, which thus undergo chemico-physical changes. How this alteration is effected depends naturally in part upon the quality of the cause of disease. It makes a vast difference, indeed, whether the tissues are burnt with sulphuric acid, irritated by the deposition of micrococci, bruised or scalded. But the nature of the object of attack is, on the other hand, so unvarying that the multiplicity of causes is far from producing an equal multiplicity of effects.

Apart from the most decided lesion, that of gangrene, the metamorphosis of cells and tissues is about the same in every instance. The state of the large active cells in the main bodily organs will be considered below. (See Parenchymatous Inflammation.) There then remain the blood vessels, nerves, and connective tissue. The condition of the fixed connective tissue cells in inflammation has been studied, in connection with artificial keratitis and dermatitis. These cells (the connective tissue corpuscles, epidermic and lymphoid cells) are frequently connected with each other by offshoots. In this case the slightest degree of inflammatory irritation is marked by temporary retraction of the rays of this star-shaped substance, and chiefly also by contraction of the cell body into a roundish lump.

A permanent contraction betokens either the death of the cell, which manifests itself later in the disappearance of the nucleus and in granular degeneration of the cell, or it signifies the beginning of nuclear and cell division, which may also occur without previous contraction of the offshoots, and may, though somewhat imperfectly, contribute to the subsequent restoration of the degenerated parts.

In regard to the blood vessels, great stress has of late been laid upon the alteration of their walls, for the reason that this is the starting point of the most important stage of inflammation, viz., exudation. It is, unfortunately, not yet possible to give any comprehensive and satisfactory idea of the inner condition of an inflamed blood vessel wall. Since the endothelia of the blood vessels are rightly looked upon as the fixed cells of the connective tissue, which shut off the parenchyma of the body from the blood, we may question how far the changes in the blood vessel walls may be compared to the above described process in the fixed connective tissue corpuscles. There appears, indeed, to be a certain sponginess in the blood vessel walls, which is coincident with the retraction of the offshoots of the network of the lymphoid cells.

Arnold and Thoma have almost demonstrated the presence of interstices in the cement-substance of the capillaries in all acute inflammations. Cell division and increase of protoplasm have been observed in chemical inflammations. But with all this the main difficulty remains unsolved. This is the more to be regretted as the alteration of the blood vessel walls determines the future course of the inflammation. Its immediate effect is the dilatation and engorgement of the blood vessels; in other words, inflammatory hyperæmia. To this is joined that escape of the constituents of the blood, known as inflammatory exudation, which is more or less permanent and especially important as an anatomical product of the inflammatory process.

(*b*) INFLAMMATORY HYPERÆMIA.—In order to gain a correct understanding of inflammatory hyperæmia, we shall do well to entirely disregard the current ideas about arterial and venous hyperæmia and their origin. The blood vessels must be considered, not as constituents of the circulatory apparatus, but as constituents of the inflamed parenchyma. If it be true, as no one now doubts, that inflammatory hyperæmia is really produced by parenchymatous changes, it may safely be called parenchymatous hyperæmia. It appears, aside from all other features, that the cohesion of the blood vessel walls is diminished in inflammation. Diminished cohesion is indicated, at least, by the above mentioned yielding of the blood vessel wall to the blood pressure, the dilatation and hyperæmization of the circulation.

The process may easily be followed under the microscope; best of all in the mesentery of a living curarized frog, which has been carefully stretched over a cork ring. In ten or fifteen minutes after the operation, the *widening* of the *blood vessels* begins. This reaches its maximum in one or two hours, and continues so during the entire process. Two hours later the dilatation is followed by a perceptible *slowing of the blood current*. When we consider that no obstacle is offered by the veins to the flow of blood, and that the arteries do not hinder the blood from coursing, as in arterial hyperæmia, more swiftly through the enlarged capillaries, we must regard this retarded flow as an especially characteristic mark of inflammatory hyperæmia.

The slowing of the blood current can lead to a temporary or even complete blood stoppage (stasis). The local dilatation of the blood vessels is not a sufficient explanation of this proceeding. Local dilatation of the blood vessels also occurs in arterial hyperæmia, which, of itself, does not retard the flow in a smaller blood vessel. We must, therefore, revert again to the alterations in the blood vessel walls. It is this factor which changes the whole power of diffusibility between the blood and parenchyma into a heightened exosmotic current. With a force foreign to normal nutrition, all the blood particles are drawn toward the blood vessel wall, and thus, among other things, the velocity of their forward movement is diminished. I say "among other things," because inflammatory exudation is a far-reaching and important result of abnormal exosmosis.

(c) INFLAMMATORY EXUDATION.—By inflammatory exudation we understand the escape of the constituents of the blood from the blood vessels of the inflamed tissues and parenchyma. The visible result is either an infiltration of the parenchyma with the escaped material, or external discharges.

All exudates are composed of different constituents of the blood, such as salt, water, albumen, fibrinoplastic substance, and blood corpuscles. In proportion as an exudate contains more of one or the other of the above named substances, it is called serous, fibrinous, corpuscular or hemorrhagic.

The *serous exudate* is closely allied in composition to the normal nutritive juices, except that the latter, while nutrition remains undisturbed, is quickly taken up by the parenchyma, which needs nourishment; whereas, the serous exudate accumulates, because the normal channels of exit are insufficient to carry off an exudate thrown out with such rapidity and abundance. There always remains, however, the possibility of disposing of it through the normal channels of exit. This generally occurs without delay as soon as the effect of the inflammatory irritation subsides, so that the serous exudate is, on the whole, of a fleeting and temporary character.

Serous exudate is, only in rare instances, the culmination of an inflammation. It is usually the forerunner of more intense inflammation, or it encircles a smaller territory where a higher degree of exudation is found, viz., suppuration. It is customary in such cases to call it "inflammatory œdema."

Finally, the serous exudate is found to be an important factor in inflammations of the skin, of the mucous, serous and other membranes. As the structure of these organs is unfavorable to an internal deposit of an exudate, the serous discharge seeks the neighboring free surfaces, where it appears in the form of an albuminous secretion, which can likewise act as a vehicle for the migratory cells which exist in the parenchyma of the skin.

The *fibrinous exudate* resembles, in composition, a spontaneously coagulated, albuminous body, which bears so striking a resemblance to blood fibrin that we are tempted to consider them as one and the same, and imagine that, in a fibrinous exudation, the denser fibrinoplastic substance leaves the blood vessels with the blood serum, and afterward hardens. This hardening, we know, needs the intervention of a second substance derived from cells. This is furnished, according to Alexander Schmidt, by the colorless blood corpuscles. The white blood corpuscles which escape at the same time with the fibrinous exudate, may take upon themselves the formation of this "fibrin ferment." This is corroborated by the histological examination of the much feared croupous membrane found on the surface of the larynx and trachea. Here, the fibrinous exudate forms a network, in whose meshes round cells are lodged, as though coagulation had centred about the cell.

The exudate itself achieves, by reason of its coagulation, a certain anatomical independence. When seen in large quantities, as in the sero-fibrinous exudation of the pleura, pericardium, etc., the fibrin appears to the naked eye as a yellowish-white, soft, porous substance, which, upon pressing out the moisture, is reduced to a body at least twentyfold smaller, but tough, thick, and inelastic. It forms shreds and flakes, occasionally also, fibres, which entwine themselves in the infiltrated meshes of the porous connective tissue, or are stretched between the surfaces of the serous sacs. The microscope shows us here fine twisted filaments, interwoven into the most delicate meshes, then, again, tough, flattened bands, which form a network, or unite into fenestrated membranes. These appearances have given rise to the term fibrin. Fibrin also occurs in the form of a granular coagulation. This appearance in the blood has given rise to much misapprehension,* because the granular bodies are here seen in a more isolated form, while in fibrinous exudates they are often massed together in an indescribable variety of shapes.

It is self apparent that the eventual removal of the fibrinous exudate is more complex than that of the serous. Even when it is present on free surfaces, as in croupous inflammations of the mucous membranes and lung parenchyma, it adheres firmly, and a certain time must elapse before the process of separation sets in. Still more, where there is a deposit of fibrin in the enclosed spaces of the body, or even in the meshes of the areolar connective tissue, is a previous chemical metamorphosis essential to its liquefaction and reabsorption. In the majority of cases, the fibrin is transformed, along with a separation of fat globules, into a sodic albuminate, which is soluble, and may even be absorbed through the walls of the blood vessels by osmosis.

It is a mistaken idea that fibrin can organize, that is, change into real connective tissue fibres. Whenever connective tissue is found in the place formerly occupied by fibrinous exudate, this connective tissue has invariably been produced from the corpuscular constituents of the exudate.

Corpuscular exudate consists either entirely of cells, or to such an extent that the occasional serous and fibrinous admixture is subordinate. These cells are originally protoplasmic masses, destitute of walls, but containing nuclei, and having amœboid motion. They cannot be distinguished from the other mobile cells of the vascular and connective tissue apparatus, viz., the colorless blood corpuscles, lymph corpuscles,

---

* Zimmermann's elementary corpuscles, Leidesdorf's syphilitic corpuscles, etc.

protoplasmic cells, etc. Experimental study of corpuscular exudation has shown that the great majority of these cells are either simply migrated colorless blood corpuscles, or are derived from subdivision of the same. The process of escape is best seen in the mesentery of a living frog. The individual blood corpuscles, as is well known, may be recognized in the veins, and here it is that they present to the observer an unusually characteristic appearance. The peripheral zone of the blood current, the original blood plasma, becomes filled with countless colorless blood corpuscles, which adhere to the wall and finally form a simple and uninterrupted layer of globular cells upon the entire inner surface of the blood vessel. This is the beginning of the migratory process. Small, colorless, button-like elevations arise on the outside of the venous wall, as if the blood vessel wall itself had produced outgrowths. By slow degrees the projections increase in size till they lie on the blood vessel like hemispheres, about half the size of white blood corpuscles. The hemisphere changes gradually into a pear-shaped body, with the large end turned away from the blood vessel, and the pointed extremity attached to its wall. The periphery of the pear-shaped body now begins to send out delicate prolongations and ramifications, and the once smooth surface becomes uneven and indented. The main body of the corpuscle recedes more and more from the blood vessel wall, and we see finally a colorless, glistening, contractile body, a wandering connective tissue cell, which is nothing more or less than a migrated colorless blood corpuscle. An individual cell often occupies more than two hours in completing this process, and as the same phenomena are taking place simultaneously, at numberless other points, it is not easy to observe a single cell in all the stages of the process.

This active amœboid movement, this restless creeping forward of the migrated colorless blood corpuscles, contrasts sharply with the passive rôle which they enact in the circulating blood. Their inclination to adhere to each other and to all stationary points, which was formerly called their cohesiveness, but is now recognized as an outcome of their amœboid mobility, is, without doubt, overcome by the same power which, in one moment, mingles the masses of blood in the heart, and in the next scatters it in a thousand directions.

This mechanical irritation contracts the leucocyte into a ball, in which shape it remains until a slowing or partial stoppage of the blood current permits their dormant elasticity to reassert itself. The cell division, which follows closely on this cellular migration, must be regarded as a further outcome of this individual activity. During the division, amœboid movement sets in, we perceive a pellucid band running transversely across the cell, giving the optical impression of an annular constriction of the surface, which often vanishes and reappears, until, at length, the separation is suddenly accomplished and the bisected halves, recoiling from each other, pursue independent paths.

Corpuscular exudation occurs in very varying degrees of intensity. Unimpeded migration and division lead to the formation of *pus*. We apply the term pus to a liquid which owes its yellowish color and thickish consistency to the suspension of numberless cells in an otherwise clear and albuminous menstruum. The cells of perfectly fresh pus are equal in size, globular in shape, have sharp outlines and a whitish protoplasm. The nuclei are not visible, but become so by the addition of acetic acid.

Pus appears (1) as a diffused infiltrate; (2) as a superficial secretion; (3) as an abscess.

The *diffused purulent infiltrate* shows us the colorless blood corpuscles and their derivatives in the first stages of their journey through the connective tissue which envelops the blood vessels, and accompanies them in all their ramifications. This connective tissue is succulent, swollen, and yellowish-white in color, the latter completely covering and changing the normal coloring of the inflamed part. The pus corpuscles are situated partly in pre-existing connective-tissue spaces, in those crevices and juice canals in which are also found the fixed connective tissue cells, and partly in the fibrils and lamellae of the basement membrane. The space occupied by them here is only obtainable by a corresponding melting away of the fibrous texture, and thus it happens that, in proportion as the infiltrate becomes thicker and richer in cells, the inflammatory product will be composed solely of cells, which, finally, upon the addition of serum, constitute a pus focus or abscess.

If the inflamed part be a membrane, for instance, a mucous,

serous, or synovial membrane, the wandering pus corpuscles, following the direction of the least resistance, soon reach the surface, where they appear as a purulent secretion. This secretion rarely furnishes pure and unmixed pus, such as is occasionally met with in purulent inflammations of *serous* membranes;* on the surface of synovial membranes, the exuded pus corpuscles are brought into contact with a large amount of fluid called synovia, by means of which the interstitial pus becomes synovial in character; while in the mucous membranes the pus corpuscles mingle with the increased mucous secretion and transform it into a muco-pus. The presence of pus, even in very trifling quantities, may always be detected from the streaked and yellowish-white coloring which it imparts to colorless fluids.

An *abscess* or apostema is a large accumulation of pus, which interferes with the normal continuity of the bodily parenchyma, as, for instance, a collection of pus between the muscles in the skin, brain, glands, etc. Pathologically considered, abscesses are also those collections of pus in preexisting cavities, such as joints, mucous and serous sacs, etc. Abscess-pus consists of cells, which, although already discarded by the organism, are still temporarily enclosed by it. This circumstance may suffice, for the present, to explain the behavior of the surrounding tissues toward the abscess, and especially that immediate tendency to reject the pus and discharge it externally or somewhere along the course of the mucous membrane. To accomplish this discharge, deep seated collections of pus often follow unusual and roundabout courses, guided in part by the law of gravity and in part following the direction of the least resistance. This latter is found in the strata composed of loose, areolar connective tissue. Generally speaking, the pus pursues a downward course through such strata, retaining, however, invariably, the tendency to pass from within outward, and finally reach the skin, which it sooner or later perforates.

(*d*) TERMINATIONS.—(a) *Secondary Arterial Hyperæmia.*— With the establishment of the inflammatory exudate we

*A moment's reflection will convince us that a moderate infiltration of the membranes in question must co-exist with the free purulent secretion, because the blood vessels are everywhere separated from the surface by more or less dense sheaths of connective tissue, and these sheaths must be traversed, *i. e.*, infiltrated, before the blood corpuscles can appear on the surface.

reach the point up to which the inflammatory cause is directly and plainly operative. The exudate, both in quantity and quality, is determined first of all by the nature of the inflammatory cause. We may, as physicians, have done our utmost to limit the quantity of the discharge; we may have tried to contract the supplying vessels by persistent cold applications; we may, perhaps, by the use of quinine and other "spanæmics," have attempted to check the migration of the colorless blood corpuscles; but all this with very indifferent results. We still have before us an inflammatory exudate, whose composition and extent can only be determined approximately, and we must console ourselves with the reflection that in most cases the cause of the disease has exhausted itself in the production of the exudate, and trust to nature and medical skill to remove the exudate and restore the normal condition.

In the matter of natural healing it is well known that nature employs no immediate means of relief. But should assimilation be impaired in any part of the organ, should there be an accumulation of substances which impede the functions and render normal nutrition impossible, there occurs, as in all physiological crises, by the intervention of the centripetal nerves, an arterial hyperæmia. The phenomena of this arterial hyperæmia are, of course, associated with those of inflammatory hyperæmia, but in character and effect this secondary active hyperæmia cannot be too sharply sundered from the genuine inflammatory hyperæmia.

The same local centre is common to both, but the boundaries of the arterial hyperæmia are extended in proportion as the surrounding arterial vascular territory is sympathetically affected. The characteristic phenomena of arterial hyperæmia, viz.: dilatation of the blood vessels, and acceleration of the blood current, are everywhere apparent. In inflammatory hyperæmia a slowing of the blood current takes place, almost amounting to stasis, and under these conditions the colorless blood corpuscles congregate on the walls and wander out. In this secondary hyperæmia, the blood flows so rapidly through the blood vessels, as not only to prevent any further adhesion of colorless blood corpuscles to the walls, but also to detach any cells already there, and, so to speak, sweep the walls clean again. When this has taken place, the most important source of exudation is cut off, and normal circulation is again restored in the inflamed part. The process of resolution can now proceed. This consists, (1) in relieving the parenchyma from the exudate, (2) in restoring the part to its former condition.

The two processes are entirely distinct. The perfect and complete restoration of the former condition is only possible when the structure of the inflamed part has suffered no injury from the exudate. But as soon as the structure of the organ is, in the slightest degree, destroyed by the accumulation of pus, the restoration can only be indirectly and imperfectly accomplished. The injurious effects of the cause of disease must also be taken into account. These consist very frequently in direct injuries, and even total death of the tissues, and we must decide, in such a case, whether, and how far, these tissues may be preserved, or whether they must be thrown off and lost.

(b) *Granulation and Cicatrization.*—The chief measure employed by the organism to effect a definite, even though incomplete re-establishment of function is the formation of *granulation* and *scar tissue*. This formation depends upon the arterial hyperæmia in proportion as the latter furnishes improved nutrition to the cells which form the blood vessel wall and those which come in immediate contact with it. The dilated capillaries are, accordingly, enveloped with young cells, which are only loosely united together, and present the histological characteristics of young, embryonic, connective tissue. If they continue to increase in such numbers that the nourishment from the mother blood vessels becomes insufficient, new vascular loops form in a very simple manner, pushing their way, first in one direction, then in another, through the densest accumulations of cells, until they finally empty into a neighboring blood vessel. To favor their development, the cells of the germinal tissue recede from each other, and, simultaneously, the blood vessel wall gives way at those points where the future blood vessels are to arise, opening the way for the arterial blood to rush in and enlarge them. This phenomenon is especially well marked at those points where the smallest terminal arteries merge into the parenchyma which they are to nourish. Hence it is, that when it occurs on a free surface, like that of an exposed wound, small, soft, bright-red warts spring up, which have been known from time immemorial as proud flesh, or granulations.

This connection with the arterial system produces in the granulation tissue a decided constructive tendency. It fills up interstices, smooths over inequalities, and often replaces, with astonishing rapidity, any loss of substance. At the same time, the granulations are, through their large and numerous blood vessels, in intimate relationship with the bodily organism, and may even be regarded as exceptionally well nourished parts of the body. But, with the abatement of the intense inflammatory process, a change occurs. The arterial hyperæmia yields, and the recently formed tissue becomes metamorphosed into fibrous connective tissue. The closely aggregated cells produce out of their fused protoplasm a fibrous substance, which differs from ordinary connective tissue by the incomplete terminations of individual fibrils, and a constant increase in thickness. This we call *scar tissue*, and speak of a cicatricial retraction, or shrinkage of the original granulation tissue. The blood vessels of the granulation tissue suffer in consequence. Many of them are obliterated, but enough remain to supply the steadily decreasing parenchyma with sufficient nourishment.

SPECIAL VARIETIES OF INFLAMMATION.

The foregoing description of the process of inflammation applies, to a certain degree, to all inflammations, but it suffices fully only for local inflammations of the interstitial connective tissue, called interstitial inflammations or phlegmon. Beyond this the course of inflammation undergoes, according to cause and locality, so many modifications, that, in order to be explicit, it would be necessary to insert at this point the greater portion of general pathological anatomy. It is not my intention to describe all known inflammations. I shall, therefore, limit myself to some of the most important varieties, which include a large number of minor types.

(*a*) *Parenchymatous Inflammation.*—Organs which consist mainly of large parenchyma cells, like the liver, kidneys, and muscles, often present peculiar forms of inflammation, which may be called parenchymatous inflammations. The chief symptoms are a moderate enlargement of the whole organ; a whitish, opaque discoloration, and a perceptible change into an inelastic, doughy consistency; but no hyperæmia, or interstitial exudation. The microscope shows that these changes result chiefly from a granular opacity and swelling of the parenchyma cells, while the blood vessel and connective tissue apparatus remains intact.

This "cloudy swelling" is supposed to be a change in the cell protoplasm, which, in consequence, looks darker by transmitted light, and more opaque by direct light; it also has exchanged its normal form for a more or less globular one. The cloudy swelling is caused by a granular precipitation from the protoplasmic juices of an albuminous body normally held in solution. This precipitation is due, in turn, to excessive chemico-physical activity, dependent upon traumatism. In most cases cloudy swelling may be compared to a cauterization which varies in depth with the amount of caustic employed, from a slight and easily healed irritation to an irrevocable, escharotic death.

Parenchymatous inflammation may be produced by a blood poison attacking the most susceptible parenchyma cells of the liver, kidneys, etc. Cloudy swelling is the palpable expression of a recent inflammatory irritation, and is, in some instances, at least, the forerunner of a general process attended by hyperæmia and exudation. The same happens in acute nephritis, and probably also in the so called idiopathic liver abscess of the Tropics.

Cloudy swelling is generally confined to low degrees of irritation, and as the granular material becomes gradually liquefied, the cell metamorphosis ceases, and the normal condition is restored. This is strongly corroborated by the frequent discovery of slight degrees of parenchymatous swelling, and the whitish discoloration of the liver and kidneys in all infectious and poisonous diseases. On the other hand, the lesion may be so extensive as to cause the cells to undergo a fatty and granular degeneration, and death to ensue so rapidly as to leave no time for the development of an inflammatory process. This occurs in acute yellow atrophy of the liver, which will afterward be discussed at length.

(*b*) *Diphtheritic Inflammation.*—Parenchymatous inflammation, as we have seen, owes its peculiar nature to certain peculiarities in the cause of inflammation. This is still more true of diphtheritic inflammation. At the present time diphtheritic inflammation is defined to be an inflammation in which the lodgment of cleft fungi has produced over a greater or less extent of surface a condition of "coagulation necrosis."

Coagulation necrosis is to be distinguished from the simple death of a part by the presence of a coagulated, albuminous liquid, which accompanies the transition from life to death in the cells and tissues. This liquid bears such a strong resemblance to coagulated fibrin that one is tempted to consider them the same; except that the microscopical and macroscopical examination proves that the coagulation is chiefly present in the interior of the cells, and in other constituents of the tissues.

The microscope shows a peculiar homogeneous tendency of the cell protoplasm, accompanied by a total disappearance of the nucleus. Thus the cells lose their sharp outlines, and become flaky masses, inclined to adhere to each other and fall into large, irregular formations of membranous consistency. The frequent wax-like appearance of these coagulations is a peculiar feature, indicating their thorough impregnation with a strong, refractive, albuminous body.

Coagulation necrosis appears to the naked eye as a distinct opaque dessication of the dead part. As all the normal tissues, not even excepting the osseous ones, are of a partially transparent consistency, and as the coagulation necrosis is generally confined to a limited area, we find sharply-defined patches, which are distinctly separated from the surrounding tissues. These, as already mentioned, somewhat resemble escharotic scabs, and are, therefore, known as scabs (diphtheritic and typhoid encrustations, etc.).

Coagulation necrosis produces, like an escharotic scab, an inflammatory irritation, which invariably results in a process of inflammation with corpuscular exudate. The process varies greatly in intensity. In a strictly diphtheritic inflammation there is a violent, reactive, inflammatory, and suppurative process, which at best leads to the throwing off of the coagulated scab, and to the formation of deep-seated ulcers, followed by scars. The diphtheritic ulcer can also, by repeated recurrence of the coagulations at the bottom and at the edges, enlarge and deepen to a considerable extent, and assume a gangrenous (phagedenic) character before it begins to heal and cicatrize.

Using the term diphtheritic inflammation in a broader sense, we may also include those analogous occurrences which, equally with the diphtheritic inflammations, are conspicuous in diseases due to cleft fungi. Such are mainly the typhoid, tubercular, and syphilitic lesions, and their accompanying processes of inflammation and suppuration.

(c) *Catarrhal Inflammation.*—The consideration of catarrhal inflammation should, strictly speaking, be limited to the simplest inflammations of such membranes as are provided with an external epithelium (ectoderm or endoderm). The slight catarrhs of the skin and mucous membranes must not be confounded with the severe purulent inflammations of the serous membranes and joints, merely on account of a distant and purely external resemblance. Catarrhal inflammation presupposes an irritated condition of the sub-epithelial, vascular connective tissue. This may be induced by external irritations, as well as by internal ones proceeding from the blood or nervous system. The result is a hyperæmia of the connective tissue strata in question, and a consequent increased transudatory action of the blood vessels.

There are *desquamative* catarrhs, in which, the outer epithelial layer being stripped off, an abundant formation and secretion of young epithelial cells ensues. There are also *mucous* catarrhs of the mucous membranes (blennorrhœa), and *fatty* catarrhs of the skin (seborrhœa), in which the increased glandular secretion is due to an over-abundaut nutritive supply.

The small number of pus cells found by the microscope in desquamative, as well as in mucous and fatty catarrhs, points strongly to the relation between them and true purulent catarrhs. In a purulent catarrh, numbers of colorless blood corpuscles escape from the dilated blood vessels of the inflamed territory. A portion of them wander into the beginnings of the lymphatics and local lymphatic glands, which in consequence begin to enlarge. A still larger number seek the surface, and force themselves through the lowest layer of the surface epithelium without disturbing its integrity. If the inflamed membrane be lined with cylindrical epithelium, the colorless blood corpuscles find easy passage to the surface, and, mingling with the outer secretion, are discharged with it. This is less easily accomplished in membranes provided with stratified pavement epithelium. Here the older and more or less adhesive epithelial strata must be first of all loosened and thrown off. In some mucous membranes, particularly those of the genito-urinary apparatus, the conjunctiva, etc., the process is more thorough, and the catarrhal mucous membrane presents a highly peculiar appearance; we see a red, easily-bleeding, spongy-porous surface lying in folds and covered with thin pus, in place of the customary, firmly-attached, pale, tender membrane.

Where the older epithelial layer is only partially thrown off, we see straw-colored vesicles filled with pus (pustules), which burst, discharge, and leave a *catarrhal erosion*. By the abundant suppuration of the exposed, bright-red, granulating connective tissue, and the maceration of the adjacent epithelial border, this erosion assumes a characteristic appearance, incorrectly called ulceration.

Such eroded and purulent spots often run into each other, and gradually cover large areas, till they appear as extensive as the purulent catarrhal mucous surfaces described above. Still, there is no actual ulceration, and restoration is consummated without loss of substance or cicatrization.

(*d*) *Croupous Inflammation.*—A croupous inflammation is any inflammation having a fibrinous exudate which is not poured out in the connective tissue, nor in serous or other closed surfaces of the body, but which forms on mucous membranes, particularly on the mucous layer of the respiratory tract. Locally, therefore, it corresponds with the catarrhal inflammation.

We have found one of the first essentials of catarrhal inflammation to be the presence of an over abundant secretion of the mucous membrane, and the preservation of at least the lower cylindrical-celled layer of its epithelium. But croupous inflammation, on the other hand, is preceded by a loss of the epithelial covering of the diseased part, so that we may assert emphatically that, wherever a recent loss of epithelium is apparent, the exposed part suffers from a fibrinous exudation.

This detachment of the epithelium may be brought about by the most varied chemico-physical processes. The least frequent is that of a mechanical injury or mechanical "excoriation;" oftener the loss is caused by chemical destruction of the epithelium or transudatory removal of the same; but the most frequent agent in epithelial destruction is unquestionably the action of cleft fungi deposited on its surface.

This is the case in the croupous inflammation of the larynx and trachea, called "croup," which usually serves as a paradigm for this form of inflammation. The exuding and rapidly-coagulating fibrin unites with the cells of the exudate into a tough, elastic, yellowish-white membrane, an exact cast of the trachea and bronchi. These pseudo-membranes readily separate from the mucous membrane, and may be coughed up, but they adhere with much more tenacity to the vocal chords, which accounts, in part, for the great danger of the disease. Also in croupous inflammations of the lungs this delayed loosening and removal of the exudate is of serious moment to the organism.

The chief danger of croupous inflammation lies, however, not so much in these mechanical difficulties as in the fungi, which, at the same time, enter the blood and cause severe fever. The appearance of fungi establishes the connection between croupous and diphtheritic inflammation. For the same fungus which destroys the epithelium of the trachea and causes croupous inflammation, also settles upon the surface of the tonsils and produces what is called *angina tonsillaris* (quinsy). In this inflammation we at first only find loss of epithelium and pseudo-membranous exudation. But as the tonsil and mucous membranes of the organs of deglutition are not provided, like the trachea, with a basement membrane which can resist the attacks of the cleft fungi, this superficial, pseudo-membranous inflammation too often runs into a deep-seated membranous or diphtheritic inflammation. Indeed, since it is now well known that there are spots on the surface of the normal tonsil where the lymphatic follicles project, so to speak, beyond the epithelium, we need not wonder that numerous depositions of pathogenic organisms occur here, causing direct diphtheritic inflammations and blood poisoning.

(*e*) *Ulceration and the Ulcer.*—We have observed above, that abscesses can only be formed at the expense of that connective tissue which serves as a nidus for the accumulation of pus. After the abscess has burst and discharged its pus, there remains a "loss of substance" (*i. e.*, cavity) in the connective tissue, which is termed an "ulcer" as long as it remains open, exposed to the air, and without epithelium. The form of this cavity depends upon its origin. Hence, we distinguish open and concealed (sinuous) ulcers; ulcers with overhanging edges; crater-like ulcers; ulcerous cracks or rhagades, and many others. In considering an ulcer, we need only describe the condition of its bottom and edges.

If the process which has caused the ulcer continues, the bottom becomes covered with a pus-like layer of dissolved and disintegrated tissues; the sides appear hard and infiltrated. If these substances are thrown off by suppuration, the bottom of the ulcer is covered with granulations which fill up the gap. Often, indeed, they protrude beyond the edges (*ulcus elevatum*), and represent an elevation, rather than a depression.

As long as the ununited condition of the connective tissue continues, there is, of necessity, a secretion of pus, which accounts for the close connection in the popular mind between ulceration and suppuration. The disunion is encouraged, and, as it were, nourished, by the presence in the bottom of the ulcer of moribund matter, which can only be separated by suppuration from the organism, and is so closely connected with it that this so-called "sequestration" is a process of time.

For this reason, ulcers of the osseous system readily become chronic, because the exposed trabeculæ and lamellæ in the bottom of the ulcer, although practically dead, are closely united with other deep-seated and living constituents of the bone. Tuberculous, syphilitic, leprous, and lupous ulcers all require a disproportionate amount of time to throw off their deep-rooted, specific products of inflammation. The worst of this is, that as rapidly as the suppurative process throws off these products, new *capita mortua* take their place.

There are still other agencies by which the ulceration may be prolonged; chiefly, by a telangiectatic condition of the diseased part (phlebectasia), the consideration of which would at present lead too far.

(*f*) *Inflammatory Connective Tissue Hyperplasia* (*Chronic Interstitial Inflammation*).—Either of the above headings applies to the inflammations caused by an inflammatory irritation of moderate intensity, which is continuous, or of frequent recurrence. The most frequent mechanical causes are pressure and tension; the chemical irritations are mostly exciting ingredients of food, such as alcohol, etc. The action of the irritants upon the tissues does not immediately threaten their stability, but it creates a want to which, according to known physiological laws, the organism responds with a vigorous and prolonged hyperæmia. This latter is arterial in character, but if an arterial hyperæmia continues, or is often repeated, permanent alterations in the vascular wall are effected, which react, not alone on the arterial, but, in a heightened degree, on the venous part of the circulation.

INFLAMMATION.

The arteries dilate and lengthen, their walls becoming thicker by hypertrophy of the muscular coat and thickening of the adventitial connective tissue. The veins, on the contrary, are, and remain, largely dilated; the elasticity of their walls is exhausted, and therefore it is not possible for them to return to their normal calibre. Whether such a condition can be rightly termed an arterial hyperæmia remains an open question.

In the further course of the disease, we usually find newly-formed connective tissue in the neighborhood of the blood vessels. This resembles granulation tissue, and may also be converted into cicatricial tissue. We may then expect considerable displacement, especially shrinkage of the organs involved (cirrhosis of the liver, contraction of the kidney). In some cases the newly formed connective tissue is more like the normal connective tissue substances, and occasions thickenings, depositions, etc.; in others, the microscope shows only a round-celled infiltration of the connective tissue, especially that forming the blood vessel wall, which does not lead to further changes.

Lastly, I would state that purely local thickening of the connective tissue without demonstrable hyperæmia, occurs as the result of slight mechanical disturbances (maculæ albæ of the pericardium).

(*g*) *Inflammatory Hypertrophy.*—Inflammatory hypertrophy is a remarkable deviation from the regular process of inflammation. It shows us how physiological growth may lead in the latter to the permanent enlargement of certain organs. The elements of the process are: hyperæmia effected by pathological irritation and local increase of colorless blood corpuscles. However, as both seem to concentrate at points where the normal growth of the involved organs is taking place, and as hyperæmia and cell formation represent in these organs the normal process of growth, we find inflammation and growth to be identical, and the result is an excessive growth hastened and increased by inflammatory changes.

Inflammatory hypertrophy is most frequently observed in the skin and bones. Active periostitis, which is important in the union of fractures, as well as in other respects, is an inflammatory hyperæmia of the bone. Elephantiasis Arabum, so called, is another example of the same. Although inflammatory hypertrophy resembles active hypertrophy (see

p. 18), it is in reality totally different, and is a diseased condition which should in no wise be confounded with the above.

(*h*) *Specific Inflammation.*—The term "specific inflammation" must be applied strictly to that process of inflammation caused by the lodgment of parasitic bodies. It produces various characteristic modifications in the course and appearance of the inflammation, which are due exclusively to its *species morbi*. The consideration of specific inflammations, *i. e.*, tubercular, syphilitic, leprous, glanders, anthrax, etc., is, therefore, not in place here, but comes properly under the head of parasitic processes of disease, which form a separate division of special pathology. I need only say that specific inflammations embrace the most varied and interesting forms of inflammation. The diphtheritic form described above may serve as a paradigm for a large number. In this we have an external attack of cleft fungi and its consequences. This attack may also be made through the blood. The minute subdivided poison is carried by the blood throughout the whole system. As the greatest amount of friction occurs where the arteries merge into the capillaries, it is here that the vascular wall is most thoroughly inoculated with the poison, and the specific inflammation thus originated is especially prone to commence as *endo-* and *peri-arteritis*. The corpuscular infiltrate invariably produced shows peculiarities depending directly upon the action of cleft fungi. Among others, there is a certain enlargement of cells with vesicular transformation of the nuclei, epithelioid degeneration culminating in the form of giant cells. Joined to this are typical forms of cell death, fatty degeneration, cloudy swelling, coagulation-necrosis and many other phases which strongly influence the future course of the inflammation, and give it a characteristic impress.

The epiphytic parasites also produce peculiar inflammations, in which we can recognize the *species morbi*, each parasite being characterized by its own peculiarities of habit and life. The detailed consideration of this subject will, however, be found in the Special Part of this work.

TUMORS.

(a) GENERAL CONSIDERATIONS.

What is a tumor? Let us consider the question first at the bedside of the patient. Here we must face the difficult problem whether the "swollen something" appearing either upon or below the surface of the body is an inflammatory exudate which will disappear in various ways, leaving the part comparatively unimpaired, or whether it is a non-inflammatory swelling, which, if left to itself, will continue to grow, and perhaps fatally involve the rest of the body.

It is exceedingly important to establish the differential diagnosis between inflammatory and non-inflammatory swellings. We know that inflammations generally arise from distinct external causes, and we are, therefore, inclined to call the questionable something a tumor, in the strict sense of the word, when it originates spontaneously. Inflammatory tumors usually develop rapidly, and are accompanied by hyperæmia, heat, and other painful sensations, while non-inflammatory tumors develop slowly, from a minute origin, are unaccompanied by hyperæmia or pain, and are at first only mechanically annoying, although their inexorable increase in size soon renders the patient restless and uneasy. From these symptoms we are able, in doubtful cases, to form a temporary diagnosis.

We have noticed before how, in inflammation, the diseased organ becomes flooded with exudate. Blood-serum, fibrin, and colorless cells rapidly take possession of a certain territory, which they relinquish, after having occupied it for a certain length of time, and disappear, leaving scarcely a trace behind them. The diseased organ is in the meantime powerfully affected; but although it may be reduced in size, changed in shape, and crippled, from the effects of the inflammation, it has of itself contributed nothing to its own destruction; it has been destroyed.

The very opposite occurs in the formation of tumors. No conspicuous participation of the blood and blood vessels is here noticed. This increase of size is not derived from without. The increase is the product of the local cells. These cells not only proliferate, but also change in character, so that when the part has lost its normal shape and color, when its size and its composition are changed, and when, finally, it is totally destroyed, we can truly say that it has worked out its own destruction.

Investigating the nature of the local changes still further, we encounter everywhere phenomena which have their natural models in the processes of normal growth. This is especially true of the elementary histological processes. Cell- and nuclear-division conform strictly to the physiological type. In most tumors, we find that complicated form of cell division which is characterized by the division of the nuclear substance into two parts, one of which refracts light strongly, the other to a much less degree. The former forms a network which resolves itself into sections; these sections then assume the shape of an equatorial plate, and finally form the amphiaster. Occasionally the new-formed cells are larger than normal, and even attain gigantic growth, although the endeavor to retain the type of the mother cell is always apparent.

This retention of the type is still more distinct when we consider, as we shall presently, the conversion of cells into tissues, and tissues into tumors. In short, the first impression received in every stage of the process is that we have before us a caricature of the process of normal nutrition. Thus we may define a tumor to be a localized growth which has overstepped normal limits; in other words, a local perverted excess of growth.

(*b*) GENERAL ETIOLOGY OF TUMORS.

When I stated above that tumors, in contradistinction to inflammation, arise from influences at work within the parenchyma, I did not intend to ignore the fact that our knowledge of the causes of their origin is extremely imperfect, nor would I spare any pains to investigate this mysterious subject.

The tendency to continuous apposition by means of assimilation is innate in living tissues. We are forced to accept this tendency, which is shown in embryonic development, and pursued until organs reach their full growth, as a preordained plan of development, apparent even in the impregnated egg, and in the local disposition of its parts. This plan of development selects, according to time and space, certain points at which more intense cell multiplication shall take place. The mechanical effect produced by one growing part upon another exerts a formative influence upon the external shape of tumors. As a part increases in size and weight, it exerts a proportionate amount of pressure and traction upon its immediate neighborhood, which in turn yields or offers counter-pressure. Numerous observations on the osseous system have proved that while traction and expansion accelerate, to a certain degree, the growth of a part, pressure restricts the same. It is only after organs attain their full growth, that a certain equilibrium of all their parts is obtained, similar to the equilibrium of the unimpregnated egg before the parts were effectually disturbed by the process of impregnation.

The individual character of the phenomena of growth appears the more marked as the part approaches its full development. Individual differences are now strongly marked when the part, having reached its definite shape and size, is subjected to a general restriction in the process of growth, which process is replaced by that of nutrition. In these two respects, I believe the function of the nervous system to be a general supervision over normal growth, and also the direction of the nutrition of each individual part. But we sometimes perceive that the prescribed limits are not preserved, but overstepped in places, and we may ascribe it to the fact that at some points the control of the nervous system over the growth of certain cells is impaired. That "local weakness" of the tissues, which has hitherto been regarded as the cause of tumors, is properly a weakening of the nervous apparatus of one part as contrasted with the whole.

The local weakness is, in many instances, a transmitted one. When we consider that cancer may attack, successively, grandmother, mother and daughter, each in the same place (uterus, stomach), and all perish, also that all, or nearly all, members of a family may be attacked on the buttock with fibroma, we are forced to conclude that it is due to local weakness in the development of an individual, which has been transmitted from mother to child.

In other instances, tumors are developed in places where, from infancy, a wart, birth-mark, or some other blemish, has betrayed a weak spot in the process of growth. Again, the organ which undergoes tumor-degeneration may not have reached the place assigned it in the normal process of development, and may stand, consequently, in exceptional relations to the common organism (testicles retained in inguinal canal).

To this category belong certain isolated and detached fragments of germinal tissue, in particular, parts of the ectoderm, which occasionally appear as the nuclei of tumors.

Notwithstanding all the evidence in favor of the hereditary nature of tumors, we cannot deny that the weakness leading to the formation of tumor often seems an acquired one. In the osseous system, sarcomata form over the seat of fractures united years before. Scars are often chosen as the seat of sarcomatous or cancerous changes. Chronic catarrhal and hyperplastic conditions of the *portio cervicalis uteri* are followed by cancer; simple gastric ulcers pass into cancer of the stomach; in short, wherever a former inflammation has left a tissue *minoris vitæ*, or a part has been weakened by a chronic inflammatory or ulcerative process, we need not be surprised to find that arbitrary growth, that wildness in the processes of assimilation, which leads to the formation of tumors.

a. General Anatomy and Nomenclature of Tumors.—Every abnormal local outgrowth leads to a circumscribed accumulation of new-formed tissue, which, judged by sight and touch, is called a tumor. The extent and shape of a tumor are determined by the resistance offered it by the surrounding parenchyma, and by its own consistency and manner of growth. If the tumor meet with a uniform resistance from the surrounding parts, as, for example, when one develops in the right hepatic lobe, it is forced to assume its most condensed shape, and appear as a sphere or node. If the resistance of one of the neighboring parts be disproportionately great, the tumor becomes flattened upon the side of the greatest resistance, but develops spherically in other directions, thus assuming the shape of a hemisphere. This is the case when a hepatic tumor develops immediately under the capsule, and is opposed, not so much by the capsule as by the firm, unyielding wall of the muscular strata of the abdominal covering, or the diaphragm. If, on the other hand, the resistance on one side be disproportionately slight, the tumor soon spreads beyond the domain of the affected organ. The shape now assumed is prescribed by its characteristic manner of growth, in as far as that is free and unopposed. A tumor starting in the papillæ of the skin is able to branch out freely (dendritic vegetation), while a tumor of the corium must first, in the shape of a node, overcome the uniform resistance, and then, when, by a process of regular growth, it has reached the outer surface of the corium, it must continue to develop in this direction, being that of the least resistance. The tumor appears as a flat tuber, which either develops into a flat, tabular swelling (fungus), or into a polypoid growth (polypus).

Deep-seated nodes are often, in the process of growth, forced to the surface, pushing the enveloping skin before them. This either causes them to be severed from the organ which has produced them, or to drag the organ with them in their growth. If this surface tendency be lacking in a deep-seated tumor, it indicates that it is becoming rapidly and more firmly attached to the neighboring organs.

All the macroscopic appearances of a tumor are embraced under these heads. The external form of a tumor affects its quality only inasmuch as the plan of development is more or less apparent in tumors growing upon free surfaces, from which fact certain general rules may be gained.

Of greater weight in the classification of a tumor are the remaining macroscopic criteria, viz., consistency, color and texture. They, however, are determined exclusively by the *minute composition* of the tumor, which we will now proceed to investigate.

Tumors, like the normal organs of the body, are composed of blood vessels and parenchyma, of nourishment and parts to be nourished.

The *vascular system* is net-like, and provided with endothelium. In other respects, there is great diversity of arrangement. There are narrow, and broad, and even varicose capillaries; some of the networks are closely meshed, while others are so wide meshed that the connections between the fine and sparsely distributed vessels can hardly be perceived under low power.

A special connective-tissue covering, to envelop the blood vessels and unite them with the insulated parenchyma, is often entirely lacking, so that the parenchyma is in close proximity to the endothelial wall, and only separated from it by interstitial space. On the other hand, the sheaths of the capillaries may become so dense that we have a coarse mass, composed chiefly of connective tissue, in which the blood-vessel lumina appear so small as almost to be imperceptible.

The quantity of the blood supply must, accordingly, vary greatly. Equally variable, of course, are the conditions of nutrition and growth which depend upon the blood supply. The necessary blood vessels are provided, but it is clear that a one-sided growth of the insulated parenchyma, and an abnormal accumulation of tissue between the blood vessels, without a corresponding expansion of the blood paths, must lead to a discrepancy between the demand and the supply of the nutritive fluid. It is true that in some tumors the formation of blood vessels is in proportion to that of parenchyma, but, in others, the latter predominates so strongly that a compression and obliteration of the vascular system is the result. Retrograde changes are now apt to set in in the parenchyma, especially fatty and cheesy metamorphoses, and also mucous softening and colloid degeneration, causing a "spontaneous though perhaps only partial retrogression" of the tumor. The detritus or the nutritive fluid may be wholly or in part absorbed, but more frequently remains for a time unabsorbed. Soft spots are visible here and there, and lead to the formation of cysts. If the tumor is superficial, an external discharge of the dead and degenerated parts ensues, and the tumor assumes the character of a suppurating abscess.

The process reacts in various ways upon the vascular system. The obliteration of blood vessels by the growth of the parenchyma has already been mentioned. If softening and discharge occur, the obliterated blood vessels are, as a matter of course, also destroyed, and their separation from the still active capillaries often occasions hemorrhage. The breaking of the tumor and the discharge of the degenerated parenchyma relieves the entire blood-vessel apparatus of the tumor, and allows the capillaries to expand. This renewed activity of the capillaries may gradually lead to hyperæmia, the originally stationary character of which is easily converted into an active and inflammatory state by the action of the suppurating decomposition in the bottom of the ulcer. Quantities of pus, granulations, blood vessels, and young connective tissue are now produced by the exposed intermediate nutritive apparatus. The bottom of the ulcer becomes partially overspread with a thick covering of the more harmless products of inflammation. These are, however, all surface products. As to the deeper parts of the tumor, the blood-vessel apparatus experiences here also a decided relief, though this is not likely to lead to inflammation, but rather to improved nutrition and a more rapid growth of the tumor. This confirms the old theory that the breaking of a tumor is generally the signal for a more rapid spread of the disease on the surface.

The relation of the *lymph current* to tumors is still a disputed point. In some tumors, as, for instance, in carcinoma of the stomach, lungs, mammæ and skin, in chondroma of the testicle, and also in cylindroma, it has been proved that the tumor forces itself into the local lymphatics, from whence it spreads by metastasis. This is, in all probability, also true of all other tumors, with the exception of the angioma. We may also suppose this to be the manner in which, in malignant tumors, injurious matter becomes mixed with the blood. Reference will again be made to this point under the head of malignant tumors.

In this early occupation of the lymphatics we must remember, (1) that normal parenchymas, like muscular fibre, ganglion-cells, gland-acini, etc., are enclosed in the lymph spaces; (2) that the lymph capillaries found in the continuity of the connective tissue are nothing more than closed canals on the outer surface of the blood vessel territory, out of which the connective tissue has grown. (Compare remarks on the Destructiveness and Malignity of Tumors.)

In considering the nutrition and growth of tumors, two points must be borne in mind; first, the accumulation of nutritive material, which must necessarily occur in the interior of the tumor from obstruction of the lymphatics; second, the influence exercised upon the growth of a tumor by the unobstructed condition of its peripheral lymphatics. Whether the endothelium of the lymphatics plays an important part in the growth of a tumor is still an open question. I myself am convinced of it, and agree with Virchow, that the endothelium of the blood vessels and lymphatics, as well as the fixed connective tissue cells which separate them, are the most important oncoplasts of the intermediate nutritive apparatus. The chondroplasts and osteoplasts are, in my opinion, only a subdivision of this great group of cells.

In the parenchyma of tumors, we meet with the following varieties of tissue: fibrous connective tissue, mucous, fatty, lymphatic, cartilaginous and osseous tissues; germinal tissue, round- and spindle-celled; nervous and muscular tissue; epithelium.

Leaving the nutritive apparatus out of the question, many tumors consist entirely of one variety of tissue, or at least of one predominating variety, so that there can be no question as to the proper classification. *Every tumor should derive its principal title from its predominating tissue.* Secondary tissue should be classed among the *epitheta*.

The Greek ending *oma* is employed in the principal titles, as: Sarcoma, Myxoma, Fibroma, Cystoma, Endothelioma, Lymphoma, Lipoma, Osteoma, Chondroma, Neuroma, Myoma, Epithelioma. In designating the epitheta, we use, beside the Greek ending *oides*, some Latin adjectives, like fibrous, cartilaginous, etc. In some few tumors, two kinds of tissue are present in such equal proportions as to make the proper appellation doubtful. This is so in Epithelioma, where the intermediate nutritive apparatus has acquired unusual activity, and produced for its blood vessels such an accumulation of connective tissue as to render the epithelial overgrowth less perceptible. Of late, however, it has been customary in such cases to attribute the beginning of growth to the epithelium, and name the tumor accordingly.

Finally, we notice a certain group of tumors in which more than two tissues are united, after the manner of an organized body, so that we are led to compare them to the miscarried germ and development of a fœtus. Virchow has applied to these enigmatical formations the name of Teratoma, thus intimating a certain connection with the province of diplogenesis. I would suggest that the Teratoma be divided into dermoid cysts and true terata; that the dermoid cysts be considered as cystic epithelioma, and the inherited tumors of the throat and coccygeal region be included among the terata known as *fœtus in fœtu*.

b. Pathological Division of Tumors.—That tumors which are accessible to anatomical investigation, and are, in general, so constituted that one particular tissue forms the bulk of their growth, should be named from the predominating tissue, is self-apparent. Equally self-apparent is the fact that this does not constitute a natural system of division. The latter must be derived from the nature of the part in question. As such an outcome we recognized degenerate growth, and must, consequently, base all further criteria upon the degree of degeneration *i. e.*, the deviation of tumors from the physiological plan of growth.

We observe here that a certain number of tumors represent merely an excessive growth of normal constituents,—a quantitative excess of normal growth, which we have previously noticed. Local irritations of organs are followed by active hyperæmia, and inflammation of such an enduring, but yet moderate character, that under their influence the process of exudation merges into a process of increased assimilation. Inflammatory hypertrophy may, therefore, be regarded as the slightest form of inflammation. Again, we have found simple hypertrophy of muscular organs to be a consequence of increased demands upon their capacity. On the other hand, *hyperplastic tumors*, which we assign to the first group, lack every external irritation, every particular excitation tending to excess of growth. Take, for instance, any spot on the bony surface of a body where, for some time, no disease has existed. The periosteum or perichondrium are constantly depositing new aggregations of their specific products, which are in a typical manner assimilated by the nutritive apparatus of the bone, and treated as if they were authorized outgrowths, tubercles, etc. This condition is customarily designated as an "outgrowth" of the organ in question; in the example cited above, we would call it exostosis, ecchondrosis, etc.

Let us now contrast *heteroplastic* with *hyperplastic tumors*. In the former, the normal law of growth is still more obscure. We find a tissue which rightfully belongs here—though in a quantity, time and arrangement disproportionate to the physiological capacity of the organ—in such large quantities that it seems no longer a simple outgrowth, but a foreign structure, which, having implanted itself in a growing organ, clings to it, invades it, and impairs its normal activity. Although nothing remains of the original structure, we are continually reminded of it by the histological character of the new growth, in which certain "characteristics of the parent tissue" reproduce themselves. The tenacity with which the latter are manifested throughout the whole disease is remarkable. We should also bear in mind that, in spite of the multiplicity of heteroplastic tumors, the same parent tissue can only produce a limited quantity of its kind, and that each part of the body possesses its own oncology; the latter fact affords a natural clue to the special consideration of the same. From all of which we conclude that the growth under consideration, although defective, is still but a caricature of normal physiological growth.

The number and variety of heteroplastic tumors is very

great. Accepting the embryonic principle of development as a standard of division, these tumors separate readily into two large groups.

The theory of His concerning the double nature of germinal tissue is constantly gaining ground among recent investigators of the history of development. His distinguishes (1) *Archiblastic tissues*, to which belong, besides the epithelial layers and investments of the ecto- and endo-derm, the nervous and muscular structures, which latter are usually associated with the mesoderm; (2) *Parablastic tissues, i. e.*, products of the vascular peripheral matrix, the *area opaca* (germinal disk, white yolk) of the embryo, which has penetrated into the archiplastic province, and serves to unite and nourish the same. All connective-tissue substances, free or fixed, belong to this class; also all blood vessels and the parenchyma forming the same.

Pursuing this theory, we divide tumors into two great groups—a division which is both useful and natural.

The *First Group* contains tumors which are the exclusive product of the intermediate apparatus of nutrition, that is of the former parablast. They are associated at their origin with the blood apparatus, and begin by establishing in the perivascular spaces an embryonic germinal tissue rich in cells. From these, following exactly the laws of physiological growth, all higher tissue types of the parablastic order may be developed, being more or less influenced by the locality where they appear. In this way arise, *Lipoma, Fibroma, Myxoma, Enchondroma, Endothelioma, Angioma*, etc.

In a large number of cases regular tissue is not produced. The new formation contents itself with the production of those unripe connective-tissue forms, referred to above as occurring in the inflammatory new-growth of the round and spindle-celled connective tissue, which we will call here *Sarcomatous tissue*.

This defective development of tissue furnishes a new criterion for the degree of degeneration and the intensity of the overgrowth, for the excess of production is in inverse ratio to the development of the tissue. The unrestrained constructive activity occupies itself solely in completing and heaping up an overpowering mass of cells, whereby the diseased organ is destroyed, and the whole body involved. This feverish activity allows little scope for the development of individual cells.

But it is interesting to note, as before mentioned, how tenaciously even the most luxuriant sarcomata retain certain characteristics of the locality whence they sprang (ossification, pigmentation, etc.)

The *Second Group* embraces epithelial tumors. Ecto- and endo-derm, either alone or in the customary connection with the paraplasts, form the essential body of the tumor. Large numbers of young epithelial cells are produced, which only exceptionally attain a higher development, but resemble the epithelial cells normally occupying their place. These form the subdivision of the *Adenoma*.

True *Carcinoma* occurs much more frequently. Here the atypical epithelial multiplication seems to have undertaken the task of producing and heaping up, in as short a time as possible, the greatest possible number of young cells. The most luxuriously proliferating cancers and sarcomata are united by this common trait into the clinical group of *Medullary Tumors*.

We are thus enabled to present the following summary of tumors:—

I. *Hyperplastic Tumors*.

They occur chiefly in the osseous system, in the skin, and in the glands.

Ecchondrosis.—The most important are the cartilaginous outgrowths of the synchondroses, of the symphyses of the pelvis, and of the synchondrosis Clivi (Blumenbachii).

Exostosis.—A hard, extensive, bony tumor of the bones of the face and of the base of the skull, in addition to the harmless, button-shaped exostosis occurring on the vertex.

Verruca.—The common wart, originating in an elongation of the papillæ of the skin. *Verruca mollis*: connective-tissue wart with a broad base and covered with a thin layer of epithelium.

Papilloma.—Cauliflower growth, tree-shaped, branched papillæ, thickly covered with epithelium. 'Apt to become cancerous.

Glandular Hypertrophies, retaining an even disposition of their parts, occur often in the lymphatic glands (Lymphoma), and in the spleen. Also in the thyroid gland (Struma hyperplastica), in the mammæ, and in the prostate gland.

Retention Cysts, so-called, are due to the partial or complete retention of secretion in glands which open on the surface. These, also, cause a certain hypertrophy of the expanded constituents of the glands. One of the most frequent is the *Atheroma* of the scalp, due to the distended condition of the entire follicular sheath of a hair; further, the *mucous polypi* of the intestines and uterus. Small outgrowths upon the ventricular surfaces of the brain are sometimes described.

II. Heteroplastic Tumors.

(Tumors in the strict sense of the word.)

A. Tumors derived from the blood-vessel and connective-tissue apparatus (*Paraplastic* heteroplasms; Virchow's Histioids).

1. Complete Development of Tissue :—

(*a*) *Fibroma*.—Consists of dense, thickly-interwoven connective tissue fibres, and has many and often large blood vessels. Proceeds from organized strata of connective tissue, from fascial membranes, from the external layer of the periosteum, from nerve sheaths, more rarely from interstitial connective tissue. The *Myo-fibroma* is an important subdivision, being the chief tumor of the uterus, where it appears peripherally, forcing its way up into the abdominal cavity; interstitially, or as a sub-epithelial tumor, the so-called fibroid polypus. If the process extend along the track of a blood vessel or nerve, it receives the name of *plexiform fibroma*.

(*b*) *Lipoma*.—Consists of lobules of fat, which are often united by means of the blood vessels, into a large round tumor. It is found almost always in the fatty layer of the true skin, especially on the shoulder.

(*c*) *Enchondroma*.—Consists of pieces of cartilage, of the size of a hemp-seed, bound together by the connective tissue into a lobulated tumor. It occurs in large numbers in the bone-marrow of the fingers, and in the joints, forming round lumps, which distend the bony cortex. On the humerus, femur, malar bones and ribs, they arise from the periosteum, and spread equally in all directions.

(*d*) *Myxoma*.—In many cases only a mucoid-degenerated Lipoma, Enchondroma, or Fibroma. Nevertheless, primary mucous tissue tumors exist, which arise in the subcutaneous connective tissue, and in the connective tissue of the nervous system.

(*e*) *Angioma.*—We distinguish *Telangiectasis*, the birthmark, which owes its origin to a circumscribed lengthening, expansion, and thickening of the capillaries. Furthermore, the *cavernous fibroma*, which depends upon a similar dilatation of the lumen, with fibroid metamorphosis of the walls and of the intermediary parenchyma, as in the formation of corpora cavernosa. Lastly, *Lymphangioma*, a local dilatation of the lymphatics, leads to the formation of macroglossus; otherwise rarely found.

(*f*) *Osteoma.*—Results from the ossification of connective tissue tumors.

(*g*) *Endothelioma.*—On a scanty connective-tissue stroma the endothelial layers accumulate and form hard, spherical tumors, particularly in the walls of the subdural space of the skull.

Tumors which are composed of a large number of muscle or nerve fibres are true Myomata or Neuromata. Concerning the origin of these very rare tumors nothing is known. What is generally termed Myoma or Neuroma are Fibromata or Sarcomata, containing muscular or nervous tissue.

2. Incomplete Development of Tissue. *Sarcoma:*—

(*a*) *Small Spindle-celled Sarcoma.*—Consists entirely of spindle cells of equal size, not exceeding in average length and thickness the spindle cells of cicatricial tissue. Arranged in bundles, they form a dense, elastic, rather exstructive tumor, arising, like fibroma, from completely developed connective tissue. (Fasciæ, membranes, periosteum.)

(*b*) *Large Spindle-celled Sarcoma.*—Distinguished by the presence of exceedingly large and often very thick multinuclear spindle cells. These form loose bundles, radiating from one or many centres. The long offshoots form a network, in which large round multinuclear cells are lodged. Fully developed connective tissue and the interstitial connective tissue of some glands form a favorite nidus for these nuclei.

(*c*) *Granulation-like Round-celled Sarcoma.*—Occurs in loose sub-serous, sub-mucous, retro-peritoneal, mediastinal, inter-muscular connective tissue; in short, in almost any interstitial connective tissue. The numerous varieties of the same are determined by the seat of their growth. *Sarcoma myxomatodes* forms in the retro-peritoneal connective tissue a tumor as large as a man's head. *Sarcoma lipomatodes* produces extensive tumors in the fatty layer of the skin, a favorite seat being the thigh. *Sarcoma melanodes* arises from the choroid coat of the eye, or from the skin. *Giant-celled sarcoma*, distinguished by the presence of giant cells containing many nuclei, occurs in the bone marrow. *Osteoid sarcoma* produces an incomplete osseous tissue, which is distributed throughout the tumor in radiated or porous masses. It arises from the inner periosteum. *Glioma* proceeds from the round cells of the neuroglia of the brain and the retina, and preserves, in a peculiar manner, the character of the mother tissue. *Cartilaginous sarcoma* is really nothing but a sarcomatously degenerated enchondroma, found chiefly in the testicles.

<small>Sometimes such a superabundance of cells occurs in tumors that the round cells resolve themselves into small and large groups, which, being emptied, resemble alveoli (*Sarcoma alveolare*). Even without the formation of alveoli, this tumor can reach the highest degree of softness (almost a pus-like infiltration). *Sarcoma medullare*.</small>

(d) *Lymphadenoid Round-celled Sarcoma*, or malignant Lymphoma, arises primarily in a lymphatic gland, but soon escapes, spreading in different directions. A large-celled variety is sometimes found.

B. Tumors whose essential constituents proceed from surface or gland epithelium (Epitheliomata. *Archiplastic* heteroplasms.)

1. *Squamous Epithelioma.*—Arises from free surfaces covered with squamous epithelium. *Epithelial cancer of the skin* consists, apart from its often very vascular stroma, of cylindrical, cancerous bodies containing only squamous epithelium arranged in layers, in the centre of which pearly bodies are found. This cancer occurs in places which are especially subjected to external irritation, as, for instance, on the hands, tibia, scrotum, lips, ears, face, penis, and vulva. It is intimately connected with cancer of the tongue and œsophagus. The former spreads rapidly by means of the lymphatics of the tongue, the latter is noticeable in the stricture produced in the œsophagus. *Carcinoma recti* is a squamous epithelioma, as also *carcinoma vesicæ urinariæ*.

2. *Cylindrical Epithelioma.*—Found along the whole intestinal tract, as well as on the os uteri. *Carcinoma fungosum ventriculi* (fungoid cancer of the stomach), which is the most common of all the stomach cancers, is distinguished by stenosis and ectasia of the stomach, later by hemorrhages resembling

coffee grounds, and by metastasis to the liver. Here, also, belongs cancer of the intestines and rectum, characterized by the production of fatal strictures.

3. *Glandular Epithelioma.*—There are, in glandular epithelioma, so many transition forms from simple and cystic glandular hypertrophies (see above), in all their stages of irregularity and imperfection, up to the most luxuriantly growing cancers, that it is no easy matter to clearly define the adenoma, cystoadenoma, cystosarcoma, cystoid, etc. The classification varies in different glands.

In the *mamma* there occurs often a true, usually double-sided, *hypertrophy* of the whole organ. *Adenoma mammæ* designates certain isolated *lumps*, in which a more abundant connective-tissue formation has taken place, in connection with a moderate increase of epithelial constituents. This new formation, when spread over the whole organ, and permeated by a leafy, papular overgrowth, which fills in the cystic dilated lumen of the lactiferous ducts, is called *cystosarcoma proliferum*, or *phyllodes*. All atypical outgrowths of the epithelium, on the other hand, are classified among the true cancers. In *scirrhus mammæ*, the epithelial outgrowths gradually fill up the connective-tissue interstices and lymphatics; in *soft cancer of the mamma*, the connective tissue yields before the powerful advance of the epithelial masses.

Adenoma in the *liver* is an outgrowth of the network of liver cells, consisting of solid or hollow aggregations of epithelial cells, the whole assuming the form of a sphere and being inclosed in a connective-tissue capsule. *Carcinoma hepatis* shows a direct transformation of liver cells into cancer cells, or (in metastatic cancer) a cell overgrowth in the lumen of the blood vessel, which, beginning at numerous individual points, results in an equal number of cancerous masses.

Three different varieties of cancer are found in the *stomach*. The first, very soft and easily disintegrated; the second, very hard (scirrhus), with a cicatricial formation of the stroma; the third, colloid, with a gelatinoid degeneration of the cancer cells.

The *glands of the uterus* produce the common cancer of the cervix and the rarer cancer of the uterus proper. Adenoma is not found here. Cancers are also found in the *prostate* and *salivary glands*, and in the *lungs*. An adenoma of the *parotid* gland also occurs.

In the *ovary* we find an exceedingly important cyst, in reality, an adenoma. Its normal structural parts being already little cysts, the cystic character found here is not surprising. True *cancer* of the *ovary*, which occurs much more rarely, readily becomes cystic, although this is chiefly due to the softening of large cancer masses. In the *testicle* the *cystosarcoma testis* resembles the sarcoma more than the carcinoma. A sarcomatous overgrowth of the interstitial connective tissue causes a partial compression and retention ectasis of the seminal ducts. Even cancers are regularly provided with a soft sarcomatous stroma, forming a combination tumor which could be called with equal justice *sarcoma carcinomatosum*, or *carcinoma sarcomatosum*.

In the *kidneys* only true cancer is found. It spreads not only to the pelvis of the kidney and its calyx, but also to the renal vein, and to the inferior vena cava, causing in the former hemorrhage of the kidney, in the latter cancerous thrombi.

The so-called *dermoid cysts* occupy a peculiar position among the epitheliomata. These cysts, as large as a man's head, are provided with a tough capsule, and are found in the ovary, testicle and connective-tissue apparatus. They exhibit the strange, genetic relationship which exists between all surface and gland epitheliomata. Upon the inner surfaces of these tumors, glandular epithelium is observed in the process of transformation into cylindrical and squamous epithelium, with all its local peculiarities, hair, etc.

This summary must suffice for the present. For a more explicit representation of tumors and of the processes concerned in inflammation, I will refer my readers to my Manual of Pathology.

(c) BENIGN AND MALIGNANT TUMORS.

Regarding tumors as local and degenerate overgrowths, I have in the preceding pages classified them in accordance with that standard, which, if it be a correct one, must serve still further to illustrate the relations existing between the tumor and the general organism.

We distinguish benign and malignant tumors. *Benign tumors* are those which, although occasioning some discomfort, may exist without positive injury to the organism. *Malignant tumors* are those which exert a baneful and constantly increasing influence upon the organs of nutrition, and, finally, bring about their complete destruction.

No tumor can, of course, be benign in the sense of healthful. A benign tumor may, from its locality, become dangerous, and under the most favorable conditions a benign tumor exhibits an intensity of growth which must, necessarily, tax the resources of the organism. This is seen in all euplastic (hyperplastic) tumors, and in those paraplastic heteroplasms whose constituent tissues reach perfect development, such as Fibroma, Lipoma, Enchondroma, Myxoma, etc.

But paraplastic tumors with imperfect tissue development, as well as most epithelial tumors, may be recognized as malignant tumors. We thus arrive at a distinct line of demarcation between malignant and benign tumors. That we do not deal here with superficial coincidences, but with a separation deduced from the nature of our classification, will appear from the following considerations:—

We found that an overpowering amount of cell production is apparently the only purpose of that intense process of degenerate growth seen in the Sarcoma and Carcinoma. This enormous productivity forces the young, new-formed cells to usurp all the available space in and around their place of origin. The young cells penetrate into every crevice, invade every pore of the structure, and infringe upon the parenchyma cells and connective-tissue fibres, which are at length crowded out and obliterated by the irresistible force of the new growth. It is, therefore, with justice, that Sarcomata and Carcinomata are designated as undermining and destructive tumors as compared with the more constructive varieties. *The especial characteristic of malignity is destructiveness.*

Very conspicuous among the interstices into which destructive tumors send their brood of young cells are the lymphatics and their beginnings. These are large enough to give free passage to the cells which reach them from the periphery, and to conduct them as far, at least, as the nearest lymph gland. Here they are arrested by the delicate reticulum of lymphadenoid tissue, but find in it a supply of nutrition admirably adapted to their growing needs. They are surrounded by a soft, porous, vascular tissue. Attaching themselves to the blood vessels, they begin at once a vigorous growth, and soon the entire lymph gland is converted into a mass resembling the parent tissue. After this the constituents of the tumor pass by means of the communicating lymph paths, unopposed, into the venous and arterial systems. The lungs are next chosen as a seat for colonies of young tumor cells, and the so-called metastatic tumors; after this all of the organs of the body, noticeably, the spleen, liver, bones and connective-tissue.

The process thus described is the typical plan of attack pursued by malignant tumors in their rude invasion of the organism. The involvement of the neighboring lymph glands, and the appearance of metastatic tumors, betokens the malignity of the tumor, and is a valuable guide in the diagnosis.

A much more dangerous and important invasion, which begins earlier and which is of greater continuity and intensity than that made upon the cells, is the admixture of the liquid products of metamorphosis which form in the tumor and are absorbed by the lymphatics. Although little is known of the chemical properties and other characteristics of these products, we may be sure that they are actively employed in undermining the entire nutritive apparatus of the patient. They are, probably, fermentative substances which act upon the albumen of the blood in the same manner as the gastric juice, dissolving it and impeding its reproduction. For the most prominent symptom of that blood cachexia, which is certain to result fatally, is the increasing impoverishment of the blood, in respect to its free and fixed corpuscular elements.

This description of the incorporation and diffusion of a malignant tumor in the system somewhat anticipates my general plan. Metastasis and cachexia are properly deuteropathic symptoms. A more complete system of arrangement will be possible in the Second Part.

II. THE ANATOMICAL DISTRIBUTION OF DISEASE.

DEUTEROPATHIC GROUPS OF SYMPTOMS.

INTRODUCTION.

The *anatomical changes* which accompany the local outbreak of disease are communicated to the adjacent organs or to the entire system. Thus arises a secondary class of symptoms, which we will term deuteropathic. The propagation of disease is, accordingly, direct and physical (anatomical), and is consummated in various ways. It is of prime importance to know whether the original seat of disease generates and throws off products, which, by the inter-communication of the lymphatics and blood vessels, are transmitted to the system at large. These products may be coarsely constituted, like aggregated or isolated cells, detached fragments of coagulated blood, etc., in which case they are liable to collect in narrow and impassable blood vessel channels and produce what is known as *metastasis*.

If, however, the products should be of a minute, liquid, or even volatile nature, we may expect them to become intermixed with the blood and juices of the body.

The reception and propagation of such a "materies peccans" from a seat of disease resembles, in many respects, the reception and propagation of organic or mineral poison, infectious matter, etc.; both processes often give rise to similar results. As one of the chief of these, we may reckon the production of *fever*. The central nervous system, being especially sensitive to blood-poisoning, exhibits certain *general symptoms of excitation and exhaustion*, which form another typical group. At last the anatomical composition of the blood begins to suffer from this constant admixture of foreign elements, and this deterioration, joined to the loss of cells and juices in the seats of disease, results in a general decline, or a *cachexia* of the body.

A local affection is also propagated anatomically through a direct attack upon the *nerves of the diseased part*. Every process of inflammation and reproduction claims a certain amount of space for its solid and liquid products. The space furnished by a closed parenchymatous organ is soon filled, and every additional deposit leads to a mechanical pressure upon the nerves of the organ. This takes place soonest in organs rich in nerves and deficient in flexibility, as in the serous membranes, periosteum, skin, etc. The local nerve irritation thus produced culminates in *pain*, and this cardinal symptom may also bring in its train a number of other nervous symptoms, ranging from the slightest sympathetic affections to the most severe neuralgias and cramps.

METASTASIS.

When a local disease, which is of some standing and unmistakably primary in origin, is followed by another similar disease in a more or less distant locality, the physician says that the disease has produced a metastasis. The same disease can form not only one, but many metastases, which, in turn, may again produce metastases, etc. This fact reveals an extensive similarity between all metastasis-producing diseases, for certain appearances are observed which are typical of certain anatomical arrangements, and result from the transmission of disease-producing fragments through the blood vessels and lymphatics.

We can distinguish sharply enough the metastases transmitted by the blood paths from those transmitted through the lymphatics. The lymphatics are so arranged and constituted by nature that they are able to take up even solid fragments, *i. e.*, wandering cells of the parenchyma. A minute subdivision of the corpuscular products in the primary seat of disease is all that is necessary to secure their entrance into and transmission through the lymphatics. The blood vessels, on the other hand, have closed walls, and, in order to effect a migration through them from one seat of disease to another, the product must have been generated within their lumen, have grown through or been forcibly introduced into their walls. For this reason metastasis through the blood vessels shows a certain sameness in the products transmitted. Most important are: blood clots, derived from the veins of the primary growth;

air and fat, which, under particularly favorable circumstances, in the case of fresh wounds, can penetrate into the veins; and, finally, intestinal worms or large pieces of tumor, which, by some accident, have broken into a vein (cancer of the veins).

(a) *Metastasis through the Lymphatics.*—It is well known that the art of tattooing, which is not confined, by any means, to Indians alone, is effected by pricking the skin with sharp needles and rubbing forcibly into the fresh wound minutely subdivided, but insoluble dye-stuffs (Cinnabar or Prussian blue.) A part of this dyestuff remains in the connective tissue, the rest reaches the lymphatics, by which it is carried further. Having gained the lymphatic gland, it even penetrates the capsule, but is then arrested. These brilliant particles remain for years in the terminal bulbs of the lymphadenoid tissue, partly closed in by cell protoplasm and fibrous tissue. The material is apparently too heavy and rough to pass unarrested through the fine and convoluted lymphatic paths into the interior of the gland. The same happens to all minutely subdivided particles which have in any way entered the lymphatic vessels at some point on their periphery. The effect of these intrusions into the lymphatic ducts is, of course, very different from the simple tolerance of the gland substance for all those unchangeable and consequently chemically bland particles, like coal-dust, iron-dust, stone-dust, etc.

Some of the wandered-out, colorless blood corpuscles are invariably carried from an inflamed centre to the neighboring lymphatic glands. In consequence of this, the local lymph paths swell so quickly and to such an extent that the secondary (deuteropathic) suffering really exceeds the primary (protopathic). The nerve sheaths being particularly pressed upon, pain results, which is increased by the slightest touch or movement of the neighboring organs.

As the inflammation diminishes, the swelling of the local glands also subsides. The cells which have wandered in have meanwhile either found their way out or been overtaken by fatty degeneration. Often, however, things do not run so smoothly. The irritated gland becomes inflamed, and the formation of pus and abscesses inevitably follows. We must, then, provide for an early evacuation of the pus, lest this metastatic centre again cause others.

We have already laid stress upon the fact that the metastasis of malignant tumors by means of the lymphatic system is very prominent.

(*b*) *Metastasis through the blood vessels.*—We have mentioned above, briefly, the conditions necessary to a metastasis through the blood vessels. The blood vessels, according to Harvey's memorable discovery, are completely closed in, and not intended for the reception of solid particles of the bodily parenchyma; hence, only such solid bodies can be transmitted from one point to another, as have been produced in the lumen of the blood vessel, or have been forcibly introduced through their walls. Whence the extreme rarity of cases of metastasis of heterogeneous substance. We will first consider the metastasis of blood clots, which have been formed in the blood-vessel apparatus, and carried away by the blood current, and also examine the doctrine established by Virchow concerning thrombosis and embolism of thrombi.

COAGULATION OF STAGNATING BLOOD.

Blood coagulates so soon as it is cut off from the general circulation and becomes stationary. If we open a vein in an animal, catch the blood in a glass, and allow it to remain stationary for a few minutes, we notice that the blood is transformed into a dark red jelly, which, in the course of a day, gradually sinks to the bottom of the glass, having diminished one-fifth in volume. In the meantime, a yellowish-colored clear liquid collects above the clot, and if evaporation is prevented, rises in the glass to the original level of the blood. The fibrin has coagulated, and with it the blood corpuscles are fixed; then, having contracted upon its contents, a portion of the blood serum has been squeezed out.

By the use of the microscope, we learn the following concerning the process:—

Let us suppose a drop of blood taken from the finger, allowed to run into the capillary space between a glass slide and thin glass cover, and placed immediately under the microscope. At once, even while the blood corpuscles are settling, we see that peculiar aggregation which leads to the formation of the well known rouleaux and other less marked shapes. In the course of ten or fifteen minutes, those groups and chains of blood corpuscles unite and form a kind of network of red bands with intermediate circular gaps. The whole resembles a coarse sponge, and it is, undoubtedly, this sponge, formed also largely in blood procured by venesection, which, by its continued contraction, presses out the enclosed serum.

Although we know that fibrin is the active principle in this contraction, we are unable to see it without further preparation. In order to effect this, we put a little of a ¾% salt solution at the edge of the cover glass, and wash the clot thoroughly by compressing it between the cover and slide. The blood corpuscles disappear in the washings and the fibrin remains outspread, resembling a veil-like tissue, between the slide and cover. Upon examination of the most delicate lamellæ, we see that the form and size of the blood corpuscles have determined the form and size of the mesh which composes the granular fibrous network. The secretion has taken place on the surface of the blood corpuscles, and united the same into a coarse, spongy structure.

THROMBOSIS IN VEINS.

When a portion of a blood vessel is cut off permanently from the general circulation, the blood within it coagulates in the same manner as when drawn directly from a vein. If the lumen of an artery is obliterated by a ligature, the whole mass of blood coagulates both upward and downward, until the first collateral branches are reached. This is the simplest form. In the study of metastases we have first to consider that stagnation-thrombosis which is produced in *un*collapsed veins when the blood current is insufficient or absent. Many organs have, by nature, veins which do not collapse. In the sinuses of the brain, for example, a considerable diminution in the force of the heart, as in extreme debility taken in conjunction with continued bodily rest, causes the blood to coagulate in certain recesses and deepest parts of the *sinus cavernosi* (marantic thrombi). In other organs a preceding inflammation furnishes the cause and material for a firm infiltration of the connective tissue which surrounds the veins and their walls. The vein wall is of itself relaxed, and can be readily compressed or folded together. If, for instance, we have amputated the leg above the knee, we expect the large veins which have been severed to collapse, and to remain firmly closed under the ligature. There exist now, as before, numerous anastomoses with the surrounding veins of the skin and muscles, but the pressure in these tributary veins is too slight to force the blood outside its normal paths of exit through the now disused paths of exit of the lower thigh. The blood does not return from the external iliac, through the crural vein, on account of the numerous valves which are there present.

This condition of things is, however, altered if a powerful and deep-seated inflammation attack the stump. I refer particularly to that extremely hard, inflexible infiltration of the interstitial connective tissue, which is produced by a diphtheritic or erysipelatous infection. This process is especially liable to locate itself in the walls of the veins, converting the same into thick, inflexible tubes (phlebitis). If these veins be divided transversely, they can scarcely be distinguished from the adjacent arteries. The veins are kept open by this dense inflammatory infiltration of their adventitia, just as the arteries, by reason of their thick muscular coat, remain open. In proportion as these changes advance, the collapsed lumen dilates anew, and is replenished with blood from the surrounding circulatory vessels. This opening up of the ends of the veins is part of the mechanism of infiltration. The blood is sucked in. Just as soon as the blood which has been drawn into the comparatively empty spaces has come to rest, coagulation takes place.*

The phenomena in puerperal inflammation of the uterus show us another modification of stagnation-thrombosis. The veins of the uterus, so long as they run entirely in its muscular structure, possess no markedly distinct walls, but are merely gaping openings separated from the neighboring bands of muscles by a thin connective tissue and endothelial

* This somewhat new description of the ætiological sequence of thrombosis in stumps applies to most, but not all cases. Often, indeed, when a venous thrombosis has been established without preceding inflammation, conditions unfavorable to the efflux of venous blood, such as, malpositions of the stump, compression of the external iliac by swollen glands, heart failure, etc., are sufficient to fill the empty venous trunks of the upper part of the thigh with stagnating blood. Coagulation now usually begins in the sinuses of one or more of the valves, and extends thence into the lumen of the vein.

We must always remember, in this connection, that when the large veins of the upper thigh are severed from their connection with those of the lower thigh, the source of the power by which they send their blood to the heart is cut off, and that henceforth these vessels are nothing but disproportionately wide, blind appendages of the circulatory system.

lining. They remain open as long as the muscular structure of the uterus is not contracted, but when contraction takes place during labor, they close, so that a well contracted uterus possesses in reality no open veins, and, in fact, only a weak circulatory apparatus. If infection and inflammation now arise, the first sign of the latter is the relaxation and renewed expansion of the uterus, causing its venous trunks again to open and blood to be sucked in from the internal iliac vein. This blood returning *a fronte* into the vessels, is wanting in *vis a tergo*, and, consequently, is disposed to stagnation and coagulation.

The above description of the two most important forms of stagnation-thrombosis will suffice. Coagulation occurs here, as in venesection, and the clot becomes dark red and soft in proportion as the circulation is more or less suddenly and completely arrested. Such properties are rarely met with, and then only incompletely, in actual cases of venous thrombi. These thrombi, if we exclude all secondary changes which may have befallen them, are generally much firmer, more highly colored, and much more irregular in shape than the clot of venesection. Hence simple stagnation does not, as a rule, cause the blood to coagulate, but under its influence certain qualities of the corpuscular elements of the blood manifest themselves, which materially complicate the process of coagulation. All the colorless blood corpuscles are active, sticky cells, their viscidity being an expression of their amoeboid movement. They are inclined to attach themselves to every firm body upon which they impinge, and having done so, to spread out, creep into small existing openings, or, if the object be sufficiently small, incorporating it bodily. As long as they remain in circulation they have no opportunity to show their adhesive tendency. They are carried along by the circulation, which rushes them rapidly, in a confused mass, first through the heart, then through the arteries and veins, and again back into the heart. As the result of such great mechanical action, they draw themselves together with a kind of tonic contraction, and assume the shape of corpuscular lumps without any apparent individual mobility. When, for any reason, the blood current is slowed, or even entirely stopped, this active stickiness of the colorless blood corpuscles reasserts itself. They collect in masses, take up into their protoplasm as many as six or seven red blood corpuscles, and glue themselves fast to the walls of the blood vessel. If stagnation thrombosis has already set in, they at once rise to the surface of the clot, forming here a continuous covering. If a new layer of blood is now deposited, the above process is repeated, which affords us an explanation of those peculiarities by which we distinguish a natural venous thrombus from one due to simple bleeding, or from a ligation-thrombus.

Those corpuscles described by Zimmermann, and which Bizzozero has recently named "blood plates" (Blutplättchen), also take an active part in this process. Like the colorless blood corpuscles, they deposit themselves upon every *caput mortuum* which appears in the blood paths, forming those considerable collections of granular material shown by the microscope to exist in all new and old venous thrombi.

This stratified arrangement of the colorless and red blood corpuscles determines not only the structure, but also the light pinkish-white color, and the relative toughness and thickness of the blood clot.

Should the new theory in regard to the secretion of a fibrin ferment by the leucocytes be established, the mere presence of a body covered with colorless blood corpuscles and located within the lumen of the blood vessel would, of itself, be an incentive to the deposition of fresh blood layers, and may be regarded as the excitant of that peculiar growth of venous thrombi, viz., *growth by continued coagulation*. It is well known that every thrombus has a tendency to grow in the direction pursued by the blood current which passes it. The growth results from the deposition of fresh clots over the whole free surface. A thrombus grows out of the crural vein into the external iliac, and often advances as far as the internal iliac. From the uterine veins vegetations derived from thrombi reach the trunk of the inferior vena cava. It is no rare thing to find a thrombus of the crural vein extending up to the right side of the heart. From such small beginnings whole areas of veins can thus, under favorable conditions, become obstructed. *Prolonged thrombosis* is a more independent link in the chain of phenomena which we are considering. In any case, it should not be treated as stagnation-thrombosis, because it arises by constant conflict with the blood current, whose paths it seeks to obstruct. Some of the most important properties of venous thrombi, and in part also their macroscopical shape, are thus explained.

The original stagnation-thrombus depends for its shape upon the shape of the veins in which it originally forms, just as, in venesection, the glass in which the blood is caught determines the form of the thrombus. Suppose, for instance, that a thrombus completely fills up the lumen of a vein, and extends upwards to the point where the vein empties into a still larger one. The first vein is entirely plugged up by an obstructive thrombus, which projects slightly into the cavity of the large vein by means of a slightly-flattened, oval head. Its further tendency is to assume first the hemispherical, then the spherical shape, by which the lumen of the large vein is rapidly obstructed. The accomplishment of this end, however, depends entirely upon the amount of blood pressure existing in the large vein. If the pressure be at all considerable, the projecting head of the thrombus is impelled towards the heart, against the side of the vessel and forced to assume the shape of a long flat tongue. It is then called a "wall-adhering" thrombus.

Wall-adhering thrombi may attain an enormous length, assuming a band-like shape. I once found a wall-adhering, band-like thrombus, 7mm. (.275 in.) in breadth, which extended from the internal iliac vein through the inferior vena cava up to the heart. This band showed, in parts, a distinct connective-tissue metamorphosis of the colorless blood corpuscles of which it was composed throughout. Generally, the wall-adhering thrombus becomes thicker and thicker, obstructing veins of larger calibre, and entirely occluding the flow of blood. Cases do occur of incomplete obstruction, where the blood current forces its way in a spiral manner along the side of the thrombus. This spiral passage is, after death, generally filled with freshly coagulated blood, while the thrombus proper is of a white or reddish-white color. It is apparent from all this that the narrowing of the blood paths in thrombosis increases the pressure and the rapidity of the blood current in the remaining parts of the venous system. In this conflict between the thrombus and the blood, it, unfortunately, frequently happens that a mechanical separation of the whole or portions of the thrombus takes place. In the former instance, the whole thrombus, being propelled by the blood, rolls itself up into a roundish mass; in the latter, small fragments are detached or broken off from portions protruding too boldly into the free lumen of the vessel. These detached fragments are rapidly swept away by the blood current, and become, when arrested in small vessels, *emboli*.

The subject of *embolism* must be prefaced with a few observations. Venous thrombi, before they are carried off by the current, often experience a series of changes which not only further the act of detachment, but influence their character to a certain extent, and determine thereby the quality of the metastatic process. These secondary changes are known as *softening* of thrombi. Before the publication of Virchow's researches, it was customary to speak of the suppuration of thrombi, as the products of this process could hardly be distinguished from unhealthy pus, being a yellowish-gray emulsion in which the microscope shows, besides granular detritus, large cells resembling pus cells. But, however definitions may vary, the fact still remains that the softening of thrombi takes place without the development of new elements, and may, in general, be regarded as a maceration of the thrombus. Only in rare cases (as in pyophlebitis) has the suppurative inflammation of veins appeared to me to furnish a predominating amount of white blood corpuscles which found their way into the lumen of the vein. In most cases, the intima of a vein, although not smooth, is dry and firmly attached to the outer layer of the thrombus, while the puriform products of softening have their seat in the axis of the latter. The centre of the clot is naturally the part most completely cut off from the general nutritive apparatus. It is the exception when venous thrombi undergo those organization changes which take place as a rule in the ligation-clots of arteries; neither blood vessels nor connective tissue are developed. Everything depends upon the external supply, and as this, under the most favorable circumstances, can only penetrate to a certain very limited depth—about one millimeter—a centripetally increasing loss of nutrition ensues, which appears in the chemical solution of the coagulated albuminous bodies. We may assume, then, that a putrid fermentation takes place in a pyæmic inflammation of a thrombus, although the process occurs without perceptible production of gas or smell.

Externally, much depends upon the layers of colorless blood corpuscles, which, as we have above observed, form the chief ingredients of the thrombus. These layers resist softening for a greater or less period of time. A consistency, at first peculiarly laminated, afterwards crumbling, precedes the complete fusion into a homogeneous mass. The color is dependent upon the presence of red blood corpuscles and their metamorphosis. The uneven, streaky redness of the fresh thrombus is replaced later, when the red blood corpuscles begin to lose their coloring matter, by a diffused flesh-red and, finally, by a dirty reddish yellow. The superficial surface of a thrombus is always firm, either white and smooth, when a layer of colorless blood corpuscles has been freshly deposited, or covered with a bright red clot. This applies especially to such thrombi as arise in the tributaries of large veins, viz., a thrombus of the saphena vein, which projects into the vena cruralis. The dome-shaped protuberance of such thrombi is firm externally, but the firmness extends scarcely a millimeter in depth; below this point, we find the centre of the softening process which produces the dome-shaped exterior. Everything is now prepared for the production of a metastasis. A sudden pressure exerted upon the vein containing this thrombus will perhaps burst the thin capsule, the rapid blood current lends its aid, and the next moment the head of the thrombus, the softened pulp, and fragments of coagula, are hurrying along on their way towards the heart.

THROMBOSIS IN THE HEART AND ARTERIES.

Next in importance to venous thrombosis, is the formation of clots in the heart and larger arteries. Endocarditis and endoarteritis produce inequalities upon the valves of the heart, upon the intima of the aorta, and the smaller arteries. Upon these inequalities tiny particles of blood settle and coagulate, colorless blood corpuscles are deposited, and we have the nucleus of a thrombus. Its development is, however, much less rapid than in the veins, because the force of the blood current in the heart and arteries not only retards the accumulation of new material, but also demolishes the thrombus as soon as it rises upon the surface of the blood vessel. Of this, thrombosis of the acutely inflamed valves of the heart is a significant example. There is, accordingly, no disease which makes as many small metastatic inflammations as acute endocarditis.

Larger thrombi, or heart polypi, never develop except when the discharge of blood from the heart is incomplete, in stenosis and when there is diminished muscular power. These polypi are often carried away bodily. A thrombus of the right auricle extends, for instance, with the blood current, into the right ventricle. The tricuspid offers no obstacle, and the thrombus, being compressed by each systole, acquires at the point of repeated compression, a constriction; in the right ventricle, however, the thrombus enlarges in a nodular manner. Finally, we have a body of the size of a walnut projecting by a comparatively slender neck from the auricle into the ventricle. Each repeated systole threatens separation, which is at last effected by a sudden acceleration of the heart's action.

Thrombi of the ventricle, after reaching a certain size, say that of a cherry, are apt to begin to soften in the centre, and when the softening extends to within half a millimeter of the surface, burst and discharge their contents directly into the heart blood.

EMBOLISM.

We have now noted the appearance of blood clots in diseased bodily organs in a number of important instances. We found blood stagnation to be the motive power for the first deposit, and the viscidity and fibrination of the corpuscular elements of the blood to be instrumental in the further growth of thrombi. We saw, moreover, how fragments of autochthonous coagulation could be detached and carried away by the blood. Their further destination is determined mainly by their starting-point; thus thrombi in the general venous system and hepatic veins traverse the right heart and reach the lungs; in like manner, thrombi in the right heart. Thrombi in the portal system are arrested in the liver, thrombi in the pulmonary veins, left heart, aorta and large arteries lodge in the systemic capillaries. The lungs, which receive thrombi from all the organs of the body, except the intestines, are the chief metastatic centres; next in frequency is the liver, which also receives arterial blood, and which should, to all appearances, share the metastases of the lungs and left heart with the remaining organs. We shall soon see, however, that this division is an unequal one, so much so that the brain, spleen and kidneys receive the lion's share, while in all other organs metastases are of exceptional occurrence.

MIGRATING THROMBI—LARGE FRAGMENTS.

Before considering the arrest of blood clots and the attendant results, we must make a more careful examination of the manner of their migration. Throw into a swiftly-flowing stream a large and irregularly-shaped block of wood, and you will see it revolve swiftly in the current, until it gains a definite position in the middle of the stream, after which it is carried forward in a linear direction. If the stream divides, the block follows the main, or most direct, branch. This hydro-dynamic picture will serve to illustrate the migration of large clots through the main arterial trunks of the body. A clot leaving the left ventricle through the aorta passes directly into the right carotid, internal carotid, and middle cerebral artery, where the sudden contraction of the lumen arrests further advance. If the clot is too large to penetrate into the lumen of the innominate artery, it follows the arch of the aorta and travels in a linear direction through the descending aorta, external iliac and crural arteries, into the popliteal, where it becomes lodged immediately above the point where the tibials are given off.

Blood clots which have reached the trunk of the pulmonary artery generally follow the main descending branches. This course may be determined by the laws of gravity, but the long radiating trunks are always preferred. Accordingly, the metastatic centres in the lungs are situated, almost without exception, superficially in the lower lobes.

THE BREAKING DOWN OF THE EMBOLUS.

Large thrombi may break down in the course of migration. Old and partially macerated thrombi are extremely brittle. When a fragment arrives at the point where a large artery bifurcates, and is too large to enter either branch, it is stopped at the point of bifurcation called by Virchow the spur. But the current breaks the thrombus, and the fragments pass both into the right and left channels. The blood often washes away small particles from a large clot into one channel, leaving the nucleus small enough to pass into the other branch. This process may be repeated until a large, simple thrombus is resolved into numberless fragments. Thus, we may easily explain the circumstance that numerous metastatic centres are frequently formed in the same lobe of the lung, in the same Malpighian body of a kidney, in the same hepatic lobe or brain hemisphere.

Small thrombi are distributed much more uniformly along the ramifications of the main arteries.

LODGMENT OF EMBOLI—PREDISPOSITION OF CERTAIN ORGANS.

We have now reached the most essential part of our subject. Every metastatic affection transmitted by the blood vessels groups its symptoms around the point where the obstruction is lodged. This act is known as embolism; the plug itself is called an embolus. The size of the embolus regulates the distance it can penetrate into any given vascular branch. This self-evident proposition is exemplified in organs where the ramifications of the afferent vessels are less regular, as in the kidneys. Here we may compare the embolism in the trunk of the renal artery with that of the arterial arch on the borders of the cortical substance, and that of the ascendant arterioles and the vasa afferentia, and find that, with a similarity of the general type, there exists a very distinct grouping of individual symptoms. (See text-books on Pathological Anatomy.)

But when the wandering clot reaches a certain size, and its diameter approaches very nearly to that of the capillary lumina, the question arises whether these same coagula can pass through one organ without hindrance and yet be detained in another. The capillaries are, in reality, of very unequal size, and the passage from the arteries to the capillaries, and from thence to the veins, is in some organs subject to so many complications that we can easily appreciate what is called the predisposition of certain organs to metastatic diseases. We might almost assert that this predisposition stands in inverse ratio to the calibre of a vessel, were it not that in capillary embolism the consequences of the obstruction are more variable than in larger arterial obstructions, the immediate allayal of the disturbance is much more frequent, and the metastasis itself less perceptible. Nevertheless, the narrowness of the brain and retina capillaries is established by the frequent presence within them of embolic centres.

THE CONSEQUENCES OF EMBOLISM.

The phenomena accompanying the complete obstruction of an artery by an embolus have been finely elucidated by Virchow in his faultless experiments in comparative anatomy, prefixed to his studies upon Thrombosis and Embolism. We now know that a perfect embolus only produces a noteworthy effect (1) when the obstructed vessel is an end artery, *i. e.*, one which can either establish no anastomosis on the other side of the obstructed channel, or, at least, one insufficient for collateral nutrition; (2) when the embolus possesses a chemically or mechanically irritating and inflammatory nature. In many cases both requisites are met with, as, for example, in metastatic inflammations of the lungs in pyæmia.

We will now investigate the mechanical effects of the obstruction of an end artery. Cohnheim's experiments on the frog's tongue furnish us with reliable information on this point, and his researches are none the less meritorious from being a confirmation of what was before only conjecture. The immediate result of withholding the blood is, of course, an anæmic condition of the part in question (ischæmia). The same phenomena occur here which we have frequently noticed in all arteries at death, viz., as soon as the blood pressure is removed the powerful contractile tendency of the artery reasserts itself, and the blood is forcibly driven towards the large, relaxed veins. In this case, the obstructed artery suffers an almost total collapse. This is, however, not a permanent condition in the artery of the living body. The original contraction soon relaxes, and presents no obstacle to the renewed influx of blood. Indeed, the blood returns in superabundance, though not *a tergo,* for in that direction the channels are blocked up, nor yet through collateral vessels, for these do not exist, but simply *a fronte* from the veins by way of the capillaries. And has not this inversion of the circulation its complete justification in the mechanical apparatus? If the blood pressure in the nearest capillaries is not great, it is, at least, greater than in the capillaries of the ischæmic territory. The latter must, in consequence, derive blood from the former, until the resistance of the overfilled capillaries and the resistance of the parenchyma surrounding the capillaries is equalized. The capillaries usually rupture, but generally not until the resistance of the surrounding parenchyma has been considerably augmented by the addition of extravasated blood serum. Thus the parenchyma does not always receive an influx of pure blood,—a hemorrhagic infarct, as it is called,—but often becomes filled with a sanious transudation or an imperfect infarction.

The appearance of engorgement of blood and hemorrhage in detached cases is of no essential value. One factor is, however, invariable. The blood does not flow on in the dilated vessels, it stagnates and imparts a fatal lethargy to the metastatic centres. Gangrene and decomposition, the fatal precursors of local death, soon set in, accompanied by an offensive odor.

So much for the direct mechanical results of the embolus of an end artery. The succeeding stages are to be regarded in the main as the reaction of the healthy surrounding tissue with its free circulation against the enclosed dead area. The latter sends out the products of decomposition in all directions, and the strongly irritating composition of these products occasion an acute suppurative inflammation, called a metastatic inflammation or metastatic abscess.

The detailed account of the inflammatory phases is reserved for special chapters on pathological anatomy. But let us remember that the hemorrhagic infarct and its accompanying results are not the sole and inevitable effects of an arterial obstruction. If the obstruction be located in the main artery of the lung, the consequence is immediate death by suffocation; if in the main artery of the kidney, it produces necrosis of the entire kidney, which is not initiated by an overloading of the blood vessels, and which converts the organ, without offensive decay, into a yellowish, doughy, anæmic mass, which suffers a tedious process of maceration and re-absorption.

If the embolus is so constituted that, by reason of its chemical qualities as a partially decomposed body, it involves the neighboring tissues in suppurative inflammation, it is naturally of less importance whether the obstructed vessel is or is not an end artery. The final result of a metastatic abscess will be the same in both cases.

FEVER.

Any noticeable and prolonged increase in the natural heat of the body, not due to external agencies, is called Fever. In fever, the body produces an amount of heat somewhat in excess of the amount it throws off, although it is not only *a priori* probable, but demonstrably true, that the escape of heat is augmented in febrile affections.

The cardinal symptom of fever is the elevation of the bodily temperature. The concomitants of fever heat are: increased frequency of the pulse and respiration; disturbances of the temperature, nerves and muscles; indigestion; diminished secretion of urine, etc. Some of these symptoms may be produced by an artificial elevation of temperature (experiments on animals in hot-air ovens). This fact might lead one to infer that all other fever symptoms are the result of fever heat. But as only a few of these symptoms can be produced by artificial means, and then incompletely, it will be safe to regard them as proceeding from the general cause of fever.

CAUSE OF FEVER.

The chief cause of fever is now held by most writers to be the introduction into the blood of certain substances which augment combustion, and hence are called pyrogenous substances. Some of these substances are generated in inflammatory centres, whence they are absorbed by the lymphatics; others are introduced into the body from without, like the inhaled poison of infectious diseases. The pyrogenous matter acts as a ferment upon the albumen of the body, disintegrates its molecules, and renders it susceptible to oxygenation. The result of this activity is soon recognized in the increased excretion of the products of disintegration. Twice the normal quantity of urea is produced, and two-and-a-half times the normal quantity of nitrogen.

The "nervous" theory of fever, as it is called, maintains that the heightened oxidation in fever may be accomplished otherwise than by the above-described fermentation or "zymosis." This theory supposes that the presence of pyrogenous matter in the blood would react upon the central nervous system in such a manner as to excite muscular combustion, and thus elevate the bodily temperature. According to this view, fever heat is not produced directly, but by the agency of the nervous system. Whether it can be produced in any other way than by the increase of oxidation will be considered under the head of disturbances of temperature, where we will also discuss Traube's fever theory.

FEVER HEAT.

In order to correctly apprehend the value of thermometrical estimates of bodily temperature, we must bear in mind that the body of the fever patient resembles, to a certain degree, any other body whose temperature exceeds the surrounding medium. As it is constantly giving off a portion of its specific warmth, its peripheral temperature is lower than that of its centre. We need not be surprised, therefore, if the temperature taken in the axilla is 0.8–1.1° C. (1.44°–2° F.) lower than that taken in the vagina or rectum. The circulation of the blood is admirably fitted to regulate such inequalities of bodily temperature, but the influence of the external cold extends to such a depth that the uniform internal heat can only be ascertained by inserting the thermometer some distance into the rectum. The temperature of the mouth is midway between that of the rectum and axilla.

The average normal temperature of the body is as follows:—

	Axilla.	*Rectum.*
In adults,	36.2° to 37.4° C. (97.2° to 99.3° F.)	36.8° to 38° C. (98 2° to 100.4° F.)
In children,	36.4° to 37.7° C. (97.5° to 99.8° F.)	37.0° to 38.2° C. (98.6° to 100.7° F.)

The fluctuations in these figures arise, in part, from individual peculiarities, in part, from the time of day when they were taken. The average daily fluctuation in the temperature of an individual is one degree Celsius (1.8° F.) The temperature is lowest between 1 and 2 A. M. Toward morning, especially after waking, it rises, and, under the influence of physical exertion and the reception of food, increases until noon; just before noon there is a slight fall, but at 5 P.M. the maximum is reached. The fall of the temperature is apparently favored by the inactivity of the muscles during sleep, so that the minimum is reached about midnight.

We might be led to infer, from the above, that the daily fluctuations were caused exclusively by muscular activity and the reception of food. This must, however, be accepted *cum grano salis*. Muscular activity and the consumption of food are undoubtedly factors which now, as always, encourage and foster the daily fluctuation. But a daily fluctuation nevertheless exists, independently of these agencies, appearing in the total absence of muscular activity and reception of food.

In fever, the bodily temperature is very soon raised 1° C. (1.8° F.); 3° C. (5.8° F.) above this is the average maximum reached in ordinary fevers. A temperature above 41.5 C. (106.7° F.) (in the axilla) very rarely occurs, and threatens a fatal termination of the disease. Yet recovery has followed a temperature of 42.5 C. (108.5° F.)

Fever temperature is, in the main, much less uniform than the normal. It undergoes a series of typical changes, which must be carefully noted in individual diagnosis. The daily fluctuation is also important in fever cases. The daily rise (exacerbation) begins a little later than in health, viz., about 9 A. M., and the acme (fastigium) is attained in the afternoon. After this, it continues uniform for several consecutive hours, and does not begin to decline (remission) until about 8 P. M. The minimum is frequently not reached until toward morning.

In slight fevers, such, for instance, as accompany simple mucous catarrhs, the daily fluctuation is 1–1½° C. (1.8–2.7° F.), the minimum being 38° C. (100.4° F.), the maximum 39.5° C. (103.1° F.) Severe fevers are distinguished, not only by higher elevations of temperature, but also by strong remissions. Fevers with slight daily fluctuations, where the fever heat fluctuates above 39° C. (102.2° F.), (*febres continuæ*), are found in typhoid fever, and other serious infectious maladies. Fevers with marked daily fluctuations, 3° C. (5.4° F.), are called remittent, and are characteristic of certain severe diseases. In malarial fevers, we have half-day paroxysms of fever, which alternate with periods of normal temperature (apyrexia). When these intermissions are of a half day's duration, the fever is called quotidian; when of one and a half day's, it is called tertian; when of two and a half, quartan. Such fevers are called intermittent.

Every fever presents in its entirety a series of changes; it has a rise, an acme, and a fall. The rapidity with which the rise and subsequent fall are effected varies widely in different diseases, and is, therefore, an important diagnostic symptom. A rapid and complete subsidence of fever is called a *crisis*. This crisis usually betokens that the system has gained the victory over the pyrogenous substances (the "materies peccans" of our ancestors), has either rejected or consumed them, and fortified itself against further inroads. The crisis is, accordingly, a process of nature, not of disease. It is apt to occur at stated intervals. The fourth, seventh, eleventh, fourteenth, seventeenth and twentieth days of the month have been the traditional critical days, a tradition which has often been verified by fact. The gradual subsidence of fever is called *lysis*.

There are also many minor fluctuations of fever heat, such as a "step-like" ascent and "terrace-like" descent, which are readily perceived by taking the temperature at intervals of five minutes, and noting the result on the temperature sheet. It seems most plausible to refer minor fluctuations to the irregular periodicity in the activity of the heat-regulation apparatus,—a subject we will proceed to consider more at length.

DISTURBANCES IN THE HEAT-REGULATING APPARATUS.

It is self-apparent that an abnormal elevation of the normal temperature affects first of all that apparatus whose function it is to regulate the escape of heat, and to maintain an average temperature $37.5°$ C. ($99.5°$ F.) A large number of fever symptoms must be regarded in this light, *i. e.*, as a reaction of the heat-regulating apparatus upon the elevated bodily temperature. First in importance among the symptoms is the *chill*, with which most severe fevers begin, and which frequently recurs in later exacerbations. A strong subjective sensation of cold is accompanied by shivering, paleness of the skin, shaking and trembling of the whole body, knocking together of the limbs, and chattering of the teeth. All the muscular fibres contained in the outer skin contract. By the contraction of the *erector pili* the hair follicle is raised, causing the so-called goose skin. Still more important is the contraction of the capillaries, in consequence of which little blood circulates through the skin, and the escape of bodily heat is thereby greatly lessened. We meet here one of the most striking paradoxes in the action of the heat-regulating apparatus. We are prepared to see an elevation of bodily temperature followed by a corresponding opening of the ventilative apparatus, a dilatation of the capillaries, secretion of sweat, etc. Exactly the opposite takes place, and we are tempted to regard the mechanism of the heat-regulating apparatus as a highly inadequate one. As it is now established beyond doubt that a chill increases considerably the bodily temperature, we can understand how Traube, an accomplished pathologist, attempted to prove that the elevation of temperature in fever was due to this cause alone.

Liebermeister has tried to explain this paradoxical appearance by saying: In every fever there exists a standard of heat-regulation higher than that of the normal mechanism, regulating the production as well as the escape of bodily heat. As the healthy body is regulated for 37.5° C. (99.5° F.), so in fever, it is regulated for 39° or 40° C. (102.2° or 104° F.) Employing the same means as those at work in a healthy man, the production of heat is increased, and the escape prevented by the contraction of the capillaries.

To accept heat-regulation as a changing apparatus possesses such a fascination for the spirit of the nineteenth century that it is with reluctance that I advance contrary views. I believe in the physiological basis, but do not think that such a clever hypothesis can be maintained. When the temperature of our blood begins to rise as the result of external heat, we endeavor, by discarding our extra clothing, to reduce our temperature to normal again. But is it really the perception of increasing bodily heat which makes us do this? Is it not rather the sensation of an insufficient escape of heat, the feeling that we cannot get rid of our warmth, that our skin is overheated? On the other hand, when a sudden fall of external temperature causes us to button up our coats and draw on our gloves, every one feels, undoubtedly, that it is done in order to prevent the too great escape of warmth. The " perception of an increased or diminished escape of warmth " incites the heat-regulating apparatus to a corresponding activity.

Our own arbitrary standard concerning the heat-regulating apparatus is fixed by the rapidity with which our body is cooled off externally,—best seen in the sudden effect of warm or cold, local or general baths. This arrangement has more than one disadvantage. It would certainly have been much better for a frozen finger or toe, had its blood vessels dilated and allowed warm blood to flow, instead of remaining contracted. But the rules of this regulating apparatus are such that when a powerful external escape of heat begins, the capillaries contract, while they open on the other hand when there is little or no escape.

We know beyond doubt that when our bodily temperature is roused by fever, the external escape of warmth is increased, the surrounding air feels cold to the fever patient, he seeks a warm bed in order to put an end to this excessive loss of bodily heat. The heat regulating apparatus is plainly in accord with the patient, for the capillaries contract, the *erectores pilorum* form goose-skin, the teeth chatter, and the patient has a chill. I consider a chill to be nothing more than an erroneous interpretation of the unquestionably increased escape through the skin of bodily heat, augmented by the high temperature of the blood of the fever patient. The heat-regulating apparatus fluctuates hither and thither, uncertain whether to lower the bodily temperature by opening up the radiating apparatus of the skin, or to prevent the escape of warmth by contracting the capillaries. This indecision often lasts for some time. As an example of this vacillation in an apparatus otherwise so complete, we might mention the sudden shiver produced by a slight breeze in a patient whose skin is burning with fever.

Whatever may be the thermal effect of a chill, there is no doubt that it preserves warmth, and that the previous temperature of the blood is increased. But since in fever, the loss of heat, in spite of the preservation of warmth, is greater than in health, the preservation of heat by a chill cannot be regarded as the sole cause of fever, but only as a secondary factor of the same. As before remarked, the gradation which is found by minutely observing the daily rise and fall of fever, is to be attributed to the vacillation of the heat-regulating apparatus.

Again, we must not forget that chills and ague fits are only temporary phenomena, and that they alternate with that totally different condition of the heat-regulating apparatus, in which, by dilatation of the capillaries, the abnormal loss of heat is still further increased. The over-irritation of the capillaries is followed by a relaxation of their muscular walls, which often lasts for some time. This is associated with a sensation of heat which often becomes almost unbearable, because the nerve filaments in the skin now record this elevation of temperature,—an office which they are only called upon to fill when the external temperature has far exceeded that of the blood.

During the entire rise and acme of a fever, this same fluctuation of the heat-regulating apparatus continues. When the crisis approaches, we often find hyperæmia of the skin, together with profuse perspiration. Under the double influence of increased radiation and evaporation, defervescence sets in, the temperature in the meantime falling to normal, or occasionally, below.

DERANGEMENTS IN THE CIRCULATORY APPARATUS IN FEVER.

Before the introduction of the use of the thermometer in medicine, the counting of the pulse and the valuation of the same were the most reliable means of diagnosing an existing fever. Even to-day the accelerated pulse may be regarded as an almost constant symptom of fever. With the rise of one degree in temperature, we may expect an increase of eight beats in the pulse, though cases in which the pulse increases twenty beats per minute are frequently found, and a pulse-rate of 120 has been observed in adults, and one of 140–160 in children.

It is not only from the number, however, but also from the quality of the beats, that the physician draws his inference. In this respect we must expect that the accelerated heart-beats, *cæteris paribus*, will cause a rise of arterial pressure. This is best seen in the hard pulse. Here the pulse feels like a cord, and gives to the finger a short, powerful beat. The hard pulse (*pulsus durus*) is often found in the beginning of a fever. If the latter has lasted for some time, the hardness of the artery gives way, and the pulse-wave, although "full," gives us a weak, elastic impression (*pulsus amplus*). The difference between a hard and full pulse does not depend upon a different variety of heart contractions, but upon the action of the coats of the various arteries. So long as the hard pulse continues, the arteries are excited to contract; in a weak, full pulse, this excitement has abated, and a certain relaxation has set in. By this relaxation, this general lack of arterial tonus, the arterial pressure is somewhat lowered, so that the systolic pulse appears unusually strong by contrast, and the arteries very full.

In the *pulsus amplus* the dicrotism of the pulse is especially well-marked, because a relaxed arterial wall transmits this disputed secondary wave better than a tense wall. Both the hard and the full pulse presuppose a faultless action of the heart, the ventricles being filled to their fullest extent during diastole, and powerfully and completely emptied during systole.

The condition of the heart in protracted fevers may be compared to that of a horse, which, from overwork and insufficient feeding, becomes tired, weak, and emaciated. Digestion fails, and with it the transmission of new nutritive material to the blood, while the process of oxidation is at the same time increased. Thus the quality of the blood deteriorates; the food of the heart is less nutritious than formerly. Add to this the excessive increase of the work of the heart, and we can easily see how the organ loses its irritability, becomes weak, and contracts only feebly. It is also possible that the rise of temperature exerts a deleterious influence upon the action of the heart, and it is by no means certain that the cause of fever does not act as a heart poison.

The direct consequence of the heart having more work to do than it can accomplish, is a decrease in arterial pressure and in the rapidity of the blood. The pulse can scarcely be felt, it is weak and easily compressed, and beats with an added rapidity, as if the heart wished to make up in speed what it has lost in force (*pulsus frequens*).

Finally, even this correction fails. The scarcely perceptible beats of the small pulse (*pulsus parvus*), which frequently cannot be counted, are no longer able to prevent the threatened fall of arterial pressure and the stoppage of the circulation. In cases of this sort, it is not rare to find a fatty degeneration of the relaxed flaccid heart muscle, which is a palpable symptom of the disturbances of nutrition which have taken place.

It is more than probable that the rise in the frequency of the pulse is dependent upon the cardinal symptom of fever —fever heat. This increased pulse, as well as the increased respiration, is found in cases where the blood temperature has been raised a few degrees by external warmth. This is, doubtless, effected through the agency of the nervous system, although the nervous influence is more marked upon the respiration than upon the heart.

FEBRILE DISTURBANCES IN THE ORGANS WHICH PRODUCE AND PURIFY THE BLOOD.

Among the vegetative functions, disturbances of digestion are first of all apparent. Loss of appetite, nausea and vomiting, together with marked desquamative catarrh of the tongue (coated tongue), denote an anomalous condition of the mucous membrane of the stomach, which is generally considered to be a slight catarrhal or parenchymatous (glandular) inflammation. The ordinary results are a complete abstinence from food, and a suspension of activity in the processes of digestion and resorption in the stomach and organs below it, which do not resume their normal activity for days or even weeks. Nutrition is thus cut off and destroyed in its first and earliest stages. The body rapidly loses in weight, on account of the increased combustion of oxidizable substances in the blood and tissue, its fat disappears, and its muscles waste away (*consumptio febrilis*).

These changes manifest themselves in the constantly increasing amount of urea thrown off by the kidneys, and of nitrogen by the lungs. Less urine is voided in fever than in health, but it is very concentrated, dark in color, and contains in proportion one-third more urea than normal urine. Uric acid is also increased, and when the urine is cold, it deposits itself in the shape of sodium urate (*sedimentum lateritium*). Phosphoric acid is also increased; in short, all the well-known products of oxidation of albuminoid substances which we find in urine are increased.

In a similar manner the function of the lung deviates from normal. A positive increase in the elimination of nitrogen occurs in fevers, where, with elevated temperature and pulse, the respirations increase ten or twenty per minute. This elimination increases at first at a uniform rate with the temperature, but presently reaches its maximum, from which it soon descends, occupying a slightly higher level than formerly.

As regards the skin, the loss of moisture by insensible perspiration is increased under all conditions as the skin becomes warmer. The sensible perspiration is commonly diminished during a fever, but appears readily as a critical phenomenon, in the shape of profuse sweat, as soon as defervescence has distinctly set in.

FEBRILE DISTURBANCES OF THE NERVOUS SYSTEM.

The central nervous system is especially susceptible to all abnormal deviations in the consistency of the blood. Nearly all dyscrasias, *i. e.*, pathological accumulations in the blood of excretory products, as well as the addition of foreign, poisonous, infectious substances, cause a general irritation of the brain and spinal cord, whose typical phenomena we will now study. In fevers, this general irritation shows itself in headache, extreme impressibility of the senses, hallucinations, and delirium, alternating with lassitude, weariness and drowsiness, to which is added the perception of perverted activity on the part of the heat-regulating apparatus, as an indescribably peculiar sensation in the external layer of the outer skin.

Our first idea would naturally be to regard the increased temperature of the blood as the immediate cause of this implication of the central nervous system. But we must not jump at conclusions. Generally, indeed, a febrile rise of temperature appears attributable to impure blood, so that we cannot state how much of this general irritation of the nervous system is due directly to this impurity, and how much to the elevation of temperature. Indeed, the occurrence of fever, without any perceptible blood changes, would denote that the elevation of temperature can arise by nervous means, and points to the so-called "nervous theories" of fever. It is a well-known fact that many of our fever remedies are at the same time nervines. I must, however, refrain to enter here into the further consideration of the question.

CACHEXIA.

There are many terms in the medical vocabulary to express a weak and depraved condition of the system, viz., decrepitude, marasmus, cachexia, consumption, etc. Each is supposed to describe the origin of the particular trouble. Of febrile consumption we have already spoken. Cachexia proper is that condition of defective quality and quantity of the blood brought about by long continued suppuration and pathological new formation. This deterioration is due partly to the appropriation of the constructive material by the massed or detached pathological cells, partly to the introduction into the blood of fermentative matter from the centres of inflammation and new-formation. We have seen (page 56) how cancerous cachexia arises in malignant tumors; in like manner arise the numerous cachectic conditions produced by the tedious processes of specific inflammation and suppuration. With these cachexias there is often associated a peculiar consequent change in the various organs of the body, which, on account of its importance, will form the theme of our next division.

AMYLOID DEGENERATION.

Amyloid degeneration is the infiltration of certain cells and tissues with a firm albuminous body, to which, on account of its present behavior toward iodine, the term "starch-like" was applied by its discoverer. If a fresh section of an organ in a condition of amyloid degeneration be washed in water, to remove the blood, a weak solution of iodine poured over it, the infiltrated spots will assume the reddish-brown color of old mahogany. Sulphuric acid added to this will produce a deeper color, shading into blue and violet, though the latter tints are soon lost in the subsequent charring process.

That the "amyloid substance" is not reparative, but is an albuminous body chemically allied to fibrin, has long been known. By studying the process of amyloid infiltration as far as possible, under the microscope, we shall see a substance which appears to be lodged in the interstices of the protoplasmic granules of a cell, or between the most minute fibrillæ of the connective tissue. The refractive power of this body is sufficiently strong to equalize all optical differences, so that the cells and fibres appear after infiltration entirely homogeneous and wax-like and are also, through the added substance somewhat larger and more rounded off, suggesting, as C. O. Weber says, "a glassy swelling." There is also an unmistakable tendency towards aggregation. The process resembles, in some respects, that of coagulation-necrosis (page 31, *a. f.*), with this difference, that, although it is difficult to form an exact estimate of the vital activity of the degenerated part, it is, at least, sufficient to preserve the part alive, and it rarely happens that an organ becomes so completely degenerated by amyloid change that it is treated by the system as "dead," *i. e.*, thrown off by suppuration, which is the case in coagulation-necrosis.

The very marked peculiarity of amyloid degeneration leads us to infer special conditions in its manner of origin. The chief of these is the extreme impoverishment in the solid, *i. e.*, cellular constituents of the blood. In all cases of amyloid degeneration of organs, the blood is reduced to one-half the average amount, and sometimes even less. It is of a thin consistency and very bright in color. If allowed to stand, the fluid becomes clear on top and deposits a thin layer of blood corpuscles on the bottom of the glass. This deposit is scarcely more than the twentieth part of the entire height, and is composed almost entirely of red cells. After some time the fluid on top coagulates into a tough buffy coat, (Brady-fibrin). If a few drops of fresh healthy blood be added, the coagulation is instantaneous.

We see that the blood has undergone decided changes. There is a lack of cells, and the fibrin generators are not in the right proportion. The chief causes of this depraved condition are suppurating diseases, especially those in which an excessive loss of white blood corpuscles occurs, and in tuberculous and syphilitic suppurations in the osseous and pulmonary systems.

The degeneration usually begins in several places simultaneously, though the preference is given to those where the blood remains longest, and there is a stronger transudation of blood-serum, as in the liver, spleen, kidneys, etc.; the lymphatics and the thyroid gland are attacked later. The capillary walls are first infiltrated, a process best observed in the kidneys. The next point of attack is the connective tissue, and then the parenchyma cells of organs. Amyloid degeneration of single cells may be finely studied in the liver cells, as well as in those of the lymphatic glands.

To sum up: the albumen of the transuding nutritive fluid appears to be arrested in the tissues through which it must pass, i. e., secreted in a solid form by a process greatly resembling the coagulation of fibrin.

IRRITATION OF THE NERVOUS SYSTEM.

It is well known that in every serious disease the nervous system becomes involved. This is accomplished by a double process. First, the central nervous system being excessively sensitive to an abnormal composition of the blood, reacts against it by periods of abnormal excitation, alternating with corresponding periods of lassitude and exhaustion. Second, the local irritation of a nerve is transmitted to the central organ where very disproportionate results are at times produced.

Before entering upon the consideration of those symptoms which characterize both general and local irritation, particular mention must be made of two phenomena peculiar to all symptoms proceeding from the nervous system. These phenomena, which have already been briefly touched upon, are: the more or less decided periodicity of nervous attacks, and the frequent disproportion in them between cause and effect.

The first, periodicity, is the outcome of a great biological law, by which all sensitive vital substances are forced to alternate between rest and activity, and to this alternation the process of assimilation is cleverly adapted. In the nervous system, however, where this sensibility of the organism finds its most intense expression, the alternation of activity and recuperation is most marked, and the two phases most antipodal. The relative difference between the abnormal processes of excitation and exhaustion may be observed in the difference between the normal conditions of sleeping and waking.

The second peculiarity of nervous symptoms, the disproportion between cause and effect, arises from the power of the central nervous system to imperceptibly gather up enormous numbers of centripetal irritations, and preserve them in the shape of tension. Thus it sometimes happens that an attack is made upon the nervous system, which, though in itself, hardly overstepping the bounds of physiological irritation, is increased by all sorts of minor irritants, such as inherited weakness, impoverished nutrition, blood poisoning etc., and we are surprised to find that the stored-up tension is suddenly released and an outbreak of the most violent emotion occurs. Let us now enter upon the subject proper.

GENERAL IRRITATION.
Delirium. Coma.

Aside from the peculiar affections of the brain and spine, the general irritation of the nervous system results oftenest from the presence of injurious matter in the blood and juices of the body. Fermentative and pyrogenous substances, which have been absorbed from inflammatory centres, have the same or a similar effect as any poison which enters the circulation directly from without. But since many of these harmful substances are of themselves fever-producing, it is not always possible to distinguish their effect upon the central nervous system from that of the increased blood temperature, and *vice versa*, to determine to what degree the constantly irritated nervous system is responsible for the febrile increase of temperature.

In what are called general symptoms, the periods of excitation and exhaustion are not sharply defined. A sensation, sometimes painful, and again almost agreeable, passes through the body and forces us to stretch and yawn. It is associated with lassitude and a sense of heaviness and depression, as well as sleeplessness and headache. The latter appears to signify a more severe implication of the central nervous system, particularly of the brain. The pain, which is at times dull and throbbing, at times violent and lancinating, results partly from the cause of disease and partly from the local seat. There follow now very pronounced indications of mental disorder, in all degrees of intensity. This is displayed in general restlessness, uneasy tossing, and hallucinations. Sounds and words are heard and imaginary substances are seen, tasted, and smelled. The patient endeavors to express these rapid impressions in incoherent words, and we then say he raves or is delirious.

This overwrought condition is followed by one of nervous depression, the degree of which appears to be determined by the preceding exaltation. The patient falls into a state of heavy insensibility (coma), from which it is difficult to rouse him. When awakened, he is in a drowsy, semi-conscious state (stupor). In extreme depression, the sleep-like insensibility is accompanied by heavy, stertorous respiration (sopor).

Eclampsia.

It has at all times appeared important and worthy of note to physicians, when the general irritability of the nervous system produces symptoms which denote an imperfect control of the will over the movements of the body. Nothing, however, conveys so absolute an impression of disease or abnormality as the abnormal contraction of individual muscles, or groups of them, which reveals to us the whole weakness of the human spirit as contrasted with the elementary forces of nature. The very first signs in this direction, like the familiar " gnashing of teeth " and " rolling of the eyes," have something terrible about them. Still more, that peculiar twitching of the fingers, known as "carphologia." The gravest of all symptoms is the onset of general convulsions—so-called Eclampsia.

A complete eclamptic attack begins with a very powerful and decided contraction of the flexor muscles of the back and the muscles of expiration. A piercing cry is uttered, the head is thrown backwards, the face upturned and a little to one side, the arms and legs become stiff, the thumbs turn in, the toes are turned out, and the soles of the feet are bent together. Then follow twitchings, which, beginning in the terribly distorted countenance, spread first to the arms and thighs, then to the forearms and legs, degenerating finally into a general convulsive struggle. A moment later, the movements become less violent, and at last cease altogether.

If the patient has not been previously unconscious, he becomes so at the beginning of the attack, and continues so for ten or fifteen minutes after it has subsided. The color of the face, which during the forced expiration was livid, gradually returns to normal, and only a few ecchymoses, the size of a pin's head, remain in the tender skin of the eyelids, to remind us of the disturbances which have occurred in the venous blood.

The great uniformity of these groups of symptoms, which reappear in identically the same shape in epilepsy, denotes that we have to consider here an abnormal excitement or rather lack of restraint in a certain circumscribed region of the brain. Nothnagel has fixed this region, which he calls the "centre of convulsion," in the floor of the fourth ventricle, in the neighborhood of the pons. We know, beside, from the beautiful experiments of Kussmaul and Tenner, that a sudden anæmia of the brain produces this "lack of restraint" in the centre of convulsion most infallibly. The same effect is also produced by the ligature of a vein and the consequent overloading of the brain with venous blood. In both of the above instances oxygen is lacking, for it is well known that no brain activity can exist without a bountiful supply of oxygen

We must also admit the possibility of a partial irritation or lack of restraint of the centre of convulsion, because it has often been observed that the eclamptic attacks appear incomplete and to a certain degree disconnected, so that the "hydrocephalic cry" or "convulsions" are the only visible symptoms.

LOCAL IRRITATION.

Pain.

A local irritation of the nervous system, produced by the continuance of a local inflammatory or new-formation process, appears in its slight degrees as a vague local impression, as of weight, pressure, fullness, etc. Then the sensation of pain begins. The whole may be likened in character to the sound produced by gently running the moistened finger around the edge of a fine glass, half filled with water, the tone being first low and intermittent, then continuous and increasing in volume until it finally rings out with a shrill and piercing noise. The intensity of pain depends, on one hand, upon the severity of the irritation, on the other, upon the sensitiveness of the sufferer. The manifold qualities ascribed to pain, such as lancinating, boring, burning, cutting, darting, depend upon factors as yet unknown. The same applies to the different paræsthesias of the skin, such as formication, itching, etc. The centre of pain, *i. e.*, which portion of the central nervous system must be most powerfully irritated in order to allow the sensation of pain to arise, is as yet a disputed point. Schiff locates it in the gray matter of the spinal cord, and to-day the majority of observers agree with him. The nerves of special sense of the brain might, however, be cited as an exception.

A distinct periodicity is observed in the course of a painful disease. Moderate pain is often followed by only a short remission, but as the pain becomes more intense, the remission is also more marked, until that alternation of strong exacerbation and complete remission is reached which we find in the neuralgias.

Pain is a prominent symptom of a local irritation of the nervous system, but is by no means the only one, because it is not the pain which is essential, but the centripetal excitement, which explains many other reflexes, which are partly of a vasomotor, partly of a sensitive and musculo-motor nature. One of the commonest reflexes is an active hyperæmia of the painful part, after which the same condition occurs in the rest of the organs. More rarely there is a convulsive contraction of single arterial twigs, followed by anæmia. Prominent among the sensitive appearances are "sympathetic affections," which first affect symmetrical, later totally distant parts. Among the musculo-motor reflexes may be enumerated conscious and voluntary movements, which serve the purpose of modifying and diverting pain, from which are to be distinguished involuntary reflexes, which consist in spasmodic contractions of the muscles. Among the latter a peculiarly typical group of symptoms deserves special mention.

Trismus and Tetanus.

The chief symptom of "lockjaw" is a continued tonic contraction of the muscles, which begins with a stiffness in the neck, passes thence to the muscles of the lower jaw and face, and finally affects the whole spinal column. When fully developed, the spinal column is bent backwards, the breast arched forwards, and the epigastrium drawn in. Everything is rigid. The jaws are closed, the teeth firmly shut, and the features distorted (*risus sardonicus*). In many instances, the tension of the muscles is increased spasmodically, whereby the body is hurled violently forward, the head buried in the pillows, and the tongue bitten. After a short duration of the lockjaw, death generally occurs, from paralysis of the lungs and heart.

A local irritation of the nervous system plays the chief part in producing these greatly dreaded symptoms. Wounds are the chief cause of tetanus, especially gunshot wounds, but all lacerated and punctured wounds may produce it. Tetanus may set in immediately after the wound has been received, during its cleansing, during suppuration, and preferably even during and after cicatrization. Improper treatment, the presence of foreign substances in the scar, and tension exerted on the nerves by cicatricial tissue, are influential. In any case a permanent disturbance of the central nervous system proceeds from the wound. This is not particularly painful, but is so peculiar, that in consequence of the cumulative irritation, increased reflex activity is permanently established. Once established, even a slight touch or a sudden draft will occasion a renewed outbreak of the above-described, powerful reflex spasms. For this reason cold has been advanced as an immediate cause of the tetanic spasm, and every one who has witnessed the outbreak of tetanus on the battle-field will admit that there is some truth in the matter.

Shock.

If a large number of sensitive nerve fibres be irritated at one time, as occurs occasionally in great surgical operations and other severe lesions, the subsequent irritation of the central nervous system resembles the effect produced by a stroke of lightning. In death by lightning, we assume an excessive and irreparable alteration in the molecular structure of the nervous system. The lesions in shock are probably of the same nature. Its symptoms are: deathly faintness, pallor of the face, weak heart and slowed respiration, resulting in immediate or gradual death. Apart from this fatal form of shock, there are a number of milder varieties; among them, the transient feeling of faintness which is produced by a slight blow on the stomach. Everywhere the process results from a concussion of the molecular structure of the central nervous system, which possesses the physiological value of an irritation affecting chiefly the centres of respiration and those which preside over the heart.

III. PHYSIOLOGICAL EXTENSION OF DISEASE.

SYMPATHETIC GROUPS OF SYMPTOMS.

INTRODUCTION.

A new series of typical groups of symptoms arises from the fact that each organ of the body plays a certain part, or does not play it, not only for itself, but also for the entire organism, whether normal or deranged.

The work contributed by the various organs differs widely in relative value, and the diseased conditions to be described in this section are, in consequence, very varied, as regards "danger to life." There is, however, no part without its function, and in every local disorder a consideration of this fact may aid us to foretell what symptoms will follow a cessation or an impairment of the function of an organ. In many instances, such consideration leads us to a well-marked typical group of symptoms; in others, again, it fails us. To the symptoms of the *functio læsa* are added additional symptoms, which arise from the desire of the organism to substitute the disturbed function by the work of the healthy parts. We must consider whether and how far these so-called vicarious functions accomplish their object, and whether the organs implicated in this unusual work do or do not suffer in consequence. We only assert that the mingling of the symptoms of the *functio vicaria* with those of the *functio læsa* produces in many cases the "typical symptoms" which are pathognomonic of disease in a circumscribed portion of the body.

A. VEGETATIVE DISTURBANCES.

Man's vegetative organs are divided into three classes: those presiding over hæmatosis; those presiding over the circulation of the blood; those which purify the blood. The effects of their operation must be considered conjointly. The organism must be richly provided with good and pure nutritive material, of a constant composition and temperature, as a necessary preliminary to a thriving nutrition. Where, however, one of the organs fails to do its work, the failure is apparent, first, in a quantitative or qualitative deterioration of the blood, or in a sluggish circulation, according as the digestive tract and the spleen, the heart and the blood vessels, or the lungs, kidneys, and liver are respectively the seat of the local trouble. The second result of the failure is a disturbance of the general function of the vegetative system, *i. e.*, the nutritive blood supply of the body and its parts. Thus we separate from the special group of symptoms a general one, which may be designated as Disturbances of Nutrition, resulting from insufficient blood supply.

I. DISTURBANCES OF NUTRITION.

This general range of symptoms takes the precedence of all others. As I write the heading, however, I feel inclined to question the manner in which it is usually employed. Are not, in point of fact, all the changes which we have considered,—inflammation and the formation of tumors, metastases and fever, indeed almost every disease,—disturbances of nutrition as well? We must, therefore, limit ourselves to those disturbances of nutrition which are such in the strict sense of the word, *i. e.*, the arrest or abolition of normal assimilation, which is the general result of poor and insufficient blood. But might they not also be the product of totally different factors, such as direct injury to the cells and tissues by chemical, physical, or other agents, or perhaps from disturbances of normal innervation? Without doubt. But we need not regard these minor considerations. On the other hand the "typical, universally accepted" character of these changes is the more distinctly illustrated, when we perceive that they re-appear in a similar manner as a result of the most varied causes.

When the skin and the visible mucous membranes are bloodless, the eyes sunken, the lips dry, the energy gone, and the weight diminished, we say a person is badly nourished, debilitated and decrepid. A portion of these symptoms may be referred directly to a decrease and deterioration of the blood, such as paleness and absence of color in the skin; others are indirectly traceable to a change in the excitability of the nervous system, and to consumption of the tissues of the body. We also foresee that a continued operation of cause and effect will, ultimately, prove fatal to the diseased body.

If we investigate the matter more closely, and examine such a body microscopically, we are soon convinced that decay is imprinted, not alone upon the prominent features of an individual, but can also be demonstrated in the individual parts. We find certain typical changes occurring in cells and tissues, which characterize the retrogression of nutrition, and perceive that these changes, appearing in certain places in the otherwise healthy body, disturb the regular process of assimilation.

The death of cells and tissues stands at the head of the cellular pathological conditions. Death is the suspension of activity in living matter, produced by an excessive alteration in the chemico-physical constituents of a part. In the abstract, death is always a sudden event, but it is possible that it may be preceded by an alteration of the living tissue, shorter or longer in duration, so that a sudden or gradual loss of function may represent a stage between life and death. Gradual decay is called "Necrobiosis," sudden death, "Necrosis." It is not, however, possible to lay down a strict line of division, because it is rarely possible to fix the exact moment at which death becomes inevitable.

(a) NECROSIS.

If a living cell be treated with various chemical or physical agents, due care being taken not to overstep a certain moderate degree of intensity, we notice that the vital mobility of the part, so far as this is visible, is excited or increased. The colorless blood corpuscles become more active, the cilia of the cylindrical epithelium lash themselves to and fro. But, on the other hand, if the cells be treated with the same agents increased in strength, if, for example, a colorless blood corpuscle be heated a few degrees higher than its normal temperature, or be placed in distilled water, dilute acids or alkalies, or subjected to a strong electrical current, we notice that it contracts into the smallest possible compass, becomes granular, cloudy and globular, then breaks down and dissolves.

In the above succession of phenomena we have the general anatomical picture of the simple death of a cell, viz., a rigidity or "rigor" (Erstarrung), followed by a breaking down of the protoplasm.

This rigidity is due to the coagulation of an albuminous substance dissolved in the living protoplasm. By interpreting it as a last tonic contraction, we accept, to a certain degree, the supposition that vital contractility depends upon a transitory consolidation of a liquid substance. This view is borne out by the fact that, under favorable circumstances, this "rigor" of death passes over, and cells which are completely motionless again resume their full activity. Motionless colorless blood corpuscles become active upon the addition of a weak salt solution, those which are inactive through excessive heat, by lowering the temperature. We can produce in the colorless blood corpuscle of a frog, by means of a solution of quinine or carbolic acid, a rigidity which may last for hours before the corpuscles again resume their activity. But if this rigidity has become irrevocable, the subsequent dissolution of the cells is only a matter of time. (See Cloudy Swelling, p. 31).

Simple necrosis acts upon all protoplasmic constituents of the animal body, as upon the colorless blood corpuscles. Modifications are produced, on one hand, by a change of external conditions, on the other, by the transformation of protoplasm into another tissue.

Red blood corpuscles appear to dissolve without previous contraction. But might not the coagulation of the blood be regarded as their death? It has never been asserted that the liquor sanguinis lives, but if we accept the fact that coagulation of the blood is prevented entirely through the influence of the living blood vessel wall, is it possible to regard this influence otherwise than as a species of vivification of those albuminous elements which, in the coagulated state, are fibrin? We shall revert to the subject.

We must admit that the hardening and contraction of the muscles of the body, which generally sets in rapidly after death, is rightly named "rigor mortis." Rigor mortis is also observed in single muscular fibres. It is accompanied by a granular cloudiness of the contractile substance. This cloudiness is somewhat increased before dissolution. A species of rigor is also observable in nerves. Probably the so-called coagulation of the nerve medulla may be regarded as such.

The intercellular substances suffer the least change before liquefaction. We can scarcely perceive a cloudiness, to say nothing of a coagulation. The calcareous osseous tissue obstinately resists liquefaction, and lasts for centuries.

Of course, the above described changes take place only when sufficient moisture is present to liquefy the dead parts, and when there is no obstacle to the chemical changes associated with the liquefaction.

Moist gangrene becomes dry gangrene by evaporation. When a dead part is completely dessicated, it lasts for thousands of years, as in the case of Egyptian mummies. Again, corpses lying on moist clay, and continually bathed with moisture, are transformed into a soap-like substance, called adipocere. This substance is also very durable, and resists decomposition.

(b) SIMPLE ATROPHY.

Simple Atrophy is that diminution in the volume of a part, which, as revealed by the microscope, is due to a corresponding wasting of the elements of the parenchyma. An atrophied muscular fibre is narrower than the normal, an atrophied fat cell contains less fat than normal; in other respects, its appearance is natural, or nearly so. We frequently observe a brown pigmentation of the atrophied cells, without being able to state in a single case where or how it was formed. The cells of the heart muscle produce a brownish-yellow pigment, which is situated in the small masses of protoplasm above and below the nucleus, the striæ being distinct as usual. In the atrophied liver-cell there appears regularly a granular, yellowish-brown pigment, shading into black. One would be tempted to attribute this to the coloring matter of the bile, if we could prove it by micro-chemical reactions. The fat in atrophied fat cells is colored brown; this can be readily perceived with the naked eye, although the origin of the color is extremely uncertain.

Simple atrophy is primarily the outward expression of a general lowering of the processes of nutrition. The immediate cause of this might well be diminution in the quantity and in the arterial pressure of the blood. Again, simple atrophy occurs in local diseases of organs, especially when these are associated with a gradual retardation of the intermediary nutritive changes, occurring in single large or small portions of the parenchyma (closure, compression of blood vessels, etc.)

(c) FATTY, MUCOUS, COLLOID DEGENERATION.

There exists, besides simple or quantitative atrophy, another series of disturbances of nutrition in the tissues, which are typified in the physiological development of the epithelial cells. As the epithelial cells continue to grow they remove farther and farther from their original place, which is usurped by their progeny, and the nutritive fluid must, in consequence, travel farther to reach them. This circumstance, combined with the pre-established law of epithelial growth, causes the structure of the older cells to undergo changes, which, being in the nature of a gradual dying out, are entitled to be styled necrobiotic. In the careful economy of the human system nothing goes to waste, and so this death and separation of the epithelial cells is put to a practical use, viz., the dessicated epidermal cells are converted into a thick and impervious crust, the horny layer of the epidermis (*keratin*). The mucus which overspreads the surface of the mucous membranes owes its origin to a mucous exudation of the epithelia of the mucous membranes and glands (*mucin*). The epithelia which cover the closed follicles of the thyroid gland furnish the colloid substance, which flows in and fills to expansion the lumen of the vesicles, a process which would very well harmonize with the suspected function of the gland. The ovary is ruptured by the discharge of a similar substance in menstruation. The fatty metamorphosis of the epithelia of the mammary glands leads to lactation; that of the sebaceous glands to the formation of sebaceous matter. Beside all these there are many metamorphoses of glandular epithelia which lead to the ferment-endowed secretions of saliva, gastric juice, etc.

Of these metamorphoses, the fatty, mucous and colloid are those chiefly met with among pathological necrobioses. All three lead to the formation of such chemical products as are soluble in water, or, at least, absorb it readily, on which account they are apt to appear to the naked eye as softenings or liquefactions. The loss of consistency proceeds by an almost imperceptible process, in which the normally tough and elastic tissue passes through various stages of pulpy maceration till it finally resolves itself into fluctuating centres of liquefaction. If this stage continue, and the softened matter is not liberated, the liquefying centre becomes by continued breaking down more and more distinct from the surrounding parenchyma, and forms a *cyst*, which we distinguish from the membranous (retention) cyst by calling it a *softening cyst*.

DISTURBANCES OF NUTRITION.

Fatty Degeneration.

Fatty degeneration is a gradual but certain liquefaction of cell protoplasm and other albuminous and albuminoid structures, which is initiated by the appearance of fat-drops in the centre of the part. Under the microscope, these drops look like small, dark points and granules. They increase by degrees, and often unite into medium-sized drops, though never into a single large one. The substratum becomes, at last, so completely permeated that it resembles a mass of dark granules.

In the degeneration of single cells, we have, at this stage of the metamorphosis, the "compound granule cell." The old cell outlines are no longer distinct, because the fat-drops penetrate to and project beyond the outer surface. The corners and edges of the normal cell have vanished, and the whole is converted into a spherical ball. The nucleus and nucleolus are not perceptible, but can be made so by treating them with carmine.

The compound granule cell is, nevertheless, not the invariable product of the fatty degeneration of a single cell. If the fatty degeneration attack a connective tissue provided with stellate cells, and the liquefaction of the cell is preceded by the usual dissolution of intercellular substance, the aggregated fat-drops are stellate, like the cells which they replace.

In degeneration of the striated muscles, the fat-drops form, at first, rows of pearly beads running parallel with the fibrils. As they multiply, and become more evenly distributed throughout the muscular fibres, the stronger refractive power of the fat-drops overcomes the optical effect of the muscle, and the striation disappears. Tiny, dust-like fat-drops form upon the muscular cells of the heart; the striation disappears here also, and is replaced by an even and finely punctated exterior.

Moderate degrees of fatty degeneration are compatible with a continuance of life, and the re-establishment of normal conditions. When, however, the degenerated tissue has become thoroughly impregnated with fat-drops, we may assume that the vital functions have ceased to act, and that the further adhesion of the fat-globules is purely mechanical.

With a sufficient amount of moisture, we may expect to see the fat-drops disorganize and emulsify into a milky fluid, called "fatty detritus." This is absorbed as readily as milk would be into the lymphatics and carried away. The condition of re-absorption must be unusually unfavorable if this fatty detritus is permitted to remain and undergo further change. The same process occurs in yellow softening of centrally-situated parts of the brain; the thick layer of brain substance surrounding the centre of softening cannot sink in, in case the fatty detritus be absorbed, neither can the skull. Consequently, the fatty detritus must remain, as if to fill in the breach. Also when fatty detritus has accumulated in the tough intima of arteries, there is no possibility of absorption. The mass, which becomes thick and doughy, and contains quantities of glistening cholesterin crystals, is called, from a fancied resemblance to gruel, " atheromatous pulp."

So much for the morphology of fatty degeneration. The most important of all its phenomena is the formation of fat by the splitting up of albuminous substance, a fact indubitably proved by physiological chemistry. We assume that in true fatty degeneration the albumen, which constitutes a part of the cell protoplasm and its derivatives, is disorganized into fatty and other products, and that the well-known insolubility of fat in a watery medium makes it visible in the interior of the degenerated part. The organized remainder acts for a time as a cement upon the whole, but yielding gradually, it becomes soluble (casein, sodic albuminate), after which its complete disintegration and conversion into a pathological milk is merely a question of time and opportunity.

Mucous Metamorphosis.

Mucin is a product of cell albumen, without sulphur, and noted for its tendency to swell up. Mucus is furnished not only by cells, but also by the matrix of the various connective tissue substances, viz., the connective tissue fibres and the matrix of cartilage and of bones. Whenever, therefore, we meet with mucin, we may be sure that it comes directly from cells or their derivates. Its manner of origin is comparatively simple. The cell protoplasm becomes homogeneous, and concentrates in constantly increasing bulk around the nucleus, where there is gradually formed a spherical drop, which increases in transparency, and upon the addition of acetic acid, shows a stringy, mucous coagulum. The drop in growing displaces the nucleus, which, after the complete disintegration of the protoplasm, breaks down into a heap of glistening fragments, which persist for some time.

The matrix of the connective tissue and cartilage becomes soft, transparent, and spongy. The addition of acetic acid betrays the mucous metamorphosis by a distinct cloudiness. Little by little the constituents dissolve, although the original shape may be retained for a considerable time by the addition of acetic acid, which produces a sort of coagulation.

The macroscopical effect of mucous degeneration is highly characteristic. Since the mucus is not soluble, it is perceptible even in small quantities. It imparts to fluids a "stringiness;" to solids, a "slippery property." When a tissue has undergone complete mucous degeneration, it assumes a "gelatinous, trembling" consistence.

Colloid Metamorphosis.

Colloid metamorphosis, called by Von Recklinghausen "hyaline," is very closely allied to mucous degeneration. The colloid substance absorbs water with equal eagerness, and yields solutions, which, though very similar, are of a more synovial character than those of mucin. The colloid substance forms with water a large number of combinations of varying consistency. One, in particular, greatly resembles partially dissolved glue, from which appearance the name "colloid" was derived. The colloid matter itself contains sulphur, and is fundamentally an albuminous body, but differs from albumen and all other protein-substances by the absence of characteristic chemical reactions. It does not coagulate when subjected to heat, and may be kept for years in alcohol without losing its translucency. It is also not acted upon by the chemical juices of the body, as, for instance, the gastric juice. Its power of resistance increases with age, but it yields, finally, though slowly, to decomposition.

Colloid matter is formed, partly in cells, partly from albumen which has been deposited in the neighborhood of such cells or elsewhere and not re-absorbed. In the latter case, there is a gelatinous formation, such as may be produced in the serum by a temperature of 69° C. (156.2° F.) In the former, the colloid drop appears beside the nucleus in the protoplasm, and, as in mucous metamorphosis, the nucleus and cell contents about it are first compressed and finally dissolved and absorbed. The large colloid masses which then arise coalesce into a hyaline contexture, in which, later, vacuoles and fissures are often perceptible.

It may be said to be almost a matter of individual taste,

whether another peculiar, albuminous, dropsical softening is to be reckoned among the mucous and colloid degenerations. An abundant permeation with stagnating blood serum leads, naturally, to a certain swelling and liquefaction of the cells and tissues, which are, however devoid of characteristic morphological characters.

(d) CALCIFICATION.

Calcification (petrifaction) is the infiltration of cells and tissues with the carbonate and phosphate of lime, together with a slight amount of phosphate of magnesium. The deposit is in the shape of the smallest, dust-like molecules, which, when placed under the microscope, appear white and glistening by reflected light, but by transmitted light are of a dark color, and disappear upon the addition of muriatic acid. As the deposit becomes more dense, the part, even to the naked eye, presents a dull white, calcareous color, and varies to the touch, from a rough, pumice-like feeling to a compact, stony hardness. With all this, the original form of the part is faithfully maintained in the calcification, and can at any time, by a judicious application of muriatic acid, be restored.

In calcified ganglion-cells of the brain, the pointed offshoots and the pyramidal form are at once recognized; in a calcified *tunica media arteriarum*, we see the transverse bundles of muscles; and in a calcified cheesy focus of the lungs, the conical shape of the phthisical lobule.

There is no doubt but that the salts of lime, which are deposited in the calcifying parts, are derived from the nutritive fluid. Except in very rare instances (as in calcareous metastases, in extensive absorptions of the osseous system), this is not the result of an unusual accumulation of salts of lime in the blood. The chemical reasons for calcification are, consequently, to be sought in the special peculiarities of the different parts. The first and foremost agency is the all but complete stoppage in the flow of the parenchymatous juices. It is, therefore, principally dead parts which become superficially encrusted with calcareous deposits. In this manner, the small round blood coagula of the vein plexuses are converted into vein-stones (phlebolithes); the cheesy lobes of the phthisical lung become lung-stones (pneumoliths); and even entire embryos, which have arrived at maturity and died in the free abdominal cavity, become petrified to a depth of one-half a centimetre (lithopædion).

Second in importance is the petrifaction of the products of pathological overgrowth, whose demands for nutrition can only be incompletely satisfied by the existing nutritive apparatus. The most simple and striking example of this is found in the calcification of the inflamed and thickened intima of the heart and arteries. The intima being, even in its inflamed condition, devoid of blood vessels, suffers from an impeded flow of nutritive fluid, and the thickest spots petrify. The calcification of certain tumors, like the enchondromata and fibromata, comes under this head.

Then follow the senile calcifications, which, generally stated, denote a deterioration of the nutritive juice current, and which gradually have for their type the physiological calcification of cartilage in osteogenesis.

II. DERANGEMENTS OF THE CIRCULATION.

When disturbances of circulation arise in the heart or large blood vessels we call them general or central; when they arise in small branches or twigs we call them local. In the neighborhood of the heart, and in the heart itself, the circulatory apparatus is limited to a single path. Here, too, the chief mechanical force of the circulation resides, hence anatomical changes occurring here influence the whole circulation, while disturbances of the circulation occurring in the capillaries or small arterial or venous territory rarely have much effect upon the general circulation.

This division is as well marked, and at the same time as illy defined, as the division of the circulation into main trunk and branches. If all the branches or only the greater portion, be affected by an anatomical change, the disturbance will, as a matter of course, be transmitted to the general circulation, precisely as if the main trunk were affected. In this manner lung disease and affections of the arteries often produce general disturbances of the circulation.

The local disturbances of the circulation have already been dwelt upon to a certain extent in connection with metastases (Thrombosis and Embolism). The following brief consideration partakes, consequently, more of the character of a scientific summary. Active hyperæmia is no disturbance, but rather an assistance, to the circulation.

LOCAL DERANGEMENTS.
ARTERIAL.
Ischæmia and Collateral Circulation.

The moment we ligate an artery leading to a certain part, the blood current is, of course, arrested, and the muscular walls of the artery, thus cut off from the general circulation, contract and force the blood for the last time through the capillaries into the veins. The part is now, as far as possible, in a bloodless condition (Ischæmia—local arterial anæmia. Virchow). The same thing happens when the artery is compressed or obstructed. Whether the entire region supplied by the artery is to remain empty depends upon circumstances. Most of the arteries of our body have collateral branches. For this reason the bloodless condition of a part only lasts for a short time, and by the so-called development of collateral circulation the endangered territory is soon provided with a bountiful supply of blood. This system has, however, its defects. It is plain that the articular branches of the knee are not sufficient to carry on the functions of the obstructed popliteal. Indeed, there are vascular areas in which the main trunk and its branches are arteries which have no collateral circulation, *i. e.*, end-arteries. It is with these as with an actual tree, when a large or small branch is broken off every thing beyond the break is lost.

The vascular territory of a small end-artery can be filled, and even over-filled, from the veins *a fronte*, especially if there is much blood pressure. The weak and distended capillary walls are now liable to burst and allow the blood to escape either into the parenchyma or externally; the part becomes excessively distended with blood—infarcted—a process dwelt upon at length on page 71 in connection with metastasis. This blood does not flow, and the interchangement of the blood particles being below normal, is nearly or wholly arrested. When a large end-artery is occluded, there ensues a permanent absence of blood in the organ, which is then followed by a rapid death.

Every disturbance of the circulation may, in reality, be regarded from two standpoints. We have thus far* only considered the condition of the territory from which the blood

---

* I again call attention to the description of the metastatic processes, p. 58, *et seq.*

has been cut off. We must now speak of the changes occurring on the other side of the obstruction.

First in importance is a general rise of arterial pressure, proportional to the size of the obstacle, and extending backward into the aorta, causing a corresponding increase in the work of the left ventricle of the heart. This rise in pressure is, however, only transient. After a short time, one or more of the pervious arteries dilate strongly, and while the general arterial pressure returns to normal, there arises in the region supplied by the above-mentioned arteries a condition called collateral hyperæmia. Those blood vessels situated immediately posterior to the obstruction are by no means those which always experience this collateral dilatation. This only occurs when these branches are able to carry, in the most direct manner, the necessary blood to the threatened parts; so, for instance, the numerous anastomosing muscular and intestinal blood vessels. But if the internal carotid of one side be obstructed, it is not the external carotid of the same side which becomes dilated, but instead the internal carotid of the opposite side. The collateral dilatation is thus determined by the need of the organism, demanding, primarily, blood for the disabled organ, and, secondarily, for that which assumes vicariously the function of that organ. Thus in the total isolation of an artery of the kidney, only one of the numerous arteries of the lower part of the body dilates, viz., the artery of the second kidney, and the collateral hyperæmia of this organ, which eventually produces a collateral hypertrophy, is sufficient to cause the secretion of all urinary products from the blood.

Here again we encounter that mysterious understanding between the organs of our body, *i. e.*, the vascular and nervous systems, which, even in active hyperæmia, awakens our well-deserved astonishment, and reminds one of the original consecutive unity of all processes, where a demand need only be expressed to be at once supplied.

VENOUS DERANGEMENTS.

Congestion and Œdema.

In order to understand the effects, as well as the non-effects, of a local interruption of the venous blood current, we must call to mind certain features of normal anatomy. First of all, we will contrast the considerable length of the venous channels with those of the arterial. Two veins of nearly equal size return the blood from a part supplied by an artery of half their common calibre. These veins, together with their small branches, form numerous anastomoses and so-called plexuses. In addition to this, there is almost everywhere a peripheral network, i. e., an arrangement on the periphery of a part, of a venous network, which can be employed in case the chief channels are temporarily blockaded or obstructed by muscular contraction. As such substitutes we may regard the ramifications of the saphenous, basilic, external jugular, azygos, and hemiazygos veins. Also in some glandular organs, viz., in the lungs, we find peripheral plexuses in the interstitial tissue surrounding the lobules. In short, nature seems to have considered the possibility that a venous trunk might sometimes become impervious to the circulation, and to have provided for the emergency by establishing numerous accessory veins, and also by availing herself of external pressure to contract the veins and strengthen the blood current. From what has already been said, we see that the pathological compression or the plugging up of any single peripheral vein is followed by little or no disturbance in the integrity of the circulation.

But it is a different matter when the majority, and sometimes all, the veins of a certain territory are completely obliterated, as we have seen in thrombosis, or when certain tissues or prominent parts are strangulated (strangulated hernia). The above conditions are easily produced by artificial means; among them may be classed acute *obstructive* or *static congestion*, or *venous hyperæmia*. The most prominent symptoms are a dark bluish (cyanotic) discoloration, a swelling which slowly increases, and a perceptible diminution in the external temperature of the congested part. The visible veins are over-distended, markedly convoluted, or spiral-shaped; the valves appear as nodules.

The microscopical appearances are best observed in the leg of a frog, after the femoral vein has been ligated. The veins, capillaries, and even the arteries, distend moderately, the blood moves more and more slowly, until the motion becomes spasmodic and synchronous with the systole of the heart. The blood corpuscles adhere so closely together that their individual contours are finally lost, and the whole appears as a continuous, red column. After the lapse of forty-five minutes, small, roundish, sacciform elevations are seen projecting from the walls of the capillaries, whereat an outwandering of the red blood corpuscles begins. They escape through the little crevices, which here enlarge to form real stomata, at the junction of the capillary endothelial cells. The blood emerges in small, round drops, and remains temporarily in the connective tissue. In the course of three or four days the red blood corpuscles lose their hæmoglobin, which, being set free, causes a diffuse and granular coloration of the surrounding fluids and tissues. This coloration will be considered later, under the head of Hemorrhage and Pigmentation.

We must at this point consider another important consequence of acute passive congestion, the so-called stagnation-œdema (Stauungsödem), *i. e.*, the escape of a certain amount of the fluid matter of the blood from the dilated capillaries. This is the direct consequence of the unusual amount of lateral pressure exerted upon the weak capillaries, and may be regarded simply as a mechanical filtration of liquor sanguinis. This exuded fluid (the transudate) contains the usual definite proportion of salts and water, but much less albumen than blood serum, so that it can be called a very thin serum. The fluid penetrates the connective tissue in all directions, fills up all the clefts, and collects in large pools in the preformed interstices of the connective tissue. Finally, it oozes out wherever possible, upon the surface, and the part in question swells up and becomes doughy. Its further fate depends upon the removal or non-removal of the obstruction to the circulation. In the former event, everything returns to the normal state, while in the latter, moist gangrene is very apt to set in.

The chronic form of venous congestion arises (1) where a permanent compression or plugging occurs in the majority but not all of the efferent veins of a certain region, so that the reflux of the blood is hampered but not completely arrested; (2) as the indirect result of general weakness and distensibility of the venous system. We know how weak an impulse venous blood receives. That imparted by the heart to the circulation is perceptible, although greatly weakened, beyond the capillaries, and, being transmitted thence to the veins gives an additional impulse to the blood contained in them. This power is, however, insufficient to propel the blood against the force of gravity from the extremities back to the heart; and were it not that valves are placed at intervals to prevent the reflux of blood, and did not occasional contractions of the muscles force the blood towards the heart, the venous circulation of the extremities would be badly off. We can, therefore, no longer wonder that abnormal collections of blood occur the moment even an auxiliary factor of the circulation fails to do its duty, and that people who are forced to lead sedentary lives, and do not use their thigh muscles, are afflicted with varicose veins and hemorrhoids. The yielding nature of the venous walls aids this dilatation, and confirms the diseased condition by making the return to normal, in time, impossible.

We are thus brought face to face with a consequence of special moment in the pathology of numerous organs, viz., we may expect that all continued or repeatedly-recurring hyperæmias, be they inflammatory, recurrent, passive, or collateral, will produce in the venous system a tendency to a permanent dilatation. This dilatation will be strong in proportion to the weakness of the vein-wall and its lack of power to contract to its normal calibre after being for a long time excessively distended. This is especially true of the sinuses of the brain; accordingly, we find a passive hyperæmia of the *pia mater convexa*, accompanied by marked dilatation and sinuosity of the veins, and by a watery exudate in the sub-arachnoid space (external hydrocephalus), the inevitable result of the most varied and prolonged hyperæmias of the brain (psychoses, alcohol, etc.) In the latter case, particularly, one phenomenon is observable which seems to characterize equally all chronic congestive hyperæmias, viz., a hyperplastic condition of the perivascular connective tissue, especially that of the veins. It appears here as a milky cloudiness of the pia mater, in other parts as an induration (kidney), and more rarely as a partial shrinking (liver).

HEMORRHAGE.

In view of the rapid advance made in medical science within the last few decades, and the many radical changes of opinion attendant upon such advance, it is reassuring to approach one subject, the views with regard to which have for years undergone no substantial modifications. Such is hemorrhage. The sudden and often fatal character of hemorrhages has always caused them to be regarded with peculiar interest both by physicians and laymen, and the comparative simplicity of the attendant conditions enables us to form rapidly a correct diagnosis.

The escape of blood always presupposes a solution in the continuity of the blood vessel wall. It may be produced 1, by locally increased blood pressure upon the otherwise normal blood vessel walls (Diapedesis, Anastomosis); 2, by normal blood pressure when the vascular walls have become weakened (Diæresis, Erosion, Rhexis). Hemorrhage is subject to certain definite laws, *i. e.*, it takes place when and as long as the blood pressure within the softened blood vessel walls is more powerful than the resistance which the escaping blood meets from without. The amount of blood lost is limited in the same manner, and this in turn determines the fatality or non-fatality of the hemorrhage.

I. The frequent occurrence of hemorrhages in hyperæmic affections is abundant proof that the mere increase of lateral pressure in any given part of the circulatory apparatus is enough to produce rupture and hemorrhage. The capillary walls are, as a general thing, so fragile that they are in many cases even unable to withstand either inflammatory or congestive hyperæmia.

Under these circumstances, the blood exudes in minute drops through fine openings in the capillary wall. This process was designated diapedesis, even at a time when blood corpuscles and their migration were not dreamed of. We should now call it "extravasation." The histological details of diapedesis were given under the head of venous hyperæmia, which section I would recommend for re-perusal. The continuation of the process depends upon what becomes of the blood outside the capillary wall. In a thick, unelastic parenchyma, like that of the brain, the extravasated blood forms at the point of rupture a small round drop 0.001 mm. ($\frac{1}{2500}$ in.) in diameter, which is not absorbed, but undergoes instead further metamorphoses. (See remarks upon capillary hemorrhage in my Manual of Pathological Histology).

When not opposed by the parenchyma, the blood corpuscles spread through the interstices of the connective tissue, and penetrate in this way the beginnings of the lymphatics, reaching also the neighboring free surfaces, with whose secretions they become incorporated, and impart to the same a hemorrhagic character. Such hemorrhagic secretions are particularly frequent in the mucous membranes of the digestive tract in people suffering from heart disease, where the induced congested state of the liver backs up the blood in the radicles of the portal vein, finding a favorable spot for diapedesis in the soft and superficial venous capillaries, which are, in reality, intended for the purpose of absorption.

The bloody stools in heart and liver diseases were known to Hippocrates as μελαινα χολη. This blood discharge per rectum frequently appears black, owing to the changes it undergoes in passing through the intestines. The blood which is vomited from the bottom and sides of carcinomatous ulcers of the stomach resembles coffee-grounds, because the blood which extravasates drop by drop coagulates immediately, and becomes brown under the action of the acid gastric juice.

• Not all blood corpuscles, however, are absorbed or excreted. A large share of them remain, as a rule, in the porous parenchyma, and lead to the formation of pigment-granules, which, after the lapse of years, still remain to testify of the extravasation. Many are of a rusty color, and give to the affected parts, i. e., membranes, a highly characteristic, yellowish-red, or brownish-black appearance. Under the microscope, we see mostly round bodies of an intense yellow color, aggregated together in clusters containing from three to ten, and attached to the external surface of the blood vessels, whose ramifications they follow. The detailed observations which have been made of late, as to the manner in which these clusters originate from the extravasated blood corpuscles, will be found recorded in my Pathological Histology. According to these observations, every yellowish-red body corresponds to a number of former red blood corpuscles or their coloring matter. Peroxide of iron predominates in these pigments above all other chemicals.

II. The second form of hemorrhage is that, where, with normal blood pressure, a deep mechanical injury to the body effects a solution in the continuity of the blood vessel wall (Diæresis). In *diæresis* we have to consider, apart from the calibre of the blood vessel, and the existing blood pressure, the rigidity or weakness of the blood vessel wall, its contractility, and the manner in which the solution of continuity takes place. Incisions into large arteries are extremely dangerous, for, although the arteries may contract forcibly on the wound, their lumen is, nevertheless, still large enough to cause, with the assistance of the blood pressure, a fatal escape of blood. In ruptures of the medium-sized and smaller arteries, the highly-elastic and contractile arterial walls contract upon themselves, and close the lumen in most cases so effectually that the hemorrhage is often temporarily arrested. I have seen, repeatedly, lacerations of the axillary artery where no great amount of hemorrhage occurred.

Wounds of veins are, in the main, less dangerous, providing they do not occur in the region of the respiratory apparatus, in which case the air sucked in through the proximal opening produces, the moment it reaches the heart and lungs, immediate death. Venous wounds are only dangerous in veins of large calibre, and in those which possess either a stiff, unyielding wall, or are attached to an unyielding parenchyma, which cannot collapse. The sinuses of the dura mater and the hepatic veins are examples of such blood vessels. Even lacerations of these, as well as of the blood vessels of a fibroma of the uterus, are extremely serious, on account of the difficulty in checking the hemorrhage.

Diabrosis is the erosion of a blood vessel by a destructive process attacking it from without. It occurs chiefly in simple or specific ulcerations, and in pulmonary and intestinal ulcerations growing in the vicinity of a large artery. The wall of the blood vessel at its most exposed point becomes infiltrated in the same manner as the surrounding connective tissue. When the infiltration has reached a certain stage, the supporting connective tissue and muscle fibres begin to dissolve, and the infiltrate, which is composed chiefly of round cells, is no longer able to resist the blood pressure. The diseased spot is apt first to protrude a little, resembling a small, pouch-like aneurism, until finally the blood ruptures the vulnerable point, and its flow, even in smaller vessels, is very difficult to check. The conditions are more favorable when the vessel is attacked *a fronte*, and not in its continuity—as occasionally occurs in gastric ulcers. When all the branches of a blood vessel are involved in such a process it often happens that the entire vessel becomes thrombosed up to its origin, and if erosion occur then, there is very little difference between it and a lateral rupture.

We now reach the laceration or rupture of blood vessels in the strict sense of the word, *i. e.*, hemorrhage by *rhexis*. Here the blood vessel wall is attacked, weakened, and finally broken down by an internal process of destruction. Atheromatous degeneration is that interesting process by which the fatty degeneration of the intima gives rise to a slight hemorrhage of the brain.

All cranial arteries are, we know, provided with unusually thin walls; the closed and bony cranium furnishes, with the aid of the intermediate parenchyma, a sufficient counter pressure for a part of the blood pressure. The adventitia is here a simple connective-tissue lamella. The muscular coat is lacking in the elastic fibres which give to the remaining arteries of the body such a high degree of elasticity and firmness. It consists only of transverse rings of smooth, muscular fibres, joined together sparingly by structureless connective tissue. Its tenacity is the result of the cumulative resistance of the intima which covers its transverse layers uniformly. The intima itself is very frail, consisting, at the artery of the fissure of Sylvius, of only six so-called striated lamellæ, while other arteries of equal calibre have at least fifteen. It is, therefore, intelligible that a process like fatty degeneration of the intima (not to be confounded with atheromatous degeneration, which it often accompanies) easily leads, in the blood vessels of the brain, to a complete destruction of the entire membrane, and threatens the integrity of the blood vessel wall, while in the aorta the same process only produces superficial inequalities of no clinical value. If a passing or perhaps trifling congestion of the brain should now set in—the result, probably, of an intoxicating drink, of prolonged and violent expiration, of straining at stool, of screaming, coughing, etc.—the blood perforates the degenerated intima, forces the transverse bundles of the media apart, and ruptures the slight and unresisting adventitia.

The above-described hemorrhage of the brain occurs in the larger branches of the artery of the fissure of Sylvius. In the smaller branches of the same trunk, especially in their anastomosing branches, it may happen that only the intima and media are ruptured, and the distended adventitia is elastic enough to retain the extravasated blood until the counter-pressure from without checks the further escape of blood (dissecting aneurism). Rhexis also occurs in the capillaries, and leads to the formation of foci, varying in size from a pea to a walnut, wherein the parenchyma is dotted with numerous distinct blood points.

In proportion to the calibre of the bleeding vessel is the danger of a rapid and excessive loss of blood, which may result either in the death of the individual, or in the destruction of the parenchyma, which is flooded, as the result of strong arterial pressure, with a large amount of blood.

In case such hemorrhagic infarcts (Hæmatomata) do not prove instantly fatal, the products of hemorrhage may be gradually re-absorbed, and a partial restoration of the injured part be effected. This happens also in pigmentation, so that, years afterwards, yellowish or brownish marks recall the original lesion. In such situations, besides other amorphous pigments, crystallized "hæmatoidin" is often found, which has latterly been proved to be identical with the bilirubin of normal bile. The granular pigments are composed almost entirely of peroxide of iron.

GANGRENE.

It has been customary to designate one of the sub-orders of local death (Necrosis, p. 93), as gangrene. When the dead part becomes very plentifully or excessively filled with blood, it soon receives from the action of the putrescent blood a diffuse coloring, shading from dark to black. The comparison with the "carbonizing" process is, therefore, not inappropriate.

The blood putrefies rapidly. The first sign of incipient decomposition is the diffusion of the coloring matter from the red blood corpuscles. First the serum becomes colored, then the vessel walls, and finally all the surrounding tissues within the limits of the dead parts. A bluish, livid coloration is visible through the epidermis, until the latter is lost, and the dark red color of the putrescent blood is plainly seen. If dessication is prevented, the color becomes greenish, which finally passes into the grayish-green of decomposition, accompanied by an offensive odor (Moist gangrene, sphacelus). If after the removal of the epidermis, evaporation is not prevented, the atrophied part dries up into a dark mass, which in reality resembles coal (Dry gangrene, mummification).

Among the local disturbances of circulation we find embolism (pp. 72, 102), frequently leading to gangrene; also the strangulation of a part (p. 104) when all the veins are compressed; also, all inflammatory processes, in which the inflammatory retardation of the blood terminates in complete stasis. An abnormal condition of the blood vessel apparatus is always responsible for this unfavorable result. In old men and women, the arteries are often hardened and calcified, and consequently incapable of that arterial congestion which is indispensable to the removal of passive hyperæmia. In other instances, the capillaries themselves are so altered by the inflammatory irritation (for instance, cold) that the adhesion of the blood to the capillary wall overbalances the motive power of the heart, and the blood "sticks," literally speaking, in the capillaries. All cases of gangrene are attributable to one or the other of the above causes. As the relation of the gangrenous part to the general organism is determined by the rules laid down under the head of cicatrization and sequestration, no recapitulation is necessary.

GENERAL DISTURBANCES.

THE HEART.

Preliminary Remarks.—The pathological anatomy of the heart shows us numerous instances of disease, in which the normal functions of the heart are impeded. The most important of these may be briefly mentioned as follows:—

Acute Endocarditis leads to an inflammatory swelling of the mitral or aortic valve, resulting, it may be, in the perforation and carrying away in fragments of the same. *Chronic Endocarditis* is a new formation of hyperplastic, indurated, connective tissue, by which the leaflets are, first of all, thickened; then follow contraction, rigidity, and even calcification. Not infrequently the diseased leaflets become adherent to each other. The valves, being now perforated, disintegrated and retracted, can, at the time when they should most offer resistance to the reflux of the blood, no longer do so, but permit, instead, regurgitation; and, being thickened, rigid and adherent, present a constricted aperture to the outflowing blood, when normally they should be closely pressed against the walls of the heart. Stenosis, therefore, resembles insufficiency in its effects, inasmuch as it impedes the flow of blood through the diseased part.

Chronic Myocarditis is a new formation of hyperplastic, indurated, connective tissue, which produces atrophy of the muscular structure of the heart, and the so-called "fibroid patch" and partial aneurism upon the anterior wall of the left ventricle. With the loss of muscular structure, comes a corresponding diminution of muscular power. Similar effects are produced by all diffused and circumscribed degenerations of the muscular structure of the heart: brown atrophy, in aged and debilitated persons, fatty degeneration, fatty infiltration, abscess of the heart, and tumors, embolism of the coronary arteries, etc. The functional exhaustion of the heart, which, after severe and protracted fevers, brings about the lethal result, is not always accompanied by visible anatomical changes in the muscular substance.

In *Pericarditis* the diastole of the heart is obstructed by the accumulation of free exudate in the pericardium. If adhesions between the pericardial layers ensue, the systole is impeded. Serous and hemorrhagic effusions into the pericardium, as well as the rare pericardial sarcomata, also prevent the normal expansion of the heart. So also do all those large tumors of the mediastinum, which exert mechanical pressure.

However varied and more or less intelligible these changes may be, their influence upon the circulation culminates in a single point, viz., the defective movement of the blood at the centre of the circulatory apparatus; in other words, weakness of the heart. This lessens and almost equalizes the difference in pressure otherwise existing between the arteries and veins—that difference which forces the arterial blood through the capillaries into the veins. The veins now become engorged, and the arteries more and more bloodless. The same effect upon the general circulation is, of course, produced by any obstacle, situated external to the heart in either of the main arterial trunks, which by exhausting the impetus of the blood, depreciates the work of the heart; always providing that the entire transverse calibre of the blood vessel be thus obstructed. Under this head are included changes in the aorta and the pulmonary artery.

Chronic endarteritis causes sclerotic thickening of the intima, which leads either through fatty degeneration to the atheromatous abscesses and ulcers, or through calcification to so-called "ossification of arteries." By all of these the friction of the blood against the arterial wall is heightened and it simpetus lessened. The same effect is noted in calcification of the muscular middle coat, which occurs simultaneously in all medium-sized branches of the aorta. The general distention of the aorta, as well as the circumscribed dilatations known as aneurisms, which are usually the result of endarteritis, obstruct the general circulation in two ways: First, on account of the great amount of blood which they require to fill them, and in a measure withdraw, from the circulation; and, secondly and chiefly, on account of the increased motive power necessary to propel the surplus of arterial blood through them.

In pulmonary emphysema most of the small branches of the pulmonary artery become obliterated. Pleuritic effusions occasionally exert upon the entire lung, including the territory of the pulmonary artery, abnormal pressure, which is detrimental to the return of blood into the left auricle.

Leaving these preliminaries, we will now pass to the consideration of those complicated symptoms which result from disturbances of the heart or equivalent conditions. We will begin with the phenomena which accompany a sudden decrease or failure in the action of the heart.

A. *Sudden Decrease or Failure in the Action of the Heart.*

a. Death from Heart Failure.—Signs of Death.

The immediate result of a definite suspension of the heart's action is death. To ascertain with certainty the death of an individual, we first feel for the radial artery, then place our hand in the neighborhood of the apex beat of the heart, and finding no impulse here, await the appearance of those phenomena which mark the gradual equalization of pressure between the arteries and veins. The first of these is the cessation of movement of the blood in the capillaries, followed by the almost complete emptying of their contents, their elastic tension being no longer overcome by the blood pressure. Other signs of death are pallor of the skin and the sinking in of the eye, *i. e.*, the collapse of the contents of the orbit, together with the eyeball itself. The eyelids remain open, and it is necessary to draw them down over the pupil. All the prominent bodily features become sharply defined, as, for instance, the nose, chin, jaw, and condyles of the joints.

As the pallor increases, the peripheral parts gradually become cold. The latter attacking first the hands and feet, nose, lips and chin, travels to the centre of the body, which retains its warmth, according to circumstances, from twelve to twenty hours.

The blood has in the meantime massed itself in the trunk and main branches of the vena cava and in the heart. The right auricle is greatly engorged, the right ventricle less so. In consequence of the higher temperature retained here for some time, and the associated prolonged vitality of the heart wall, the blood coagulates very gradually, and the blood corpuscles have time to sink, by virtue of their specific gravity, to the bottom of the liquor sanguinis, leaving above them a considerable zone of clear yellow fluid, which, after coagulation, leads to the formation of the gelatinous buffy coat.

Another link in the chain of post-mortem blood changes is the appearance of discolorations (*livores mortis*). The blood being a heavy fluid seeks the lowest level, just as soon as the heart ceases to oppose this tendency. At death the sinking occurs throughout the general circulation. Livid purple spots appear in the dependent portions of the body, which present at their borders the appearance of discolored marble.

A greenish discoloration starting in the abdomen and jugular regions must not be confounded with the *livores mortis*. The former is indicative of approaching decomposition, and begins in the contents of the ileum, which are abundantly infiltrated with bacteria.

Respiration does not always cease with the beats of the heart. Often single deep inspirations occur after the heart is entirely motionless. In rare instances the respiration is prolonged for some minutes, and this tenacity of the respiratory apparatus may often bridge over short intermissions in the action of the heart, as the aspiration and expulsion of the blood by the lungs is an important addition to the mechanical power of the circulation. Upon this circumstance are based the customary efforts at resuscitation by artificial respiration, which are often followed by astonishing results.

The loss of sensibility and motility are the least reliable among post-mortem symptoms. These are only criteria after the muscular structures become perfectly hard and stiff, which is usually coincident with complete coldness of the body. The rigor mortis of individual groups of muscles may, upon occasion, be overcome, but never that of the entire muscular system.

β. Collapse.

Another group of symptoms which often terminates fatally, proceed from a weakening of the heart's action, which is so sudden and decided that the arterial pressure no longer suffices to sustain general circulation. Pulsation in the radial artery and in the heart may possibly be felt, but it is extremely feeble. Capillary circulation is arrested at the periphery of the body. The hands and feet, and even the nose and ears, become cold. The skin becomes pale and lifeless, and adheres closely, as in death, to the underlying parts, the condyles become prominent, the lips recede from the teeth, the eyelids from the eyeballs, and the jaw drops (Facies Hippocratica). Collapse is generally sudden and calls for vigorous measures, the use of stimulants, friction, etc., in order to restore the suspended activity of the heart, and avert a fatal result.

γ. Hypostatic Congestion and Œdema of the Lungs. Apoplexy and Paralysis of the Lungs.

If after a long and exhausting illness the heart is no longer able to contract properly and force the blood into the lungs, it by no means follows that the important influence exerted by inspiration upon the thoracic circulation is removed. Every breath that is drawn sends fresh amounts of venous blood through the right heart into the pulmonary vessels, where, by the effective operation of the valves of the pulmonary artery, and its well-known power of resistance, not a single drop of the aerated blood returns into the right heart. The consequences are self-evident. Following the law of gravity, the blood sinks into the most dependent parts of the lungs, filling them to engorgement (hypostatic congestion). The momentum of the blood steadily decreases and lateral pressure is increased, until a mechanical infiltration of the liquor sanguinis is inevitable. The transudate which, from the admixture of red blood corpuscles, is of a light red color, appears on one side in the pleural cavity, on the other into the alveoli of the lung. In the latter the presence of air is revealed upon auscultation, by crackling râles. After the air is excluded there is a flat percussion note, by which the height of the œdema can be determined with exactitude. When about one-half of the respiratory tract is thus affected, life usually passes away with a few deep inspirations.

Lesser degrees of hypostatic congestion appear as intercurrent symptoms; these either disappear, or form the basis of a future inflammatory affection of the lung. There is, doubtless, a slight degree of local hypostatic congestion in even an ordinary pneumonia, as it is impossible to imagine a large accumulation of blood in the lungs which would not be more or less affected in its distribution by the laws of gravity.

B. *Gradual Weakening of the Heart's Action.*

The great number and complexity of the symptoms accompanying the gradual weakening of the function of the heart are due to the fact that the heart, more than any other organ, is able by its own action to neutralize the effects of unusual and abnormal disturbances. By its function and nutrition it is essentially adapted to cope with the most varied abnormal conditions. Thus we see, side by side with the symptoms of functional weakness, the phenomena of equalization, which often bring about complete compensation for the existing defect. This compensation, although not permanent, often exists for a long time.

a. Compensatory Symptoms.

As it is universally conceded that it is the province of the heart to maintain, by its contractions, normal blood pressure in the systemic and pulmonary circulations, it is evident that an accelerated heart beat will constitute one of the symptoms under discussion. The blood pressure in the aorta and pulmonary artery is directly increased by this acceleration. Palpitation, therefore, is one of the first and persistent signs of impaired activity of the heart. Important, also, is simple hypertrophy of the myocardium, where the heart performs an excessive and abnormal amount of work. In chronic endarteritis, the orifice of the aorta is occasionally so contracted that one can scarcely determine through what crevice or imperceptible aperture the blood passes into the aorta, and yet, by the powerful hypertrophy of the left ventricle, the heart is able to force through continually the requisite supply. The same process is repeated in stenosis of the right and left auriculo-ventricular valves, although there are here auxiliary forces at work.

The direct consequence of every obstruction of the blood paths is naturally an aggregation of blood at the point of obstruction, and a corresponding increase of pressure in the affected portion of the circulatory apparatus. Increased pressure leads to increased dilatation and tension of the blood vessel wall. If, by reason of an insurmountable obstacle, the blood cannot regurgitate, it is plain that the heightened tension of the blood vessel walls in the dilated territory will give a favorable impetus to the forward movement of the blood. This is a decisive factor in the compensation arising from a defective mitral valve. The heightened tension of the pulmonary circulation finds an excellent point of support in the closely-shutting valve system of the pulmonary artery, and its beneficial effects are apparent even in view of its serious concomitants, viz., hyperæmia of the lungs, dilatation of the capillaries, brown induration, and the danger of hemorrhagic infarcts, not to mention the constant and annoying bronchial catarrh. The healthy mitral valve is also a firm point of support for the development of a compensatory dilatation of the left ventricle, in cases of defect of the aortic valves. Without this, the existing muscular hypertrophy would be insufficient to supply the aorta with blood, especially when, on account of an insufficiency of the valve, there is a certain diastolic regurgitation of aortic blood. This, however, implies that the dilatation be retained within certain limits, which, if overstepped, would shut off the possibility of a perfect systolic contraction, and thus destroy compensation.

The tricuspid valve is unquestionably the weakest valve of the heart. If, therefore, the right ventricle be distended with blood from the lungs, or from any other source, its hypertrophy will immediately ensue. Although equally prompt, this hypertrophy is never as powerful and beneficial as that produced in the left ventricle by stenosis of the aorta, because the dilatation of the ventricle is followed immediately by such an extension of the right auriculo-ventricular valve that the tips of the tricuspid valve are unable to fill in the intervening space. Thus is produced that momentous condition of relative insufficiency of the tricuspid, which so often proves the fatal element in heart disease; the blood is projected directly into the venous system, and finds in its broad paths not a single point of support where an effective equalizing tension might be established.

β. Cyanosis and Dropsy.

We have indicated above that the compensatory power of the circulatory apparatus may oppose the impending decrease of arterial pressure, up to a certain point. When this point is temporarily or permanently overstepped, compensation becomes imperfect, and the abnormal accumulation of blood in the venous system manifests itself equally in two diseased phenomena, viz.: Cyanosis and Dropsy.

Cyanosis in its lightest form is apparent as a marked injection of the superficial veins at the periphery of the systemic circulation. The ears, nose, lips, cheeks and chin are overspread with a bluish discoloration. In continued cyanosis the capillaries protrude more and more, in the shape of delicate, convoluted, stellated figures, which appear to lie immediately under the epithelium. The cuticle of the arms and legs is similarly affected, but here the subcutaneous veins are especially prominent and abnormally engorged. The sinuous course of these veins, which in the normal body are visible through the integument, becomes now more sharply defined, and finally terminates in knotty dilatations, known as varicose veins.

The engorgement of the venous system leads, sooner or later, to the much dreaded extravasation of blood serum from the dilated vessels, which we call dropsy* (hydrops). This effusion, being serum mechanically pressed out, is called a transudate, as opposed to exudate, whose inflammatory nature involves the tissue in active participation.

The dropsical fluid is either colorless, clear or pale yellow, alkaline, and possessing an insipid, salty taste. It consists of from 92 per cent. to 95 per cent. of water (although it may contain 99 per cent.) and of albumen; the latter being less abundant than that contained in the blood serum. This varies, however, with the age of the transudate, which becomes more albuminous as the dropsical condition is prolonged. It is not unlikely that certain chemical changes take place, such as the conversion of the sero-albumen into a peptone, resembling that produced in digestion. The presence in the transudate of the more easily diffusible, extractive matters of the blood of urea, for instance, is *a priori* to be expected. It is likely that other constituents of the transudate, as, for example, fat and mucus, have been formed like the albuminous peptones, by secondary changes.

The external phenomena of dropsy proceed so directly and

---

* The term œdema is applied to a dropsical parenchyma (from $οιδεω$, to swell); a dropsical cavity is termed hydrops. Anasarca (general dropsy) is an œdema of the skin and areolar tissues. Ascites is a dropsy of the peritoneum.

simply from the effects of mechanical infiltration, that they can be easily reproduced by artificial injection of the parts with a salt solution. It is a well-known axiom that among stereometric bodies the sphere embraces within the smallest circumference the largest amount of space. When, therefore, a cavity is forced to receive and surround the largest possible volume of fluid, it assumes naturally, whatever its previous shape might have been, that of the sphere. This tendency manifests itself strikingly in severe forms of dropsy of the abdomen (ascites). The characteristic sign produced by gently tapping (percussion) with the finger such an accumulation of fluid is an important diagnostic symptom. A concentrically spreading fluctuation is perceptible, and, upon increasing the tension of the wall, a similar short vibration of the latter is felt.

Parts especially rich in coarse connective tissue, become, when œdematous, greatly disfigured, viz., the eyelids, prepuce, scrotum. The folds of soft skin which characterize these parts are replaced by round, pouch-like masses, of a smooth, lustrous, sometimes transparent, appearance, which, however, hang heavily and are inelastic and doughy to the touch. The impress of the finger remains for some time in the cold, waxy surface.

When the skin is stretched to its utmost capacity, the texture gradually gives way, exhibiting a system of uniform water lines, which show us that the normal, invisible texture of the skin is really composed of individual territories of nutrition. The skin may at last burst and discharge the dropsical fluid. Notwithstanding the excessive abnormality of this condition, it may be compatible for a long period with the maintenance of life, and under favorable circumstances the fluid can be very readily absorbed. This can be easily shown by taking a piece of excessively œdematous skin, and noting with what ease it can be restored to its original condition by merely pressing out of it the serous fluid.

In a gradual weakening of the function of the heart, cyanosis and dropsy furnish criteria for determining the gravity of the situation during the equalization of pressure between the arterial and venous systems. Death results usually from over dilatation and paralysis of the myocardium, occasionally also from paralysis of the lung.

III. DISTURBANCES IN BLOOD-FORMATION.

All the nutritive matter which the various organs of the body demand and consume is supplied to them by the blood. The most important of these, *i. e.*, oxygen and fat, are only temporary constituents of the blood, since they are only taken up in the alimentary canal and lungs in order to be again given off to other organs. The same is true in part of albumen, although this does not hinder us from considering it as one of the integral constituents of the blood, and its regular supply as one of the chief factors in the normal production of blood. The more permanent or so-called tissue constituents of the blood, the blood corpuscles and the liquor sanguinis, depend also so largely upon these temporary substances for their duration and constant renewal that we cannot fail to regard the reception of such substances as the basis of normal formation of blood.

We shall, accordingly, designate as disturbances of blood formation (1) the insufficient supply of nutritive matter from the intestinal tract; (2) the insufficient restoration of the constituents of the blood by means of the "blood making organs," *i. e.*, the bone marrow, spleen and lymphatic glands.

DISTURBANCES IN THE NUTRITION SUPPLIED BY THE INTESTINAL TRACT.

The pathological changes in the digestive apparatus, which bring about disturbances of the nutrition, are both numerous and varied.

Among the diseases of the organs of mastication and deglutition, we will only mention stricture of the œsophagus, which, be it cicatricial (sulphuric acid) or carcinomatous, renders the passage of food to the stomach impossible.

Among stomachic troubles, catarrhal gastritis holds the foremost place, appearing either as an independent disease (injurious ingesta, drinking cold water, when the body is heated), or as the concomitant of more serious complications (fevers, serious affections of the digestive tract, etc.)

It is undoubtedly true that there is an insufficient secretion of gastric juice in gastritis; and, when fever is present, also a lack of muriatic acid. This also would suffice to disturb the processes of solution and subsequent resorption of the nutritive material, without taking into account that the muscular coat of the stomach is so far involved in the hyperæmia and swelling of the mucous membrane as to be unable to contract with vigor and purpose. The peristaltic action of the stomach becomes imperfect and painful, so that the gastric juice is not properly mingled with the food. This feature is intensified in proportion as the food is surrounded by a hard exterior or by difficultly soluble fats, which render it less permeable to the gastric fluid. Digestion is furthermore impaired by the copious secretion of catarrhal products, which by their own alkalinity neutralize and render inefficacious a portion of the acid gastric juice.

In conclusion, therefore, in catarrhal gastritis a large share of the contents of the stomach—albumen, carbo-hydrates and fat—remain undissolved. Such a condition, it is clear, must initiate another series of disturbances, which not only still further compromise the digestive functions, but also inaugurate very serious dangers of another kind. Leaving the effects of the gastric acid to a certain degree out of the question, we find that the undigested ingesta are now in a condition to begin individual processes of fermentation and even decomposition. These soon set in, as the necessary temperature, moisture, and other promoters of fermentation, are all at hand. There is no lack of ordinary yeast cells; these latter are not rarely accompanied by small, quadripartite cubes, known as sarcina. Under their influence lactic and carbonic acids and hydrogen are produced. There is a feeling of oppression, heart burn, and water brash, which is especially characteristic of a disordered stomach. The stomach, in particular, becomes gradually dilated as the result of gaseous fermentation. At this stage the disorder undergoes a decided change for the worse.

We noticed above how the contractility of the muscular coat of the stomach is impaired by the concomitant hyperæmia and œdema. No sooner is there a positive counter-pressure established in the stomach, than the contractility is completely overcome, and there follows a gradual dilatation of the organ, which assumes a more permanent character, as "gastrectasis," and presents an independent chain of symptoms. Every stomach must yield to gastrectasis, if its peristaltic action is not equal to the demands made upon it. We may also expect this condition, when there exists in the pylorus any mechanical hindrance to the emptying of the organ; such, for example, as a strongly protruding or a circular constricting carcinoma. In this case gastrectasis is the first result of the primary affection from which there is developed in reversed order, as in catarrhal gastritis, first stagnation, then decomposition of the contents, and lastly catarrhal inflammation and disordered secretion.

Gastrectasis is furthermore entitled to be classed among independent diseases, inasmuch as it grows from causes within itself, finally threatening even the life of the individual. The liquid and solid products gravitate naturally to the bottom of the stomach into the greater curvature, and drag with them into the lower parts of the abdomen this portion of the stomach, which is by nature less firmly attached. The passage into the pylorus becomes more and more abrupt, and the normal discharge of the contents more difficult. At length, the greater curvature sinks to the top of the symphysis, and the steady development of gaseous products of fermentation brings about, besides an abnormally distended abdomen, a complete stand-still in the regular reception of food, and a dangerous general decline in the processes of nutrition.

When we look back upon the close and logical sequence of these symptoms, and perceive how, at times, a disturbance, of itself trifling, leads to serious results, we cannot fail to admire the wise provision of nature by which the contents of the stomach are thrown off and the ascension of the *scala vitiosa* prevented.

Vomiting is caused by a reflex contraction of the abdominal walls, accompanied by a simultaneous relaxation of the circular muscular fibres of the stomach, together with a perceptible shortening of the œsophagus. The latter involves also the œsophageal end of the stomach, for it must be remembered that the longitudinal muscular fibres of the œsophagus do not terminate at the œsophageal opening, but extend some distance upon the surface of the stomach. The angle at which the œsophagus originates in the stomach is also the starting point of longitudinal muscular fibres, which radiate here in a stellate manner and soon are lost. It cannot be doubted that these fibres are concerned in the shortening of the œsophagus, and that they, by virtue of their origin, strive to change the angle of origin by several degrees, *i. e.*, they open in a funnel-shaped manner the cardiac orifice, whose circular muscular fibres are completely relaxed, and thus afford the greatest possible facility for the discharge of the contents of the stomach.

The act of vomiting, as before observed, is a beneficial interruption in the *scala vitiosa* of the disturbed digestive process, although, as is easily seen, it only assists indirectly in supplying the blood with nutritive material, by cleansing the resorption territory.

The act of resorption is as often abnormally disturbed beyond the pylorus as in the stomach. For not only is the preparation of carbo-hydrates, albumen and fat, which depend upon a sufficient secretion of intestinal and gastric juices and bile, interfered with, but especially is the reception of the dissolved nutritive material into the blood and chyle easily disturbed. Here, as in the stomach, the real cause is found to be the superficial position of the mucous capillaries, which, in turn, is demanded by the participation of the blood vessels in the work of resorption. It is clear that as the blood vessels, especially those of the venous apparatus, approach nearer to the surface, they become more and more subject to the various injurious influences there present; and if we are correct in locating the salient point of inflammation, as an alteration of the vascular wall, we must be prepared to find upon the exposed surface of the mucous membranes all possible forms and degrees of inflammatory hyperæmias and exudates. We are not mistaken in this expectation. Pathological anatomy chronicles here a long list of simple and specific inflammations, catarrhal, croupous and diphtheritic, tumors and abscesses, all of which are found in the mucous membranes. In every decided inflammation, the capillaries, as a matter of course, cease to absorb, and the diametrically opposed process, that of inflammatory exudation, sets in.

Great caution must, however, be used in determining any form of enteritis. No organ of the body is as subject to the action of functional hyperæmia as the mucous coat of the digestive tract, therefore we must not ignore the fact that the irritation of the ingesta brings on functional hyperæmia, and with it an increased peristaltic action. The latter, besides promoting resorption by pressure upon the intestinal contents, causes: (1) an accelerated movement of the contents downwards; (2) a more abundant secretion of intestinal juice from Lieberkühn's follicles. As the intestinal irritation and its accompanying hyperæmia become more and more intensified, the process of resorption is subordinated to an increased secretion of intestinal juice, and rapid descent of fecal matter. We have now a condition which oversteps the limits of functional hyperæmia in an inflammatory direction, but is yet, by no means, an inflammation in effect. Its pathognomonic symptom is *diarrhœa*.

The phenomenon of diarrhœa is, in some respects, similar to that of vomiting; more especially in regard to its result, viz., relieving the stomach of injurious ingesta. Both, therefore, furnish a valuable hint for the physician, who should not hesitate to employ emetics and cathartics, whenever there is danger that the intestinal contents might, by their continued presence, act perniciously upon the intestinal wall and general organism. In the bowels, as well as in the stomach, an unusual detention of the contents threatens danger to the organism. Constipation is always accompanied by slight processes of fermentation and decomposition. These are attributable: (1) to the numberless fermentation and decomposition fungi, whose presence in the fæces is easily demonstrated; (2) to the final exhaustion of the protective action of the gastric juice and bile, against fermentation and ordinary putrefaction furnished by their admixture with the intestinal contents.

The formation of gas (flatulency), due to hydrogen gas and its combinations, is an almost invariable accompaniment of such decomposition; then follows pain, and soon there can be no doubt but that an inflammation of the intestinal wall has set in. It is at first of a catarrhal character, and it is at this stage that the disease should, if possible, be checked, either by natural means or by artificially removing the contents of the intestines. In default of this we may expect to see this inflammatory process advance, penetrate the layers of the intestinal wall, and reach, finally, the peritoneum (peritvphlitis, stercoraceous peritonitis). The muscular coat now becomes inflamed, œdematous and completely paralyzed; the intestine is distended to its utmost by the accumulation of gas (meteorism); the abdomen is greatly swollen, the diaphragm is raised and ceases entirely or in part to exert its influence upon respiration. The crisal symptom of this disorder is stercoraceous vomiting which is apt to appear when the intestinal canal becomes permanently obstructed by intussusception, cancerous or cicatricial growths, strangulated hernia, etc. By it we understand a discharge of the entire intestinal contents by the mouth, which occurs when the distended intestines have lost their power of contraction, and no longer oppose abdominal pressure, which causes the contents of the bowels to be expelled by vomiting.

The fatal termination is hastened by the appearance of fulminating purulent peritonitis, which sets in as soon as the contents penetrate the intestinal wall and spread themselves over the peritoneal surface.

In proportion as the hyperæmia of the mucous capillaries assumes, instead of a temporary, a more permanent character, the blood vessels cease to absorb the nutritive material, as far as normal digestion and blood formation is concerned. For this reason absorption is greatly impaired in diseases of the heart and lungs, when there is a permanent hyperæmia of the mucous membrane of the digestive tract. The absorption of chyle is also somewhat disturbed, as the flow of chyle depends upon the precision and regularity of a number of factors, such as an intact epithelium, a regular contraction and erection of the intestinal villi, an undisturbed and powerful peristalsis, and an exact and well-timed filling of the blood vessels. It is clear that every serious inflammation must interfere with the action of one or more of these factors. A normal condition of the mesenteric glands is also necessary to the further progress of the absorbed chyle. An inflammatory, cancerous, or tuberculous intumescence of these glands imperils the process of absorption, just in proportion as the intra-glandular lymphatics are more or less effectively obstructed.

Marasmus, Defective Nutrition.

The evil effects of any serious disturbance of nutrition in the digestive tract are apparent to all: hollow eyes, thin and emaciated limbs, pallid and withered skin,—such are the sequelæ of this condition. Marasmus or the result of a prolonged loss of food, has already been sketched, where especial stress was laid upon the diminished quantity of blood and the loss of flesh.

Physiology teaches us how the hungry body, robbed of its food, subsists at the expense of the muscles and fat, until, after the lapse of two weeks, it can no longer, by preying upon itself, avert the deadly suspension of sensibility, and thus perishes, of complete exhaustion.

DISTURBANCES IN BLOOD CORPUSCLE FORMATION.

The most important constituents of the blood are the red blood corpuscles. They alone possess the power to take up oxygen in the lungs, and conduct it in loose chemical combination to the tissues of the body. This power of the red blood corpuscles is due to hæmoglobin, a peculiar reddish-yellow substance which they contain. Hæmoglobin is readily resolved, by the action of alkalies and acids, into an albuminous body, globulin, and into the coloring matter of the blood, in its restricted sense, hæmatin. This separation is more rapidly accomplished by ozone, especially with high temperature. When we picture to ourselves the unceasing action of the inspired particles of oxygen upon the red blood corpuscles, we can comprehend the rapid changes which the molecules of hæmoglobin undergo in the body, changes whose magnitude may be estimated by a comparison with the quantity of pigment secreted by the bile. No one now questions that bilirubin is identical with transformed hæmatin, but nothing is known of what becomes of the globulin. At any rate the disintegration of the hæmoglobulin calls for a rapid restoration of the blood, and just here our knowledge of the formation of blood is completely at fault. We do not know to what degree the hæmoglobin-changes are identical with those of the red blood corpuscles, nor whether the blood corpuscle yields up its hæmoglobin individually; whether there is a shedding of hæmoglobin, or whether for each amount of bilirubin secreted in the bile a corresponding number of red blood corpuscles are withdrawn from the circulation.

Nature displays a certain extravagance with red blood corpuscles, and slight losses of blood seem easily repaired. Still we meet here with individual differences, and the formation of the red blood corpuscles is, and will doubtless remain, one of the most difficult problems of our science. Little is known of the remote conditions or the locality and the histological process concerned in the origin of the red blood corpuscles.

In the red marrow of the bones and in the splenic pulp of the mammalia, we find nucleated red blood corpuscles, which resemble exactly embryonic corpuscles (hæmatoblasts). Processes of nuclear and cell division may be easily observed in these cells. I also believe I have demonstrated that these cells, by expulsion of their nuclei and mechanical remodeling of their shape, are converted into the well known bi-concave, non-nucleated discs.

According to the above, the production of the red blood corpuscles would be the function of the splenic pulp and the red marrow of bones, and disturbances in the formation of red blood corpuscles would be referable to disturbances in the above sources—a hypothesis which entirely agrees with observed pathological facts. So we shall for the present consider essential anæmias as disturbances of splenic or medullary hæmatosis, without attempting an exact definition of the process or dwelling upon the post-mortem studies relating thereto.

Essential Anæmias.

An essential anæmia is a decided and prolonged proportional diminution in the number of red blood corpuscles in the blood, which is not produced by loss of blood and nutritive fluids, like cachexia, nor by the destruction of the red blood corpuscles by means of poison. One of two things operates to produce an essential anæmia, viz., an insufficient formation and supply of red blood corpuscles on the part of the hæmatoblastic tissues, or a premature disintegration and destruction of the formed or partially formed cells.

Thus essential anæmias fall into two classes. The type of the first class is the so-called pernicious or progressive anæmia. In a few months this disease, in the face of all known remedies, reduces the blood, especially its hæmoglobin constituents, to $\frac{1}{8}$ or $\frac{1}{10}$ of its normal quantity. The nutrition of all the tissues is thereby impaired; the cardiac parenchyma undergoes fatty degeneration and death is caused by paralysis of the heart. In dissecting, we are astonished at the paradoxical condition of the bone marrow. Everywhere, even replacing the fat marrow of the long bones—the femur, tibia and humerus—we find an intensely red marrow containing numberless nucleated red blood corpuscles; in other words, an advanced state of development of those cells in which the blood is deficient. What is the meaning of this? Why was the formation of red blood corpuscles arrested just before completion? And why did they not enter into the blood? Pernicious anæmia is of rare occurrence. It is only found among the badly nourished of the poorer classes of society.

An anæmia called *chlorosis*, which is generally of a temporary character, prevails frequently in young women of all classes. Here, too, we can trace a loss of one-half or more in the coloring matter, *i. e.*, of the hæmoglobin. The complexion becomes very pale greenish, and many disagreeable symptoms make their appearance (dyspepsia, anomalous menstruation). The spleen and bone marrow require some assistance in their function of blood making, and this, fortunately, we possess in iron, which, if properly prescribed, restores the normal condition with comparative rapidity.

In some of the other forms of essential anæmia, the lack of red blood corpuscles is to a certain extent overlooked in view of the highly singular attitude of the colorless blood corpuscles. Pseudo-leucæmic anæmia, which often terminates fatally, shows a diminution in the quantity of the blood, accompanied by an immense accumulation of colorless blood corpuscles in the lymphatic glands. These corpuscles cluster together and form large-sized tumors. Splenic anæmia is coupled in the same manner with an astonishing increase in size of the spleen and decidedly leucocythotic in character.

An advocate of the view that the hæmatoblasts arise, not only from cell multiplication, but also from white blood corpuscles, would infer from these combinations that the swollen organs were depriving the blood of the constructive material residing in the red blood corpuscles. In a case of splenic anæmia in which I made a post-mortem examination for Griesinger, it appeared to me as though all the blood of the body were retained in the spleen; the spleen weighed over twelve pounds, and the blood vessels were entirely empty.

The most enigmatical conditions are found in leucæmic anæmia, or leucæmia. The loss of red blood corpuscles is concealed by the simultaneous gain in colorless blood corpuscles. In blood extracted from the finger of the patient, we can count one white to every twenty, ten, or even two red blood corpuscles. The blood is of a raspberry color, and seen in bulk, appears streaked with white. The white blood corpuscles are of considerable size, and not rarely multinuclear. Their preponderance in the blood leads, in many places, to extensive migrations, occurring either diffused or in masses. These migrations are as much entitled to the name of extravasations as exudates, or even new formations of lymphatic parenchyma, for they are often accompanied by exhausting hemorrhage of the mucous membrane of the nose and intestines, and by a constant and excessive enlargement of the spleen, *i. e.*, of the lymph glands (leucæmia lienalis or lymphatica).

In studying the formation of red blood corpuscles I have arrived at a theory of my own concerning leucæmia. I am of the opinion that the hæmatoblasts, instead of becoming red blood corpuscles, are converted into certain large, colorless cell-elements of the marrow. The latter appear in moderate quantities in normal blood marrow, and are found in leucæmia in enormous quantities, not only in the bone marrow but, as before noticed, in the blood as well.

The second class of essential anæmias result from a premature destruction of red blood corpuscles; or rather, I should say, appear to result, for at this point our knowledge is most defective and uncertain. We know that the normal disintegration of the red blood corpuscles gives rise to a brown pigment, the coloring matter of the bile. Furthermore, we know that certain brown and blackish pigment substances are formed from extravasated blood, that the same or similar substances are found normally in the spleen and marrow, and also in great abundance in the spleen of the frog, where it has been formed from the disintegration of red blood corpuscles. We are thus led to consider a rapid destruction of the red blood corpuscles as the cause of such essential anæmias as are accompanied by a conspicuous formation and deposition of pigment. Although the spleen and the marrow of bone preside over the formation of the red blood corpuscles, they are also the chief seats of the pathological disintegration of the red blood corpuscles, and, in consequence, also of the formation of pigment. To say that the hæmatoplastic substance is at the same time the birthplace and the deathbed of the red blood corpuscles appears like a surprising assertion. But this assertion, made thirty years ago in the manuals of histology, has ever since maintained its ground, being supported and confirmed by recent pathological researches.

The best known anæmia is probably *melanæmia* or, more correctly, *anæmia melanæmica*. Severe and protracted intermittent fevers are often followed by intense anæmia, and the spleen is frequently excessively pigmented or even entirely black. The pigment consists of dark brown and black granules, strongly impregnated with iron and of irregular-shaped flakes, lying loosely in the splenic pulp. Certain particles of this pigment are, little by little, washed away by the blood current and deposited in the liver, brain and kidneys, where they give rise to considerable disturbance of function, especially in the brain. If there be a renewed attack of fever, causing a temporarily-increased hyperæmia of the spleen, we shall also find, during the attack, more pigment in the blood of the melanæmic patient. Little definite information can be had as to the condition of the marrow in this unusual disease. Were I to assert that there is in melanæmia a premature disintegration of red blood corpuscles in the spleen, and that this is the cause of the grave anæmia which terminates the life of the patient, I should certainly assert more than I am able to prove. Notwithstanding this, there are, at least in melanæmia, more data from which to draw conclusions than in the succeeding groups of symptoms which we now approach.

Melanosis, so called, presents an inevitable and rapid decline of vitality, in conjunction with a proportional formation and accumulation of a brown, or deep, sepia-colored pigment. This is distributed partly in solution in the blood, in which case it is found in the urine, which, upon exposure to the air, acquires a dark gray to a black color, and partly as granular deposits, occurring at different parts of the body.

In the summer of 1881 a case of melanosis came under my notice, in the Julius hospital of Würzburg, in which all the bone marrow, which is normally red, *i. e.*, the marrow of the vertebræ, ribs, sternum, etc., instead of being red, was black. The same was true of the spleen. The liver also showed diffused pigmentation, which, under the microscope, was seen to have attacked all the vascular and many of the investing cells, both of which contained brownish-black flakes of pigment.

The resemblance which is thus far traceable between melanosis and melanæmia ends here; the quantity of the pigment alone brings about a radical difference. Melanæmia-pigment is a body rich in iron, which, combined with muriatic acid and ferrocyanide of potash, yields a beautiful Prussian blue. Melanotic pigment, on the other hand, belongs to those pigments as yet chemically undetermined, which are formed normally in the choroid coat of the eye and the rete mucosum of the skin. If, therefore, in the above-described case of melanosis, we are to consider the bone marrow and spleen as the breeding place of pigment (just as in melanæmia), they have, undoubtedly, assumed a function usually accorded only to the choroid coat of the eye and the rete mucosum of the skin.

Another consideration is the fact that melanosis is, in the greater number of cases, associated with melanotic sarcoma, hence it is difficult to disprove the assumption that melanotic dyscrasia is the result of a pigment tumor of the eye and skin. This, however, has always been a disputed point. Virchow, otherwise so decided as to the primarily local nature of tumors, is forced, in melanosis, to accept at least the possibility of tumor-formation preceded by dyscrasia. He calls attention to the fact that melanosis generally attacks those persons who are by nature inclined to an abnormal formation and deposition of pigment. Also, that gray or white (albino) horses are especially and even constitutionally subject to melanosis, so that it would almost appear as if the missing pigment of the eye and skin were vicariously secreted in these black tumors. In the case I have spoken of as coming under my observation, I found, both in the liver and spleen, a soft, spherical, black tumor of the size of a walnut, a section of which showed a puffy, protruding surface. Each nodus was imbedded to such an extent in the diffusely blackened parenchyma, respectively of the liver and spleen, that they could only have been secondary formations.

In the liver are scattered throughout the entire organ numerous points, marking the starting place of microscopically minute nodes, growing out of the proliferated endothelia of the blood vessels. The latter were everywhere of a brown or black color, in all gradations of shades, from a light, diffused brown, to a paranuclear deposit of deep black granules and flakes. From such a soil the tumor had formed.

There is, furthermore, a melanotic dyscrasia, *i. e.*, the blood, having an abnormal constituency of diffusible coloring matter, gives it up to the endothelia of the capillaries, which condense it into black pigment granules. When a certain stage is reached in this disposition, the endothelium in question begins to divide and form sarcomatous tumors. It is possible that the coloring matter reaches the blood by means of the premature disintegration of the red blood corpuscles, and that the decay really takes place in the spleen and bone marrow, but this is, as yet, mere supposition.

Finally we must note, at this point, a very singular group

of symptoms, characterized by local, dark gray discoloration of the skin, and anæmic debility, with which is often associated a degenerated condition of the renal capsules. This disease, first described by Addison, has received the name of Addison's Disease.

IV. DISTURBANCES IN BLOOD-PURIFICATION.

The purification of the blood, which is, strictly speaking, the removal from it of the retrograde products of metamorphosis, is, as we know, entrusted mainly to the three chief organs of the body, *i. e.*, lungs, kidneys and liver. Each of these organs may be hindered in the exercise of its especial function by all sorts of pathologico-anatomical changes, and excretory products, may, in consequence, accumulate in the blood. Thus, we find an accumulation of carbonic acid, urea, and biliary products in the blood, and may, with propriety, regard these accumulations as the leading phenomena of the groups of symptoms due to derangements of these organs respectively.

The functional disturbances of the excretory organs, however, rarely present themselves in so simple a form. For the lung is not alone intended to throw off carbonic acid, but for the reception of oxygen as well. Therefore, we find in the symptomatic picture of the disturbances of respiration, that the lack of oxygen plays at least as important a rôle as the poisoning from carbonic acid. The most important of the affections of the kidney is nephritis. Nephritis not only threatens the destruction of the epithelium that secretes urine, and thereby the organism with uræmia, but almost invariably produces changes in the capillaries of the Malpighian tufts, in consequence of which the albumen of the blood passes into the urine, and albuminuria becomes a prominent symptom. There is still much doubt as to what substances the liver extracts from the blood, in order to form bile; but as we find decomposed hæmatin thrown off with the bile, we are thus inclined to look upon the remaining constituents of the bile as products of the disintegration of the red blood corpuscles. Chlolæmia does not signify, by any means, a retention of the formative material of the bile, in the sense of a retention of carbonic acid and urea, but only a resorption dyscrasia, brought about by the reabsorption of the bile from the biliary ducts. If we are correct in defining hæmatogenous jaundice as caused by blood pigment which has disintegrated in the blood (independently of the liver), it must be regarded as an exception to the above. It is not impossible that similar discoveries yet remain to be made as regards the other elements concerned in the production of bile, although the function of the liver cells does not appear to be readily disturbed. It is most astonishing how protoplasm will still continue to secrete, even when almost obliterated by an immense fat drop, and how an amyloid liver, not possessing a single normal liver cell, will continue to furnish the requisite quantity of bile. But the facts speak for themselves. It is only when, by some few anatomical changes (such as gallstones, catarrh of the efferent ducts, etc.), the discharge of bile is hindered, that the bile passes into the blood, and a characteristic dyscrasia is produced.

Alongside of this incongruity between a defective purification of the blood and a general disturbance of function in an organ intended for the purification of the blood, another circumstance forces us to increase the number of typical groups of symptoms associated with the organs concerned in the purification of the blood. For it sometimes occurs that there is an accumulation of excretory matter in the blood, far exceeding the capacity of the organ designed for its removal, and this without any apparent pathological change in the latter. This condition, however, only arises (1) when there is produced an abnormally large quantity of the substance in question; (2) when it is a chemically slightly diffusible body, which appears normally in small quantities, and which the glands are, therefore, unable to secrete in large amounts. Of such substances uric acid and glucose are the most important. The retention of these in the blood produces uric acid- and sugar-dyscrasias, which will be considered more at length under the head of the non-excretory dyscrasias.

DISTURBANCES OF RESPIRATION.

There is perhaps no organ in the body which undergoes so many and so varied pathological changes as the lung.

Almost all of these changes are detrimental to absorption, to a greater or less degree. Inflammatory exudates fill the alveoli and prevent the atmospheric air from coming in contact with the blood of the pulmonary capillaries, cellular infiltration of the connective tissue of the lungs compresses the pulmonary capillaries and hinders the blood from coming in contact with the air in the alveoli. A similar effect is produced by hemorrhagic and liquid transudations, which flood the organ of respiration over a more or less extended space; and also by the emphysematous atrophy of the alveolar septa, and the compression of the lungs in the pleural cavity by means of inflammatory or non-inflammatory effusions. But whatever the original cause may be, we must always remember that a defective supply of air and a defective supply of blood to the lungs lessens or prevents that contact of air and blood which is necessary to perfect interchange of gases. We must, therefore, include under difficulties of respiration, not alone those diseases which are peculiar to the lungs, but everything which acts injuriously upon the air and blood paths, either in the main trunks or in their ramifications. Foreign bodies, compression of the trachea, spasm or œdema of the glottis, pseudo-membranous (croupous) accumulations in the larynx and trachea, catarrhal secretions,—all have their effect upon the respiratory process. So also have various defects in the valves of the heart, and embolism of the pulmonary artery and its branches. Even an imperfect composition of the blood affects respiration. A deficiency of red blood corpuscles indicates a proportional loss of hæmoglobin. Too few red corpuscles represent a proportionate deficiency in the gas-exchanging hæmoglobin, and when in cholera the watery secretions of the mucous membranes of the digestive tract has produced the dreaded inspissation of the blood, there is an immediate decline below normal in the interchange of gases contained in the blood.

There are many other causes of disturbed respiration which ought to be enumerated, and this variety in the causes contrasts singularly with the monotony in their operation. The result is invariably the same; on the one hand, a lack of oxygen in the blood, on the other, an excess of carbonic acid.

We know, from various experiments performed on animals, that a deficiency of oxygen is felt, first of all, in an increased excitation of the respiratory centre. A lack of oxygen is, therefore, correctly regarded as the prime instigator of all those modifications of respiration which have for their object a heightened interchange of gases and blood in the lungs, which are known under the generic name of dyspnœa, short-breath, or still better, difficulty of breathing.

The heightened excitation of the respiratory centre is only possible as long as the blood contains a certain proportion of oxygen. With the loss of this, the excitation of the respiratory centre ceases, and, after a short expiration, breathing is suspended.

An excess of carbonic acid in the blood works like a narcotic, at first rousing then rapidly stupefying the entire nervous system. Its effect is, therefore, not unlike that produced by a deficiency of oxygen.

Both agencies appear in intimate association in every imaginable degree of intensity, forming, in connection with their respective phenomena, an extensive and characteristic chain of symptoms, the most prominent of which we will now proceed to consider.

Disturbances of breathing, in their slightest forms, are synonymous with those general circulatory disturbances described (p. 118) under the head of cyanosis. Persons troubled with emphysema, or affections of the heart, are notably disinclined to violent bodily exercise, to mounting stairs, walking rapidly, etc. Experience has taught them the necessity of a quiet deportment, *i. e.*, the least possible consumption of oxygen and the avoidance of unusual respiratory exertions, the infringement of which rule is sure to bring on an attack, even though slight, of dyspnœa.

Dyspnœa, or difficult breathing, is, next to restriction in the consumption of oxygen, the only but also effective means employed by the organism to restore normal interchange of gases. Difficult respiration implies in all cases more powerful inspiration. The increased power is derived from more than one source. A deep breath and an accelerated breath lead to the same result. As these conditions cannot be conveniently combined, they are employed alternately, the preference being given to one or to the other according to circumstances. Where a deep breath is painful, as in pleurisy, we find a rapid, superficial respiration. In general, however, the deep breath is, in spite of the unavoidable retardation, the most efficient correction of a disturbed gaseous interchange in the blood.

The altered rhythm of respiration is aided on occasion, by various expedients. Thus, inhalation is expedited by dilating the nostrils, and by stretching the head and neck. Accessory muscles are called in play. In inspiration, the intercostal muscles, and the sterno-cleido-mastoids; in expiration, the diaphragm and the depressor muscles of the shoulder, which, through the weight of the upper extremities, exert a lateral pressure on the thorax.

In accordance with the well-known action of the respiratory mechanism upon the circulation, dyspnœa accelerates not only inspiration and expiration, but also the blood changes in the lung, so that it is, in fact, the best alleviation for the trouble. Its operation, aided by the will power of the patient, is, in slight attacks, very thorough; so much so, that the aim is sometimes overshot, and an excess of oxygen accumulates in the blood, a condition which is, naturally, only of short duration. Soon the ever-active cause of the disturbed respiration again occasions defective blood purification, and dyspnœa is once more established. Thus it is that dyspnœa is prone to return periodically, and in this phase is called asthma. Much effort has been made to ascribe the periodicity of asthmatic attacks to other causes, viz., to a neurosis (asthma nervosum), or as the result of a periodical accumulation of certain small crystals in the bronchial secretion (asthma crystallinum). When the impeded respiration steadily grows worse, and is not to be overcome by dyspnœa, there appear, sooner or later, the symptoms of gradual suffocation. The leading phenomenon in this group of symptoms is the impaired sensitiveness of the respiratory centre, which is due to the increasing deficiency of oxygen in the blood. The breathing and the circulation grow weaker, the latter appears almost suspended, and asphyxia is the result. The narcotic properties of the over accumulation of carbonic acid become more visible. The patient succumbs to a general apathy, stupefaction and somnolence, associated with convulsive twitchings of individual muscles.

In the group of symptoms of gradual suffocation there is occasionally found a most ill-omened appearance, viz., intermittent breathing, known as the Cheyne-Stokes respiration. In this an entire cessation of breathing, lasting from three or four up to thirty or forty seconds, will be followed by respirations which rapidly grow deeper and stronger until a pronounced dyspnœa is established; these, in turn, become suddenly slower and less deep, until they are at last again entirely suspended. This paroxysm may be repeated from one to five times in a minute. There is a diversity of opinion as to whether this intermittent irritation of the respiratory centre arises from a lack of oxygen or an excess of carbonic acid, but all are agreed that it denotes a gradual crippling of its activity.

Sudden suffocation is occasioned not alone by the hangman's rope, but equally well by spasm of the glottis, by obstruction in the trachea, by pressure on the trachea in goitre, or even by hæmoptysis in consumptives.

The painful struggles which in these cases precede death are due mainly to the withholding of oxygen from the blood. The proportion of the latter decreases inside of thirty seconds from 15% to 2.6–1.5%. By this means all the centres situated in the brain become violently excited; the respiratory centre, the vascular centre, the centres that preside over the dilatation of the pupil, the pneumogastric centre, etc. The unfortunate individual gasps vainly for breath, and a general bodily uneasiness is followed by twitching and convulsions, which violently distort and rack the body. At last respiration ceases. The tonic contraction of all the small arteries rapidly raises the blood pressure to a temporary height of 160 mm., the pupils dilate to their utmost, and the irritation of the pneumogastric causes first a slowing, then a complete cessation of the cardiac contractions. After a few moments death ensues.

DERANGEMENTS IN THE FUNCTIONS OF THE KIDNEYS.

(a) *Uræmia.*

The office of the kidney is, as we know, to separate the superfluous water from the body and also to cast off all the bodily products of disintegration which are soluble in water. From the surface of the intestines there passes throughout the entire body to the surface of the kidneys a continuous stream of water, moving now rapidly, now slowly, washing out the organs of the body and uniting the products of their disintegration to form urine.

The epithelium which invests the convoluted uriniferous tubules possesses a specific attraction for substances peculiar to urine, such as urea, uric acid, etc., and, in fact, for almost all organic substances which occasionally pollute the blood. The latter are extracted by the epithelia from the blood of the capillary vessels which invest the tubules, and are then precipitated into the watery current, which, coming from the Malpighian tufts, flows in a rapid stream through the uriniferous ducts. The secretion of the tuft consists, mainly, of water and salts. In quantity, it is regulated exactly by the rapidity of the blood current through the Malpighian tuft. The secretion of the kidney is consequently increased by every active hyperæmic condition of the organ. The urine becomes, at the same time, abundant, clear and watery. The relative amount of the solid constituents diminishes, but the absolute quantity remains uniform, or is, perhaps, slightly increased. Renal congestions are chiefly traceable to the presence of urinary matters in the blood, especially in the renal epithelia. It cannot yet be proved whether there is a nervous centre, which, being especially sensitive to attacks from such substances, reacts against them by dilating the renal arteries. The appearance of the so-called watery diabetes (Diabetes Insipidus) would thus be referable to a further irritation of such a centre.

When the secretion of urine is suddenly and completely arrested, there results at once an accumulation of urea in the blood, known as uræmia. Epileptic convulsions are followed by profound insensibility (comp. Eclampsia, p. 86), which, after several attacks, often ends in coma and death. These symptoms can be produced in animals by ligating the two ureters. An analysis of the blood of such animals shows 0.040–60 gramme of urea to 100 grammes of blood, while, in normal blood, there is at most 0.016–20 gramme of urea. The increase of urea is distinctly demonstrable in the muscular juices, as well as in all the bodily parenchymas. This abrupt and complete stoppage of the secretion of urine is rarely found in man. Accordingly, the phenomena of uræmia are only seen at long and disconnected intervals, between which the blood poisoning is only manifested in an apathy and an abstracted, sleepy condition, sometimes joined to severe headaches.

Vomiting and diarrhœa, the frequent concomitants of uræmia, are generally regarded as the result of vicarious secretion by the digestive tract, because in both evacuations the presence of urea is readily shown. It is, however, a question whether these symptoms have not in some way to do with the watery secretion which accompanies that of urea, and which must in some way find an escape. That this over-accumulation of water causes certain local œdemas of the skin (eyelids), a frequent symptom in uræmic patients, cannot be doubted, although the theory of Traube, which attributes uræmic convulsions to an œdema of the brain, has not yet been confirmed.

Hemorrhages are also included among the symptoms of uræmia. They arise from the unusual blood pressure in the arteries and occur partly from large-sized vessels whose resistance has been already weakened by disease, and partly from capillaries and arterioles, as punctiform hemorrhages. These latter are best observed in the retina of the eye. The complete but often only temporary blindness of those suffering from uræmia is not owing to any local affection of the eye, but to paralysis of the centres presiding over vision.

The symptoms of uræmia are to be dreaded in proportion as the epithelia of the convoluted uriniferous tubules are unable to perform their functions. This is the case (1) when the urine cannot be discharged from the tubules, (2) when the epithelia themselves are injured and incapable of their function, (3) when the kidneys are imperfectly supplied with blood. One or more of these conditions are generally present in nephritis, and thus nephritis produces, next to ischuria, due to obstruction of the large urinary passages, the greatest number of uræmic symptoms. There exist, however, so many varieties, degrees, and stages of nephritis, that the danger from uræmia cannot be accurately foretold. The following group of symptoms, which are apt to appear in kidney disorders, present quite a different aspect.

(b) *Albuminuria and Hydræmia.*

A local dilatation of the renal blood vessels in the Malpighian tufts causes a local increase of lateral pressure, which although moderate, suffices for the continued transudation of that quota of the watery portion of the blood which constitutes the water of the urine. The quantity of urine produced is in proportion to the amount of blood flowing through the kidneys; in other words, the more the motive power of the arterial blood is expressed in rapidity rather than in lateral pressure and friction, the greater is the quantity. This regulation presupposes a free and unhindered flow of blood through the renal veins, and also a perfectly intact condition of the relatively weak vascular wall of the Malpighian tuft. Many well-established experiments have shown the results produced by a defective fulfillment of these two conditions, which have been confirmed by observations at the bedside.

By obstructing the renal vein, we produce albuminuria and a decrease of urine, which continue until the obstruction is removed. In this case, the retarded blood changes lead to a diminished secretion of water, and the increase of lateral pressure, on the other hand, to the filtration through the walls of the Malpighian tuft of one of the less diffusible constituents of the blood, viz., the sero albumen.

A half-hour's exclusion of the blood, by ligation of the renal artery, will effect an alteration in the nutrition, *i. e.*, the chemico-physical composition of the blood vessels in general, and of the Malpighian tufts in particular. What follows? The urine diminishes in quantity and is found to contain albumen; the kidneys pass through all the changes of genuine nephritis; the epithelia of the convoluted uriniferous tubes undergo fatty degeneration and are thrown off in the shape of compound granule-cells or fatty detritus. The parenchyma around the pyramids of Ferrein collapses and gives the surface of the organ an uneven, granular appearance. There occurs at the same time a cellular infiltration of the connective tissue, succeeded by shrinkage and a permanent condition of granular atrophy.

The heightened friction of the blood, exerted upon the inflamed walls of the Malpighian tufts, is in this instance responsible for the retarded circulation, the intensified lateral pressure, and the albuminous infiltrate. The changes in the uriniferous tubes may eventually produce uræmia. Every secretion of albumen in the urine (albuminuria) which occurs in kidney diseases proceeds from one of two factors, viz., venous congestion or changes in the vascular walls of the Malpighian tufts. To trace how first one, then the other of these factors leads to albuminuria and to the other typical groups of symptoms, not only in the various form of nephritis, but also in the congested kidney, in amyloid degeneration, in partial obstructions of blood vessels, etc., would lead us too far. Such a consideration belongs to the province of special pathology. Only with albuminuria proper are we to concern ourselves.

The albumen, having penetrated the walls of the tortuous vessels, reaches the investing space of the Malpighian capsule, which latter is the pouch-like commencement of a uriniferous tubule. If in animals where an artificial albuminuria has been produced, the kidney be ligated, removed and boiled, the

Malpighian tufts are found enveloped by a capsule of coagulated albumen, which fills the investing space.

In the further passage of the albuminous secretion into the uriniferous tubules it takes up the secretions of the urinary epithelia, and becomes more and more acid. In proportion as this occurs, the secreted albumen displays a tendency towards coagulation which, at length, develops into the "fibrinous casts," of the uriniferous tubules. This term is applied to certain delicate-shaped hyaline coagula, which slowly collect as a sediment in the urine, and are recognized microscopically. A study of these casts convinces us that they are thrown off from the uriniferous tubules, and that, while their ends are still growing by apposition, their middle portions are loosened, compressed, and rounded off by the urine.

The amount of albumen contained in the urine varies from the most minute quantity, which, upon boiling, produces an almost imperceptible cloudiness, up to 2, 3 and even 4%, which yields upon boiling a cheesy coagulate.

Albuminuria signifies a corresponding loss of serum albumen on the part of the blood, which, in its normal condition, contains 8 to 9 parts by weight of the latter to 1 to 2 parts by weight of salts, fats and extractives, and 90 of water. The blood would thus become more and more watery, were it not for the thorough compensation effected by the additional supply of nutritive albumen. The results thus produced are really astonishing. In nephritis, for instance, the daily loss of albumen amounts to five, six, or seven grammes, or even more, although it is well known that patients suffering from nephritis are not necessarily poorly nourished nor hydræmic. With the exception of an acute watery composition of the blood, caused by suppression of urine, hydræmia does not appear until the assimilation of the nutritive albumen has been checked by a simultaneous prostration of gastric and intestinal digestion. This, it must be acknowledged, occurs often in diseases of the kidneys.

The thinness of the hyrdæmic blood, although not the only, is the chief predisposing cause of the much to be dreaded renal dropsy. Even Hippocrates comments upon the foamy, *i. e.* albuminous, urine of certain dropsies. We now know that the appearance of dropsy is secondary to the albuminous condition of the urine.

If hydræmia furnishes the most important predisposing cause, we find in the weight of the blood the most important localizing factor of this form of dropsy. Appearing first in the most dependent portions of the body, it not unfrequently changes its seat according to the position of the patient. The feet are favorite seats, although at first an elevated position of the limbs is all that is required to cause the dropsy to disappear.

In addition to the weight of the blood, various other local causes might be mentioned, for example, local irritations of the skin. It has been asserted that a particular kind of endermic medication will attract water to the spot in question and thus imitate a local dropsy.

The later stages of renal dropsy are identical with those of cardiac dropsy (see p. 119).

(c) *Glycœhæmia. Diabetes Mellitus.*

Normal blood contains a very slight amount (ranging in the decimals of a thousand) of grape sugar. The greater part of this sugar, after having been converted into lactic acid, becomes oxidized and is finally eliminated as carbonic acid and water. The small remaining portion is excreted by the kidneys, and appears as one of the normal constituents of the urine.

As much as a half per cent. of sugar is found in the blood in diabetes. Sugar is present in all secretions and parenchyma juices, and, in fact, in all the nutritive fluids of the body.

Saccharine matter causes an increased concentration of the blood, and this, in turn, produces the same effect as profuse perspiration or highly-salted food, viz., extreme thirst, leading to excessive drinking and increased urination. In diabetes mellitus, accordingly, large quantities of water are imbibed and subsequently secreted by the urine. Six to ten and twenty pounds of urine are sometimes voided daily. This urine is pale, slightly cloudy and feebly acid, somewhat foamy, of a stale odor, and sweet taste. It contains from three per cent. to ten per cent. of sugar. Its specific gravity ranges from 1.025 to 1.040. Its viscidity is sometimes one of the first indications of glucosuria.

A small amount of albumen is frequently found in connection with the sugar in diabetic urine. Of greater importance is the invariable increase in the excretion of urea. Although the proportion of urea in diabetic urine is comparatively small, we find that the amount secreted within a period of twenty-four hours is double and treble the normal quantity.

Thus we perceive that this continuous washing out deprives the body of much organic matter, which, in the normal process of oxidation, serves as valuable combustive material or as products of decomposition. Assimilation is, undoubtedly, greatly and abnormally increased. In order to maintain a proper equilibrium, corresponding nutritive supplies are eaten. A person suffering from diabetes will, if he can afford it, eat two or three times as much as in health. This additional supply, although sufficient to restore the balance in slight cases, does not meet the demands of a more severe attack. The organs, instead, emaciate and atrophy. Especially striking, in view of the corpulency by which it is generally preceded, is the loss of fat. The muscles tire easily, the movements are languid, the contractions of the heart lose their vigor, and the pulse beats feebly. All the glands are reduced in size, and the genital glands become sterile.

The disturbed nutrition is apparent in the skin, in various ways. It becomes thin, shriveled, dry and pale, and the hair follicles drop out. It exhibits, also, a peculiar vulnerability, manifested in a tendency to all sorts of inflammations, paronychia and furunculus, which are apt to be prolonged and to terminate in gangrene. The fatal termination of diabetes is usually due to tuberculosis of the lungs, supervening upon a prolonged bronchial catarrh.

The origin of the excess of sugar in the blood in diabetes is, unfortunately, as yet involved in doubt. The oldest and most plausible theory attributes it to "non-combustion" of the carbo-hydrates which have been introduced by the mouth and to the "hoarding up of the same in the blood." This is, however, an insufficient explanation, because the sugar formation and excretion cannot always be obviated by resorting to a meat diet. In support of this hypothesis, it is noticeable that when the patient has taken much sugar and other carbo-hydrates there is a perceptible increase of sugar in the urine, while a pure diet of meat produces a decrease in the same. This fact is at any rate plainly evinced, that from whatever source the sugar is supplied to the blood in diabetes, there is an incapacity to utilize it properly.

It appeared at one time as though the diabetic centre discovered by Cl. Bernard, and his investigations concerning glycogen in the liver, were on the point of clearing up this difficult problem. But it has been proved (1) that the temporary diabetes, as well as the other heterogeneous phenomena, produced by irritation of the diabetic centre, is not identical with the permanent diabetes of glucosuria; (2) that glycogen, about which, following the initiative of the French investigator, countless experiments have been made, does not exist alone in the liver, but in almost all parenchyma, especially in the muscles; furthermore, that it is a product of the splitting up of albumen, occupying in this respect a position similar to that of fat, and that these two substances in their deposition and subsequent use present much that is analogous.

As to the practical gain from this discovery, it teaches us at most to assume that there is in diabetes mellitus an excessive consumption of bodily albumen, and that the disintegration of the latter, with the probable assistance of glycogen, forms the sugar. In order to understand this storing up of sugar in the blood, we must supplement the above assumption by still another, viz., that, for reasons as yet totally unknown, the diabetic patient is unable to assimilate in a physiological manner the sugar which has accumulated in the blood. Lest this lack of adaptability should suggest "non-combustion," we must bear in mind that there are still other metamorphoses of sugar known to us, and we must also be cautious about attributing the supposed non-combustion to an imperfect supply of oxygen.

A certain amount of acetone has been recently proved to exist in the urine of diabetes mellitus. Urine containing acetone exhibits, upon the addition of the chloride of iron, a dark red coloration. The presence of acetone in the urine presupposes it also in the blood, constituting acetonæmia, although disturbances especially characteristic of acetonæmia are not known.

(d) *Uric Acid Diathesis.*

We have found the phenomena of diabetes mellitus to centre, not in the saccharine urine, but in the blood containing saccharine matter. This is equally true of what is known as uric acid diathesis.

Uric acid is a product of urinary excretion, which is more or less largely secreted according to individual conditions which are very imperfectly understood. As the excretion of uric acid in certain animals takes the place of that of urea in man, there appears to exist a certain "supplementary" relation between them. Such a relationship could be easily interpreted if we were able to prove that the uric acid is converted within the body, sometimes in a greater, sometimes in a lesser degree, into urea. Outside of the body, indeed, we are able to resolve uric acid into urea and such substances as may be considered urea, and in which certain hydrogen atoms are represented by acid radicles. But it has not yet been established that uric acid is also converted into urea within the body. It seems rather to be of extreme stability and to be thrown off finally only as uric acid. This fact, on account of its insolubility, leads to peculiar phenomena, which progress from a condition of perfect health up to the most aggravated diseased states.

The "over production" of uric acid either during or after a fever is well established. The *sedimentum lateritium* (brick-dust sediment), consisting of sodium urate, is well known in the cooled urine of fever patients. Again, this over-production of uric acid appears among people who have been subject all their life to rheumatic fevers, so that it would seem as though certain cell districts of the organism (brain, spleen?) persisted in the over-production of uric acid as a bad habit contracted during fever. Another cause, which is still more important and widely prevalent, is the habitual use of alcoholic drinks and excessive consumption of meat. Still the origin of uric diathesis is not entirely clear. With many it is hereditary, and, once acquired, reappears with stubborn persistency from one generation to another.

There is but one mode of escape for this superabundance of uric acid. Like the normal uric acid, it must be extracted from the blood by the epithelium of the uriniferous tubules, must be mixed with the secretion of the kidney and thrown off through the larger urinary passages. Unfortunately this mechanism is not always equal to the task assigned to it, and both the extraction from the blood and the elimination from the urinary passages may be imperfectly performed. Hence we have gout on the one hand and gravel (lithiasis) on the other, representing the most important results of the uric acid diathesis.

Gout (arthritis) is a very painful inflammation of one or

more joints, due to the deposition of urate of sodium, urate of calcium, or pure uric acid in the cartilages, ends of bones, synovial capsules and ligaments. The paroxysmal recurrence of gout is usually assigned, not so much to a periodic increase in the formation of uric acid as to a periodic decrease in its excretion from the kidneys. It almost appears as though the renal epithelia became exhausted by the continuous and excessive excretion of uric acid, and suspended temporarily their activity, for it is a well established fact that the proportion of uric acid in the urine is lessened during gout.

Notwithstanding all this, there is much that is obscure about the disease. The deposition of uric acid in the joints,—tophus formation—is due chiefly to the insolubility of the uric acid. It is only soluble as a basic salt. If one-half of its base be withdrawn by any acid salt, e. g., bibasic phosphate of sodium, there results a crystalline precipitate of acid urate of sodium or calcium. The question now arises, in what degree are these conditions fulfilled in the deposit of the secretion within the cartilages of the joints, etc.? Is there an acid reaction on the part of the nutritive fluid? Certainly not in a normal condition, but it is possible that in the uric acid diathesis, the impeded flow of nutritive fluid, especially in the joints, may afford time for the slightly alkaline fluid to become completely acid.

A much more simple process is the formation of gravel and calculi in the urinary passages. The acidity of healthy urine is due to the acid phosphate of sodium which it contains. When, therefore, there arises, as the result of the increase of uric acid, a quantitative disproportion between acid and base, the insoluble uric acid precipitates itself in the urinary passages, and the concrements thus formed are called, according to their size, gravel or calculi.

Urinary gravel, or sand, consists of yellowish-brown granules, of the size of a pin's head or smaller, which, upon examination under the microscope, prove to be a conglomeration of uric acid crystals. The smallest conglomerations of this kind are found ultimately in the kidneys themselves, especially in the broad excretory ducts of the renal papillæ. From here they pass into the renal calyx, and thence, growing gradually larger, into the pelvis of the kidney and bladder, from whence they are discharged. Unfortunately matters do not always run thus smoothly. As the ureters on the one hand, and the urethra on the other, do not arise from the most dependent portions of the pelvis and bladder, both of the latter are particularly favorable seats for the reception and retention of some of the heavier concrements. Remaining in this position, and increased by new additions of uric acid and urate of sodium, such a mass becomes, finally, a large kidney- or bladder-stone, the natural discharge of which is accompanied with agonizing pain (renal colic), if, indeed, it is possible to discharge it at all.

(*e*) *Disturbances in the Secretion of Bile.* (*Icterus. Cholæmia.*)

There are very few general observations to be made concerning functional disturbances of the liver. This is owing, in the main, to the great tenacity of the hepatic cells in the discharge of their function, even under the most unfavorable circumstances, and also to the broad underlying basis of this function, *i. e.*, the abundant blood changes in the organ. Although an easily verified fact, it still seems hardly conceivable, that the requisite amount of bile can be secreted by a liver in which each separate cell contains a fat drop, so large that it can scarcely be encircled by the normal protoplasm, or that an amyloid liver can still perform its functions without possessing a solitary intact cell. Whether and to what extent the protoplasm of the hepatic cells is capable of abnormally increasing its activity, is a pertinent question. It is certain that when numbers of liver cells undergo degeneration, as in syphilitic disease, the remainder subdivide and thereby avert the threatening disturbance of function.

It is only in acute yellow atrophy of the liver that there is an unquestionable suppression in the formation of bile. Apart from this affection, which will be considered hereafter, the medical vocabulary defines a disturbance of the biliary secretion to be exclusively an impeded discharge of the bile which is already formed, from the biliary passages into the intestinal canal. It gives the name of hepatogenous or resorption icterus to that dyscrasia which is produced by the resorption into the blood of the individual constituents of the bile, especially the biliary coloring matter.

The most frequent cause of suppression of bile is a catarrhal swelling of the *ductus choledochus;* sometimes, but more rarely, it is due to gall stones obstructing the lumen of the same. The resorption of the watery matter of the bile and the bilirubin contained in the same, dates from the moment when the lateral pressure of the accumulated bile becomes greater than the pressure which forces the lymph current into the adjacent lymphatics. The biliary salts are absorbed in small quantities, the cholesterin not at all.

That this resorption has taken place is soon apparent, for all the visible parts of the body, which are normally white, and the least colored by the blood, assume first a light, then a deeper, shade of yellow. The sclerotic first betrays the fact that the blood serum is no longer colorless. The skin then becomes tinged with all shades of yellow, finally becoming brown, and even black.

The parenchymas of the body become, of course, also jaundiced. Only nerve tissue and cartilage remain white. The passage of the biliary pigment into the urine is of especial note, as it is only through this means that it can eventually be removed from the blood. The urine becomes dark brown or almost black, it exhibits a yellow froth, and upon being carefully mixed in a test-tube with strong nitric acid, shows a brilliant play of colors which betrays the presence of the biliary pigment.

We may safely conclude, from the diminished frequency of the pulse in icterus, that the blood receives not only the coloring matter but the biliary salts as well. These have also been traced in the urine, although in such insignificant quantities that we need feel no great alarm at the presence of substances otherwise so poisonous and of such destructive effect upon the blood corpuscles.

Much more serious phenomena than those produced by the resorption of the biliary constituents into the blood, are caused by the accompanying non-discharge of the secretion of the liver into the digestive tract. It is of little consequence in jaundice if the intestinal contents remain uncolored, *i. e.*, of a clayey-white color, but it is a rather more serious affair when they become actually decomposed and productive of offensive gases. Gerhardt has discovered in them enormous quantities of tyrosin crystals. The bile, we know, possesses anti-putrefactive properties and aids in the assimilation of fat. In icterus, accordingly, the assimilation of fat is also impaired, which undoubtedly must and does exert a pernicious influence upon general nutrition.

Ordinary jaundice is, generally speaking, a condition which, notwithstanding some unpleasant features, may continue for weeks or months without injury and with a reasonable certainty of ultimate recovery.

It is only when the obstructions of the ductus choledochus are unusually firm, obstinate and persistent that simple cases of icterus develop into a very serious complication called *icterus gravis*. The pulse, which until now has been slow, becomes first of all strikingly accelerated; after which there follows a depressed, sleepy, and finally comatose condition. From time to time the patient exhibits restlessness and a desire to rise; he talks incoherently, and at last becomes so delirious that he can with difficulty be held in bed. Hemorrhages from the nose and anus also take place, and if an autopsy be made we find extravasations in many of the organs, as well as in the loose connective and fatty tissues, and in the cerebral and serous membranes. There is, likewise, a fatty degeneration of the myocardium, of the renal epithelia, and especially of the liver cells, as far as they are visible.

As the result of much personal experience, I do not hesitate to attribute the cases of icterus gravis (cholæmia, in its strictest sense), which have been developed from simple icterus, to a biliary liquefaction of the liver cells, although I am not as yet prepared to assert whether this cholæmic admixture of the blood is induced by resorbed bile, by re-absorbed products of degeneration of the liver cells, or by the storing up in the blood of biliary constituents.

This precaution is a necessary one, in view of yet another mode of origin of the symptoms characteristic of icterus gravis, viz.: their appearance in connection with acute yellow atrophy of the liver. In this disease there exists neither an obstruction of the biliary passages nor a preceding stage of simple icterus. A man in perfect health is suddenly struck down with this severe form of jaundice. In the few hours which elapse before death, the physician perceives a distinct diminution in the area of dullness of the liver, which is explained by finding at the autopsy a marked diminution in the size of the organ, caused by the dissolution and resorption of liver cells. Is it possible that there is here a resorption of bile? The biliary passages, it is true, are empty, and contain in place of bile a colorless mucus. We get the impression that they are empty, because they have for a long time received no influx of bile. In this case, the scarcely-formed bile must have been re-absorbed from the intercellular biliary capillaries—a very bold hypothesis. There remains then only the supposition of a primary transformation of the liver cells, the nature of which is unknown to us. Is it a .cloudy swelling resulting from a poisonous inoculation, which is analogous, and possibly at times even identical, with the action of phosphorus on the liver cells? We only know that the liver cells degenerate with surprising rapidity, and that their products of degeneration are rapidly transferred to the blood. I am, accordingly, much inclined to attribute icterus gravis to the action of the re-absorbed debris of liver cells. This action is apparent in one direction by the dissolution of numberless red blood corpuscles, and the metamorphosis of the liberated coloring matter of the blood into biliary pigment; in another, in serious irritation of the central nervous system and the general dissolution of the blood, leading to hemorrhage.

In the present imperfect state of our knowledge, we can neither deny nor prove that the formative matter of the bile, which during the suspended activity of the liver cells must naturally be retained in the blood, has some share in producing cholæmia. On the whole we may conclude that this matter is of a more harmless nature, such as albuminous bodies, fat, etc. This for the present disposes of the question as to the existence of a retention-dyscrasia of the biliary constituents—corresponding to the retention of urea or carbonic acid in lung and kidney diseases—and of a pollution of the blood by non-secretion of possible "bile-constituting" excretory substances. Such an idea must, on general principles, be rejected, although the denial in the case of the biliary pigment should be accepted *cum grano salis.*

There is an abnormal state in which large numbers of red blood corpuscles undergo dissolution, whether as the result of poisonous matter which has entered the blood and caused the dissolution (protoxide of carbon, picric acid, poisonous fungi), or, as is oftener the case, as the result of an extensive extravasation where the extravasated blood has been dissolved out and gradually re-absorbed. In both instances the liberated coloring matter is often retained for some time in the blood serum, and becomes only gradually converted into biliary coloring matter. The latter lends to the skin and sclerotic precisely the same yellowish and brownish hue as that produced by the biliary pigment which is absorbed from the biliary passages in "resorption icterus." We have, accordingly, some authority for contrasting this hæmatogenous icterus with the often-described hepatogenous form. Bilirubin appears also in the urine, and is generally termed urobilin, and the disease designated as *urobilinuria*. No investigations of any note have as yet been made regarding the non-secretion of this bilirubin by the liver, although the question is probably within the range of experimental investigation.

B. ANIMAL DISTURBANCES.

The apparatus of animal sensation and locomotion possesses no arrangement by which it, like the blood in the vegetative organs, can generalize every local change and sympathetically affect the entire body. It consists of many parts, brought into communication with each other by nerve fibres, which unite them into an anatomical whole. This connection makes a diffusion of local disturbance possible, in the sense of anatomically-continuous sympathetic affections. We have already noticed, in the deuteropathic group of symptoms, that an irritation of a peripheral sensitive nerve may assume astonishing proportions, and it is self-evident that the individual anatomico-pathological changes are equally capable of diffusion. In other words, wounds, inflammations, hemorrhages, tumors, etc., centering in the nervous system itself, are able to produce symptoms of local and general irritation which, through the anatomical agency of the nervous system, may be propagated from every possible seat of disease. This is, however, not our present point of view. We have now to consider the generalization of a local trouble by the local disturbance of function and the participation of the general organism in the same. By studying the individual diseases of the sensory-motor system in this light, we shall arrive at very different results.

We are struck, first of all, by the extraordinary diversity in the operation of the pathological changes of the sensory and motor apparatus upon the general organism. Their value and significance depend partly upon the locality which is attacked, partly upon the manner in which it is attacked. The slightest change in the floor of the fourth ventricle may produce an instantaneous stoppage of respiration and death by asphyxia. Equally dangerous are all the acute exudations into the ventricles and sub-arachnoid spaces of the cerebrum, and also hemorrhages which lead to extensive destruction and compression of the organ attacked.

On the other hand, the brain possesses an unusual power of accommodation for all small and slowly-increasing pathological effusions and new formations. And not in the brain alone, but in the entire sensory-motor apparatus, do we find a thorough development of the principle of vicarious performance of function. Accordingly, when a local trouble does not at once produce death, we may be prepared to see it last for some time.

This latter fact explains why diseases of the sensory-motor apparatus appear to be of less intense interest to a physician than those affections of the vegetative organs which place the life of the patient in more immediate jeopardy, although there is, undoubtedly, no other branch of pathology which offers to the thoughtful student a richer field for sagacious deliberation and diagnosis.

The groups of symptoms may be subdivided into those concerned (1) with the phenomena of anatomical change, (2) with the disturbances of function, produced by the same, (3) with the vicarious functions themselves. These three divisions, studied as a whole, present, we may truly say, a mathematically correct and characteristic expression of the disease, and one which is applicable to each part of the apparatus. Yet how difficult it is, in many cases, to analyze and define, not only the *nature*, but also the *seat* of the disease! And it is these two points, as we have said, which are of prime importance in estimating the pathological value of every lesion.

In considering the seat of disease, we must recollect that the various members of the sensory-motor apparatus are combined into a harmonious whole. Thus, the pathological symptoms which come under our notice are, equally with the normal symptoms of the apparatus, the external manifestations of an extended or limited series of phenomena, which have been propagated through legitimate paths from the seat of disease. The fact that a joint sometimes remains immovably flexed may be due to various causes: (1) to a degeneration of the joint itself, (2) to a contraction of the flexor muscles, (3) to an irritation of the motor nerves belonging to these muscles, (4) to centric disease, which is either situated at, or acts upon, the centre where these nerves originate. Many other causes might be enumerated. It is easily possible that such a contraction might be produced by reflex action of a peripherally-irritated, sensitive nerve, as we often see in hysteria. Generally, however, we do not go so far out of our way, but content ourselves with establishing a very sharp division between centripetal and centrifugal phenomena. This distinction is especially of value in view of the fact that in all the larger animals, as well as in man, there is in the brain a marked capacity for receiving and retaining impressions transmitted from without. Accordingly, in people gifted with unusual brain power, the majority of these impressions terminate, for the time being, in the brain. Does not the entire psychical life of man depend upon this mediatorial office of the brain, with its retarding influence upon the processes of sensation and motion? What we call mental faculties are merely the different divisions of the road which leads into, through, and again away from the brain. These divisions are centres which are neither purely sensory nor purely motor. They represent, rather, various transitions and mixtures of sensation and motion, which we call perception, imagination, fancy and will. In perception, the motory element is the weakest, the sensory the strongest. This is reversed in will, while in imagination the active and passive preponderate alternately.

The brain, therefore, with all its individual functions, occupies the middle ground between the centripetal and centrifugal phenomena. This circumstance, while it justifies a marked distinction between the two, necessitates at once an especial category for the psychical disturbance of function.

To establish the nature of disease is another task which presents far more difficulties in the realm of the sensory-motor apparatus than elsewhere. The number of pathologico-anatomical changes occurring here is unusually large. We meet with acute and chronic inflammations, and with tumors of every variety, both in the brain and spinal marrow and in the peripheral nervous system. In vivid contrast with this multiplicity is the unvaried monotony of symptomatic expression, arising very naturally from the uniform aim of the system to produce either sensation or motion. In these two directions, therefore, and only in these two directions, we may see the effects of functional disturbances; and all anatomical changes, call them what you will, produce exclusively motor or sensory disturbances. It is impossible to judge from the quality of the functional disturbance of the quality of the disease.

There is still another consideration. Within the range of the sensory-motor disturbances we may perceive conditions of abnormally increased and abnormally diminished activity; on the one hand *hyperæsthesia* and *hypæsthesia*, on the other, *hypercinesia* and *hypocinesia*. A closer study of these four elementary forms of animal groups of symptoms is next necessary. It would appear as if with the aid of this classification we might perhaps establish a qualitative diagnosis. But such is not the case. Most of the local affections of the sensory-motor apparatus produce, first of all, a slight injury, which, acting as an irritant, produces in the sensitive nerve fibres an abnormally increased or unnatural sensation, and in the motor nerves convulsions and contractions. Letting the matter rest here, we see that the severest functional disturbances, the most terrible convulsions and neuralgias, are caused by anatomical changes so slight as to be indistinguishable, and we are thus forced to concede the existence of *neuroses sine materie*. But we find instances where the anatomical disorder assumes constantly increasing proportions, and is more and more prejudicial to the performance of the functions. We then see plainly how the phenomena of abnormal irritation pass into those of paralysis, and how a disease which in its early stages caused pain and convulsions now deteriorates into anæsthesia and paralysis. Thus we lose still another diagnostic prop, and the cases are in the minority in which, by the growth of anatomical changes, there is a sudden and abrupt arrest of function, a condition which renders diagnosis materially easier.

It is not entirely satisfactory to apply the term "sympathetic," which signifies an involved condition of the entire organism, to the sensory-motor group of symptoms, because the importance of the diseased spot in relation to the general organism is so very varied. It cannot be denied that severe injuries of the brain and spinal cord, reacting upon the circulation and respiration, bear this general character. And the less severe cases may also be construed as functional disturbances of the whole body. Such a conclusion finds abundant anatomical support in the universality of the nervous system, and the intimate connection between all parts of the body established by the same.

The term "typical" has a different application. Here we must recollect that the symptomatic picture which betrays a local affection of the sensory-motor apparatus corresponds exactly to the intensity and extent of the disease, and is characteristic of the same. But under the head of typical groups of symptoms, *i. e.*, those recurring frequently and uniformly, we can only class the general phases of irritation and paralysis, which appear in the centripetal parts of the apparatus as hyperæsthesia and hypæsthesia, in the centrifugal as hypercinesia and hypocinesia, in the brain, as psychical irritation and paralysis. An appendage to these is found in the neuro-vegetative disturbances, which represent irritated and paralyzed conditions of that part of the nervous system which projects into the vegetative system.

Before, however, proceeding to the special consideration of these four species, we must throw a cursory glance upon a further peculiarity of all nervous symptoms, and one which has already been alluded to (p. 84), viz.: periodicity and the disproportion between cause and effect. It is "the inclination to recurrence of a condition of excitation which has several times existed," which, once established, becomes habitual, and, independent of the permanent irritative cause, gives rise to a group of symptoms by which an independent hereditary disease is established.

If we are willing to admit that the vital substance contains, besides assimilation and sensibility, still another fundamental element, it is undoubtedly memory, recollection. Every movement of protoplasm is more easily executed the second than the first time. It thus appears that there are certain regulations of matter which arise in order to facilitate the first movements and which remain in force for some time, and become more and more established in proportion as their activity is called into play.

It is, of course, not my purpose to discuss this momentous principle which plays so important a part in Darwin's evolution theory. It is sufficient here merely to call attention to the fact that in the individual only the faculty of memory residing in the central nervous system is involved. The delicate fibrous nervous network of the gray substance must be regarded as the anatomical substratum, which, in its delicate construction, accommodates itself to the often repeated impulses constantly passing through it, until it finally reproduces them involuntarily upon the slightest provocation. The smoother the path, the easier the traveling.

The point is at last reached where the action, having become habitual, appears spontaneous, and the trifling incitement which has caused it entirely eludes our observation. It is, in truth, of very little consequence from what quarter the slight impulse comes. It is unimportant whether the ripe fruit has been shaken from the tree by a child or by the motion of the wind. It is the result alone which concerns us.

This relative separation between the phenomenon and its cause becomes a "habit" of the nervous system, which, associated with diseased processes of sensation or motion, is entitled to be called a "bad habit." It has become a fixed function of the central nervous system, which, by frequent repetition, grows more and more persistent, and assumes, when repeated as local outbreaks, the form of an independent disease—in short, a neurosis.

When we come to consider in the Special Part those diseases which arise by "pathological development," we shall have occasion to refer the "heredity" of disease to the singular stamp imprinted upon all protoplasm, in especial that of the central nervous system, by an abnormal and habituated activity. In this connection we shall also discuss the heredity of neuroses.

HYPERÆSTHESIA.

As sensibility is a function of the central nervous system, and especially of the gray matter of the cerebro-spinal system, it is natural that an excess of sensibility or lack of the same, should be due to the excess or lack of those changes in the gray matter which accompany those functions and make us conscious of sensation.

Confining ourselves first to the excess of sensibility, to hyperæsthesia in its broad meaning, we find that we are already familiar with its chief appearance, viz., pain, which is produced by the peripheral irritation of sensitive nerves (p. 87).

It is likely that all nerve fibres which are functionally related have a common origin in the central gray substance, which is distinguished by a more dense accumulation of ganglion corpuscles. The so-called centres of origin of the brain nerves are, for the most part, well-known. But upon careful examination and comparison of sections taken from different parts of the spinal marrow, we are inclined to admit the existence of "centres" for the spinal nerves as well, which vary in length and extent, according to the size of the organ supplied. If this is correct, we may infer that the sensation of pain, apart from its later diffusion throughout the central nervous system, consists, first of all, in an abnormal excitation of the centre of origin of a closely-related group of sensitive nerve fibres. Whether the irritation of the nerve fibres occurs actually at their peripheries, or at some point of their course, is really of small importance. The manner of the irritation determines the character of the pain, in all its varied forms, pricking, throbbing, lancinating, etc. The intensity of the pain is likewise graded according to the various causes. The seat of the pain is, however, invariably situated at the peripheral terminations of the irritated nerve-fibres.

We may even go so far as to assert that the diseased irritation of the central nerve nucleus is also consciously transferred to the periphery, even when the irritation is not produced by the centripetal nerve fibres (law of eccentric projection). The central nerve nucleus may also, as we know, be irritated by diseased conditions of the brain or spinal marrow, of which it forms an integral constituent; thus, it is very plain that we ought to distinguish these pseudo-peripheral sensations, which are in reality central, from those which are generally peripheral.

Over-sensibility, or hyperæsthesia, is not, strictly speaking, real pain. It is a certain additional mobility of the whole or a part of the sensory apparatus, by virtue of which very trifling irritations are enabled to produce acute sensations. In fever we find a general and frequently occurring hyperæsthesia, which is rarely lacking when the fever is at its highest.

There are also local hyperæsthesias which are situated in the peripheral ramifications and terminations, as well as in the centres of origin of individual sensitive nerves.

Neuralgia.

Local hyperæsthias especially invite our attention, because they furnish the basis for a very important variety of oversensitiveness, viz., *neuralgia.*

By neuralgia we mean an acute pain which attacks the trunk and all the ramifications of a given nerve in an intermittent and irregularly recurring manner. The pain is felt along the entire course of the nerve, although there are certain spots known as pain centres. These are fixed undoubtedly by the anatomical construction of the nerve trunks, as they are generally the same in each. Like every other violent pain, neuralgia affects sympathetically the sensory-motor and neuro-organic apparatus. Its effect upon the latter will again engage our attention when we come to speak of trophoneurosis.

Leaving out of the question the great number of predisposing influences, conspicuous among which is heredity, we may define neuralgia to be the result of a persistent, uniform, although not always powerful, excitation of that point in the brain or spinal marrow where the nerve in question originates. Whether the excitation comes from without, or is produced internally, is of small consequence in the symptomatic picture. After it has existed for some time, an over-sensitive condition sets in, in the shape of slight pricking and throbbing, the premonitors of pain, after which the first neuralgic attack ensues. Thus the gradually habituated excess of sensibility is converted into a permanent and periodically recurring function of the gray matter, a neurosis of sensibility.

By molecular lacerations (nerve stretching), or cutting out portions of the nerves along whose paths the neuralgia is situated, we can temporarily arrest the physiological centripetal irritation, and thus proportionally lessen the irritated condition of the nerve nucleus. The probability of a permanent cure depends upon the nature and seat of the cause of disease.

ANÆSTHESIA.

Almost all the organs in a healthy body are entirely devoid of sensation, or we realize at most their presence in an indefinite and vague manner. A further diminution of sensation, or its complete absence, can, therefore, not be interpreted as disease.

Only the skin and the adjacent portions of the mucous membrane constantly convey to our consciousness impressions which we are accustomed to class with the perceptions of the higher senses, calling them sensations or feelings. It is the diminution or absence of these which give rise to anæsthesia. Defects of sight, hearing, taste and smell, belong, strictly speaking, also to the anæsthesias, but it is customary to classify blindness and deafness, at least, separately, while cases of anosmia (loss of smell) and ageusia (loss of taste) are so rare as scarcely to merit a detailed description.

Anæsthesia is the typical symptomatic expression of an abatement of function in the sensibility of the skin and other membranes. Physiology, as we know, subdivides this extensive territory into the sense of touch, feeling of pressure, perception of heat, and also the sense of locality, whenever a definite irritant acts upon the skin. Many ingenious methods have been employed in order to ascertain the degree of acuteness of the skin in different cases of anæsthesia.

The sensation of touch is tested by the slightest touch applied to the skin, that of feeling by applying small weights or the "baræsthesiometer;" that of temperature by the use of differently heated plates of metal or the "thermæsthesiometer;" and lastly, that of locality by Weber's calipers. We find by these experiments that the different varieties of membranous sensibility do not always diminish uniformly, although generally they do.

A person suffering from anæsthesia of the skin is generally conscious of "numbness and formications." He does not feel the contact of his body with his clothes, nor of his fingers with any object which they may grasp. In locomotor ataxia, where the lower extremities are perceptibly paralyzed, the patient feels in walking as though he were treading upon air, so that his eyesight is in constant requisition. In addition to these purely negative phenomena, we have usually those pricking sensations of formication and itching (paræsthesias), which penetrate the paralyzed sensibilities like electric shocks, acting as very imperfect and unwelcome representatives of normal perception. The general sensitiveness of the skin is also implicated in the impairment of the senses. The anæsthetic organ is more or less incapable of experiencing pain (analgesia), and is insensible to pin pricks, burning, pinching or electrical irritation. On the other hand, we not rarely find cases of anæsthesia dolorosa, *i. e.*, disturbances in the course of certain sensitive nerves, caused chiefly by tumors, where there is a growing and finally complete paralysis of sensation, alternating with periodic attacks of violent pain.

In conclusion, I will allude to a series of trophical disturbances resulting from anæsthesia, and which we shall consider hereafter in connection with trophoneurosis, paralysis after neurotomy, etc.

The chief cause operating to produce anæsthesia is the anatomical oppression of the central receptive organs by all sorts of local changes, inflammations, degenerations, atrophies and tumors of the brain and spinal cord. The minor causes are the rarer but very diverse disturbances in the peripheral radiations of the sensitive nerves, such as the extremes of temperature, caustics, traumata, pressure upon nerve-trunks, etc.

HYPERCINESIA—CONVULSIONS.

In studying the construction and functions of the sensory-motor apparatus in different animals, we shall find, I believe, that the great progress from lower to higher life is due to the constantly-increasing ascendancy of the segments of the brain over those of the body, the functional independence of the latter being limited by the former, which constantly absorbs a large share of segmented excitation, and confines the direct control of the same to a segmental centre. The subordination of the segmental centres to the brain finds the fullest development in man. Reflex action, the last remaining vestige of the autonomy of the segmental centre, is here represented in its weakest form. The only noticeable exceptions to this rule are the centres of automatic movement, respiration, heart's action, contraction of the iris, etc. This is, however, easily accounted for by the constancy and uniformity of the producing cause. The periodical functional irritability is forced to yield, and we see, as the result of the compromise, the well known rhythm of the pulse and respiration.

Leaving the automatic movements out of the question—a thing we can the more readily do, as they are pre-eminently a part of organic man—the main point remains unaltered, viz., that in man the sensitive centres of the spinal cord yield up a large part of their excitation to the brain, where it is transformed, and either no motor expression at all is given off, or it manifests itself at some other point. Thus, under ordinary circumstances, the principles governing the local connection between the sensitive and motor division of the same centre are almost wholly abolished.

A higher secondary effect of this anatomical centralization of the nervous system is the well-known consciousness of individuality. The power of the brain to retain the centripetal emotions which reach it, and either convert them into action or suppress them, appears to us as the leading characteristic of our own individual will, the expression of that free power of volition which underlies all law and nature. Natural philosophy readily accords to the will the sovereignty over the chief muscles of the body, and pathology, in particular, looks upon a muscular contraction which takes place against the will as the first undoubted sign of disease. Such contractions, which differ from voluntary movements in their aimlessness and unnecessary exercise of strength, are termed "twitchings," or "convulsions." In other respects their manner of experience is exceedingly dissimilar. The ancient classification of convulsions is into tonic and clonic. A tonic spasm is a single, prolonged, violent and often painful contraction, in which the muscles are stiff, board-like and rigid. Clonic spasms are contractions which follow each other in quick succession, either in individual or collective groups of muscles.

Tonic convulsions are subdivided into: (1) cramps, which attack a muscle or muscles for a short space of time (bather's cramp); (2) tetanus, which extends over almost the entire muscular system (p. 89); (3) *flexibilitas cerea*, which exhibits all the muscles in a moderately contracted condition, and the antagonistic ones with a complementary increase of nervous power, so that a position once forced upon the patient is inflexibly retained; (4) contracture and painful and frequently permanent rigidity of a muscle or muscles, terminating at last in atrophy.

Clonic convulsions, which are classified according to the number and force of the involuntary movements, present an ascending scale of varieties, from trembling (tremor), shaking (agitatio), knocking together of the limbs, involuntary grimaces when the convulsions affect the facial muscles, up to the most aggravated form of convulsive contractions of the entire body and horrible facial distortions.

Let us now inquire into the causes which produce convulsions. The first of these is, naturally, the weakening of the incomparable mastery wielded by the brain over the incoming and outgoing sensibilities of the nervous system. This is the only explanation of the "suspension of consciousness" which we find in epilepsy and other severe convulsions. The actual sources of this weakening are not definitely known. In many instances it is chargeable to a natural imperfection of the brain, due either to inheritance or disturbed development; in others, again, it is an acquired anomaly, an intercranial inflammation or tumor, it may be, which has deprived the brain of its restraining power over the conditions of excitement.

To produce these convulsions, which have their centre in the brain, does not require, as a general thing, any strong, centripetal irritation of this organ. The physiological irritations to which it is exposed are abundantly sufficient. This does not, however, apply to that variety of convulsions which originates within or without the brain—regarding the sensory-motor apparatus as a whole—to what are known as direct and reflex convulsions. Muscular contractions produced by direct irritation of a muscle or a motor path, outside of the brain and spinal marrow, are generally of a tonic character. If the irritation attack a mixed nerve trunk it will be accompanied by corresponding sensitive and other disturbances. It is, however, worthy of note that the motor nerve fibres are not capable of offering much resistance to the irritation just mentioned, so that a convulsion is very soon converted into a paralysis. This is especially true of all mechanical irritations. A prolonged convulsion is much more likely to be produced by a cumulative inflammatory process, discerned by the pathologico-anatomist with difficulty, as a slightly overgrown nucleus in the nerve sheaths.

In regard to the "reflex convulsions" there can be no doubt that the great intensity of the centripetal excitation is sufficient to break down the intracranial restraint, and through the agency of the centres of the spinal cord, bring about a reflex twitching. It is however, much oftener the case that "reflex action" is heightened and reflex convulsions are produced, not by the superior force of centripetal irritation, but by the defective construction of the intra-cerebral limitations. For since the intra-cerebral regulation apparatus is based, as we have seen, so largely upon the conveyance of the centripetal irritations to the brain, it follows that everything that impedes the course towards their reception in the brain must cause the irritation to recoil upon the adjacent centres of the spinal marrow, thus producing at this point a reflex movement.

The rise of reflex activity in a decapitated frog vividly illustrates this simple process. Whether certain poisons like strychnia increase reflex activity by paralyzing the reflex centres is an undecided point. The history of tetanus proves that this may be accomplished in other ways. In tetanus the way is prepared for the reflex action by excessively powerful centripetal irritations, or there exists a slight but prolonged and uniform irritation proceeding from one source. This irritation need not be consciously perceived, *i. e.*, it is confined to the centres of the spinal marrow, where it gradually creates a condition of heightened irritability, which vents itself at last in powerful tonic contractions of all the muscles of the body (compare p. 89). Of similar origin are the numerous other reflex convulsions, in the region of individual nerves; for example, trismus, *i. e.*, lockjaw in the region of the trifacial or fifth verve; tic convulsive and blepharospasmus, in the region of the facial muscles; torticollis and *caput obstipum*, in the region of the accessorius; spasmodic hiccough, sneezing, yawning, hysterics, in the territory of the respiratory muscles; writer's cramp, in the region of the flexor digitorum; and many others. Under this head may also be classed what is known as tetania, a spasmodic tonic contraction of the muscles of the forearm, in which a heightened electrical irritation of the motor nerves is perceptible. Tetanus and tetania are transition stages of motor neuroses.

Motor Neuroses.

We have already studied the nature of "neurosis" (p. 157), and have found in neuralgia the most important variety of sensory neuroses. The motor neuroses are much more numerous and varied. The symptomatic expression is much more complex than in neuralgia, because the latter appears only subjectively, while all convulsive contractions are visible objectively, and display according to the individual muscle or muscles very changeful pictures. Moreover, there is a typical contraction of the entire muscular system, which is designed to release the body from the bent position assumed *intra uterum*, or during sleep, and to restore it to a straighter and more natural attitude.

There appears to be one particular spot in the floor of the fourth ventricle (convulsive centre), whose only function consists in this complicated movement. It appears likewise as if there were an enormous reserve force of power waiting to take part in this movement (cerebellum?), and further that where the restraining power of the brain is intact, these forces are carefully and judiciously employed in the desired movements, but where the restraint is impaired there is an irregular, extravagant, and exhaustive use of this pent-up power.

The eclamptic convulsion has been studied elsewhere. In it is exhibited the typical process of contraction above mentioned in its most unrestrained and exuberant expression. If our conception of neuroses did not include the idea of acuteness, eclampsia might be termed acute neurosis. As it is, such a designation is not allowable, and we have only to remember that the typical contraction in question may appear as a neurosis.

Epilepsy.

An attack of convulsions differing in nothing from the eclamptic spasm described on p. 86, is the most prominent feature of epilepsy. This attack recurs at intervals ranging from a few hours to a whole year, although it generally occurs every few weeks. The mind and temperament are affected somewhat according to the natural disposition of the patient, but on the whole in proportion to the frequency of the attack. The memory and imagination are mainly affected, which would imply that the attacks had impaired the integrity of certain delicate regulations in the gray substance of the brain, which are formed by individual mental growth, and facilitate the repetition of impressions which have been once experienced.

In searching for the cause of epilepsy we shall find that more than one-fourth of all cases are to be traced to the hereditary predisposition which underlies the "epileptic change in the nervous system." And at least one-half of all cases are chargeable to the same agency when we include under this head of predisposing causes not only epilepsy proper, but all serious neuro- and psycho-pathic conditions in a progenitor.

We are still in ignorance of the nature of the permanent alteration in the central nervous system which manifests itself periodically in an epileptic attack. The conclusion of one attack furnishes a starting point for another, which, as soon as the requisite force is accumulated, breaks out in such parts of the central nervous system as are in possession of the abnormal condition. Hence we are inclined to view this as a condition of abnormal excitability, which, induced primarily by some local irritation, becomes finally domesticated and independent of the exciting cause, and constitutes an independent, transmissible disease.

This view is favored by the results of experiments on animals as regards the primary origin of epilepsy. In guinea pigs, namely, the "epileptic change" is brought about, and the first epileptic attacks occur in from four to six weeks after lesions of the spinal marrow, medulla oblongata, crura cerebri, or corpora quadrigemina, as well as after section of one or both sciatic nerves. We know, furthermore, that epilepsy thus produced in guinea-pigs is often transmitted to their young.

In very many instances medical observation is able to refer the origin of the epileptic change to a local irritation of the nervous system; to external violence, especially upon the skull, to wounds, scars and tumors on the peripheral nerves, to tumors of the female genital apparatus, to intracranial exostoses, to the pressure of an abnormally protruding *dens epistrophei* upon the anterior surface of the medulla oblongata, etc.

Pursuing this line of investigation and experiment, we are led to seek the essential cause of this malady in the abnormal excitation of the reflex centres of the spinal cord and pons varolii. Acquired or transmitted defects of the brain, by which it is rendered incapable of exerting normal restraint upon the activity of these centres, might be adduced in support of this theory—which, however, is far from being established. We must not forget that the epileptic fit is invariably associated with a suspension of consciousness and a sudden anæmia of the cerebrum. No one will deny that these two features are intimately associated with the outbreak of convulsions. The advocates of the irritation theory say that the irritation of the convulsive centre, and the simultaneous excitation of the neighboring vasomotor centre, occasions a contraction of the cerebral blood vessels, resulting in the phenomena above mentioned. Any one who has had occasion to witness the entire course of an epileptic attack, although he may concede the possibility of such a connection, will not forget that the pallor and the unconsciousness precede the convulsions by two to ten seconds, and will, in consequence, be apt to attribute the excessive action of the reflex centres to a lack of restraint on the part of the anæmic brain. The breaking down of the cerebral restraint, considered as a variety of brain exhaustion, would also be a cumulative force, which, when the maximum was reached, would lead to an acute prostration of consciousness and a simultaneous discharge of motor force.

I say "would be" and "would lead," for I am unwilling to overthrow an hypothesis. I can, however, plead as an excuse the many well established cases where epilepsy has resulted from toxic irritation of the brain, as in drunkenness, or from functional over excitement, as in fright or insanity. The manifold fluctuations in the quantity of blood contained in the cerebral blood vessels can very readily pass into the incipient stages of cerebral neurosis, where they constitute the leading element. We shall some day, perhaps, learn to discriminate between reflex and cerebral epilepsy. The fact that the etiological characteristics of both are interchangeable admits a large number of intermediate varieties.

Catalepsy and Hypnotism.

Closely allied to epilepsy is catalepsy, which is distinguished by paroxysmal attacks of cataleptic convulsions, such as described on page 162. Here also we find the abnormal activity of the convulsive centre associated with complete or partial loss of consciousness. That brain exhaustion is primarily concerned here is proved by the recent careful investigations into the nature of hypnotism, commonly called somnambulism. In these experiments catalepsy is produced artificially. The individual chosen for the purpose is made to gaze steadily at some shining object—the head of a scarf-pin, let us suppose—which is held motionless a few inches away from the eyes. This fixed scrutiny in a short time exhausts the brain to such a degree that a mesmeric sleep ensues. While in this condition the body is insensible to bodily pain, to pricks, burns, etc.; conscious movements are replaced by the cataleptic state. The mind can only be reached by the higher organs of sense. The responses which can be evoked from a hypnotized person by addressing them distinctly, displaying certain objects, and conveying impressions of smell and taste, are not clear and conscious utterances, but merely a mechanical reproduction of familiar perceptive processes. Charcot has very aptly called them psychical automata.

Chorea.

A weakened brain and an incapacity to control the movements of the motor centres of the spinal cord are the prerequisites for choreic spasms. Under the name of chorea minor it appears before puberty as a transient neurosis; as chorea major it constitutes one of the most dangerous and severe varieties of anatomical lesions of the brain.

In chorea minor, the weakening of the brain is relative, inasmuch as this organ has not kept pace with the rapid development of the genital apparatus and the many excitations reaching it from that source. In chorea major, the impaired brain activity is absolute and degenerates into complete paralysis. The spasms in chorea are twitchings of individual groups of muscles, attacking first one point, then another, with lightning-like rapidity. The arm is bent, the hand undergoes first pronation, then supination, the fingers are spread out, the shoulder raised, the head is thrown back, the eyes distorted, the tongue projected and immediately drawn in, the teeth are ground together, the knee is suddenly raised, so that the sufferer is thrown to the ground. The patient is unable to feed himself, as it is impossible to control the motions of the hand and arm. In chorea major, the movements are even more powerful, amounting to twistings and contortions of the entire body.

The movements are entirely beyond the control of the patient. He feels, on the contrary, that even voluntary movements must be carefully guarded, lest their exercise should give free rein to those which are uncontrollable. His mind is weary and confused, and memory, appetite and sleep are disturbed.

HYPOCINESIA, PARALYSIS.

More simple in appearance and origin than the arbitrary contractions of the muscles, is their more or less pronounced inability to respond to the will, as seen in paralysis or paresis (partial paralysis) of the muscles. Everything which influences the musculo-motor apparatus to such a degree as to cause an impairment of function is expressed symptomatically as a paralysis of the muscle or muscles in question. The result is the same whether the point of attack be in the very first beginnings of the apparatus—in the laboratories of the will situated in the cerebral cortex; or in the intra-muscular nerve-terminations, or the muscular substance itself. These lesions are of the most diverse nature. In order to limit their territory, it has been customary to make a distinction between the strictly-speaking nervous paralysis, and the inaction of the passive organs of motion, the bones and joints, as well as the disturbances of purely muscular function. Although this division, as we have repeatedly remarked, is incorrect in view of the strict continuity between these parts and the nervous system, we will adopt it for the sake of convenience, and only speak of paralysis proper in connection with lesions of the nervous system.

(a) PERIPHERAL PARALYSIS.

Whether, independent of the well known effect of the American Indian arrow poison, woorara, upon the intramuscular nerve terminations, there is still another form of paralysis which is confined exclusively to this portion of the musculo-motor apparatus, remains a doubtful question. On the other hand, the entire peripheral course of the motor nerve fibres, from the brain to their entrance in the muscles, is exposed to countless traumatic lesions. Such lesions are: contusions and lacerations from gunshot and sabre wounds, from fractures, and dislocations, compression from inflammatory new formations and tumors, leading to complete or partial destruction of nerve fibres and to corresponding paralysis of the attendant muscles.

Experiment has shown that motor fibres offer an astonishingly slight resistance towards all mechanical injuries. A pressure of eighteen or twenty inches of quicksilver, for a space of fifteen minutes, is sufficient to interrupt motor impulses for a considerable period of time. Section of a nerve is followed by instantaneous and total paralysis of the muscles concerned. If reunion of the two sections is impossible, the paralysis is permanent, but if they are successfully approximated, it disappears gradually but completely. The anatomico-physiological changes which the peripheral nerve endings and their muscles undergo at such a time are so typical and so valuable in forming a prognosis that they are worthy of especial mention.

First, as regards anatomical changes. We distinguish (1) a series of degenerate processes, occasioned by section of the nerves; (2) a series of regenerate processes, which facilitate the union of the sections, check further degeneration, and repair the injuries already received.

Degeneration sets in at once after section. A portion of

the nerve medulla exudes from the cut ends of the nerve fibres, and the tubular membrane is cleft apart some distance along its course. In this cleavage appear cylindrical flakes and round drops, to which are added, after the seventh day, ordinary fat granules, which congregate in spots, forming a sort of compound granule-cell. All the products are reabsorbed by degrees, leaving only a narrow, pale, ligamentous substance behind, consisting of the axis cylinder and Schwann's sheath (tubular membrane). In this manner the fibre is preserved for weeks and months, waiting to be restored by innervation.

The paralyzed muscles remain intact somewhat longer than the motor nerve fibres. It is only after the expiration of some weeks that there is a decided atrophy of the individual muscular fibres, with obliteration of the transverse striæ. This atrophy, betraying itself macroscopically in a corresponding emaciation of the belly of the muscle, leads at last to the degeneration and total loss of contractility.

Side by side with these purely degenerative changes, and following like them immediately upon the solution of continuity, are restorative processes which are calculated to regenerate the disturbed nerve-paths and the muscles which have been threatened or already injured by atrophy.

A young, soft connective tissue, well provided with cells, is deposited in the interstices between the nerve-filaments. Conspicuous among the cells are certain large, spindle-shaped ones, whose polar offshoots follow the longitudinal axis of the severed nerve, thus effecting a protoplasmic union of the detached and sundered fibres. This establishes a bridge between the central and peripheral trunk, which in process of time is converted by corresponding development into a genuine nerve-fibre. This favorable termination can, of course, only be expected when the gap between the central and peripheral nerve trunks is not too great. If, however, it is once completed, all abnormalities of the nerves vanish by degrees, and the paralyzed muscle regains its former volume and firmness, together with its full contractility. The manner in which this restitution of the muscular substance is brought about depends upon the degree of the previous degeneration. The muscular substance appears capable of restoration as long as the striation is preserved. When that is lost, and the muscular substance disintegrates into certain homogeneous, shiny, waxy flakes, a complete reconstruction of the contractile cylinders becomes necessary. The material for this is doubtless furnished by the non-degenerated and rapidly proliferating muscle corpuscles.

Complete degeneration of the paralyzed muscle is the inevitable result where there is a failure to re-establish continuity between the central and peripheral nerve-ends. It is associated with vasomotor paralysis produced by section of the vasomotor nerve-paths. The immediate consequence of this vasomotor paralysis is an arterial hyperæmia, which, however, after the prolonged dilatation and ultimate relaxation of the vascular walls, takes on a more lasting character, and like the venous hyperæmias, furnishes the basis for a slowly increasing proliferation of connective tissue. The atrophied muscular fibres are entirely destroyed in the progress of this growth, and the bellies of the muscles are transformed into a tough, ligamentous, fibrous mass, whose otherwise homogeneous surface is varied by occasional striæ of adipose tissue and rows of fat cells.

So much for the anatomical changes which we must expect to meet in all peripheral paralysis of the nerves and muscles. Their main features have long been known. But modern science points out certain physiological characteristics, by means of which we are able to recognize with almost absolute certainty a peripheral paralysis, and discriminate between it and most paralyses of central origin. I allude to the so-called "reaction of degeneration" in the paralyzed parts, *i. e.*, to the effect produced upon them by electric currents, which is at times very striking. For either a faradic or galvanic current, applied to the *nerves* of the paralyzed muscle, produces a gradual fall and a subsequent rise of excitability, which is exactly proportioned to the processes of degeneration and restoration described above. But in applying electricity to the paralyzed *muscle* itself, the same effect can only be produced by the irritation of the induced current of short duration. On the other hand, galvanism produces in the second week, after the occurrence of the paralysis, a very marked rise of excitability, which continues to augment, during the next week, and disappears only gradually, whether a cure be effected or the paralysis become permanent. Electro-muscular contractility does not take place suddenly, as in the healthy muscle, but slowly, although vigorously, and with a pronounced tendency towards prolonged muscular tonus. The law of contraction undergoes here a quantitative alteration. Strong contractions are not produced by the cathodic (+), but by the anodic (—) *closure*, while on the other hand, the weak and very soon extinguished *opening* contraction is greater with the cathode than the anode.

It can scarcely be doubted that this phenomenon proceeds from the determined opposition of the so-called idio-muscular contractility to the neuro-muscular. Further discoveries must show us the relation of this to the incipient degeneration of the muscle.

(b) SPINAL PARALYSIS.

When the spinal marrow is subjected to any of the more extended pathologico-anatomical changes, which involve the entire transverse section, the paralysis thereby induced involves all the motor nerves arising below this point. It is always on both sides of the body (paraplegic), ascending, and complicated with paralysis of the bladder, because the nerves of the latter arise from the lowest section of the spinal marrow. The participation of the symmetrical muscles of the lower extremities, trunk and upper extremities is regulated by the seat of the disease, according as this is located in the lumbar, thoracic, or cervical regions of the spinal cord. Sensibility is destroyed in the same proportion, although experience has shown that sensation is by no means as easily interrupted as motion. One peculiarity of spinal paralysis is the sensation as of a girdle or belt fastened around the body. This "feeling of constriction" is associated with abnormal sensations, formications, etc., in the feet.

Reflex action below the seat of the injury is at first heightened, afterwards also impaired.

A more complicated variety of spinal paralysis is found in those anatomical lesions which produce a partial but never complete suspension of function at many different points of the spinal cord. Most cases of so-called gray degeneration of the brain and spinal cord belong to this class. As the name indicates, the white substance becomes discolored, and presents a reddish-gray aspect, resembling outwardly the ordinary gray matter of the brain. The diseased part exhibits at the same time a considerable decrease in volume. The true action of this process is as yet unknown. The name of "gray degeneration" is well chosen, inasmuch as the gray coloring is mainly determined by the loss of the white, shining and oily myeline of the medulla of the nerve fibres. The name, therefore, emphasizes that change which without doubt furnishes the immediate cause of the disturbed function. So soon as the nervous conduction loses the isolation, which is effected solely by the stability of an intact medullary sheath, the clearness and independence both of simultaneous sensation and simultaneous motor impulse becomes imperiled, if not abolished. While there is, on the one hand, a constant increase and fusion of the sensations appertaining to the sensibility of the skin, so that conscious sensation is entirely overcome or replaced by a chaos of paræsthesias, we see, on the other hand, a remarkable separation of the combined motor phenomena into their elements—the so-called *ataxia motoria*. A healthy person executes voluntary movements by a single impulse, because of the well drilled co-operation of individual contractions in the muscles concerned. The axis cylinders which guide the motor impulses are probably lodged in close proximity to each other in the medullary substance of the brain, and even more in that of the spinal cord ; but, as long as they are properly enveloped in myeline, the isolated condition of the attendant motor impulses is assured. In the absence of the myeline stratum, an effect, to be produced at all, must be the result of individual action on the part of each motor impulse, while the co-ordinate motion resolves itself into a succession of heterologous, and, in part, antagonistic movements. The simplest instance of a loss of co-ordinate power is seen in the trembling palsy (Intentions-Zittern), which appears characteristically in those suffering from repeated scleroses of the brain and spinal cord. In a reclining position this is hardly perceptible, but no sooner does the patient attempt to walk, stand, or grasp anything, than he is overtaken by a trembling and shaking which is strong in proportion to the energy of the intended action. Similar appearances accompany movements of the tongue, lips and eyeballs.

Real ataxia, which presents an especially typical phase in tabes dorsalis, does not confine itself to mere trembling and shaking of the limbs. The movement of the limbs in walking is jerky, irregular and uncertain, the abrupt extension of the knee brings the foot down solidly upon the ground. All the movements are zigzag, and must be controlled by the eye, otherwise, on account of the lack of the sense of position, the aim is overreached. Even in attempting to stand with closed eyes, the patient will stagger and fall.

Besides these unmistakable lesions of the spinal cord and its disturbed function, there is an extensive group of so-called reflex paralyses, which are the result of peripheral irritation. On this account, partly, and partly on account of the double nature of their appearance, we are led to seek the origin of these paralyses in the spinal marrow. They are most frequent after severe disorders of the abdominal organ, after dysentery and diseases of the bladder and uterus, painful delivery, etc., and are of a progressive and often incurable character. They resemble the above-described reflex convulsions to a certain degree, the former being the result of an abnormal irritation of the reflex centres, the latter of an over-excitation and complete exhaustion of the same. A tangible basis for all these changes is greatly to be desired. In some cases of reflex convulsions, and also reflex paralyses, there have been found distinct traces of inflammatory hyperæmia, or infiltration, and even hemorrhage and softening in the spinal cord itself, or in the outposts of the central gray matter in the intervertebral or basal ganglia. An ascending neuritis has even been remarked, affecting finally the entire reflex system. All these instances, however, are of a casual nature, although no case of tic douloureaux, of convulsions, or reflex paralysis should be allowed to leave the post-mortem table without a careful anatomical and histological scrutiny of the involved centres.

(c) CEREBRAL PARALYSIS.

Cerebral paralyses must be divided into those which are produced by a palpable lesion of the main channels of the will power, and into those which are properly central, having their seat in the part impressed by the will, the cerebral cortex. These cerebral paralyses (due most frequently to hemorrhages, softenings, inflammatory and non-inflammatory new formations) are, as a rule, hemiplegic, *i. e.*, they affect only one side of the body, and that the one opposite the injured hemisphere. The upper extremities are usually most severely affected, then the face, which on the paralyzed side is smooth and flabby, the tip of the tongue also when protruded inclines towards the diseased side.

About purely central paralyses there is little to be said.

The mind is characteristically affected by a simple or excitable weakness of the combined powers of sensation, imagination and will, which is liable to end in total imbecility (progressive paralysis, paralytic imbecility). Besides this we find total and semi-paralyses of widely divergent motor paths, especially of the muscles employed in phonation. They develop rapidly up to a certain point, after which they increase slowly, remain stationary, or even retrograde. In many of them the anatomical· position of the disease may with reasonable certainty be located at a particular point in the cerebral cortex, since experimental pathology has lately pointed out the localities where the will power appears to concentrate in order to execute certain co-ordinate movements.

The anatomical changes which lead to central paralyses are due chiefly to chronic inflammations, with connective tissue proliferation and subsequent contraction. Although irreparable in themselves, the disturbances thus caused are up to a certain point capable of equalization, owing to the superior capability of the brain for the performance of vicarious functions. Beyond this point the extended nature of the disease makes equalization impossible and the paralysis becomes permanent.

PSYCHICAL IRRITATION AND PARALYSIS.

There are certain pathological changes which attack the whole or a part of the cerebral cortex. Although their postmortem appearance is only that of a protracted hyperæmia and its results, we need not be surprised to meet pathological symptoms which resemble those of a mind which, though over-excited, or it may be totally exhausted, is still normal. This resemblance is sometimes so close that we are led to question whether it will ever be possible in every instance to discriminate accurately between the irresponsible demeanor of an unscrupulous person, and the same actions in a lunatic. The judges in such a predicament are constrained to consult the physician. The latter, if sufficiently authorized by the facts, need not pronounce the condition one of mental health, but one of mental derangement. The chief criterion of the psychical anomaly presents itself as follows:—

A sane individual displays in his perceptions and emotions, as well as in his thoughts, words and deeds, a well proportioned relation to preliminary circumstances and conditions. The tranquil course of this mental activity, from the external impulse through all the stages of psychical life until it finds motory expression, is interfered with by the anatomical change in the cerebral cortex, which either increases its irritability in the most surprising manner, or paralyzes it. The symptoms of this irritation are psychical. They associate themselves with the emotional and imaginative life, sometimes in harmony, sometimes at variance with the will, but differ from the physiological processes in that they are executed under the pressure of an irresistible inner impulse, "without sufficient psychical motive." The source of this compulsion is the diseased condition of the cerebral cortex.

Much stress has been laid upon the "element of excess" in psycho-pathological symptoms. But when we consider what an enormous amount of power the physiological brain is able to exert, we soon come to the conclusion that the psycho-pathological appearances appear excessive only because they are entirely disproportionate to the preliminary causes, or else have no apparent cause at all. Indeed, the "illogical, forced, compulsory" element in psychological processes is the only really fundamental feature by which they can be discriminated.

The typical groups of symptoms are quite varied, although three principal groups may be mentioned, (1) those of moderate irritation; (2) those of stronger psychical irritation; (3) those of psychical paralysis.

Moderate psychical irritation exists only as long as the patient is able to give vent to his inner agitation in a corresponding degree of expression (hyperthymia, hedonia, mania). The mind is full of images, following each other without logical sequence (hallucinations). The images are expressed in words, the words in deeds. In this excitation the first symptom is an aimless rushing hither and thither and purposeless activity; the next is continuous chattering, singing, dancing, boasting, and unseemly actions (nymphomania), until the crisis is reached in wild shrieks and cries, blind violence and destructiveness, and powerful and astonishing exhibitions of muscular strength (frenzy). All this is in strong contrast to the trivial nature of the external irritation which appears to have occasioned such abnormal effects. On the other hand, the perception of the most insignificant objects is wonderfully heightened. The patient sees and hears everything, and appears exceptionally bright and happy. The easy transition from ideas to words, from desires to deeds, causes at first an intensified enjoyment of life, such as only those can appreciate who have themselves felt the inspiring and energizing power of healthful activity.

It may to many appear paradoxical to class frenzy, which is assuredly not mild in character, with the moderate psychical irritations. But although it may appear to the uninitiated as the "mad raving" of a lunatic, the alienist is well aware of its inoffensive nature.

We are authorized to assume the presence of increased psychical irritation whenever the patient is no longer in a condition to convert the impressions which throng in upon him into action; when, realizing his powerlessness, he relapses into deep spiritual depression (melancholia). The images which pass through his mind are feeble and fluctuating. His paucity of ideas is painfully apparent even to himself. Fresh irritations, which reach him from without, leave no trace upon his stupefied senses. Every hope and wish, every desire and ambition, seem paralyzed. In connection with the most advanced stages of psychical trouble there is often an absolute lack of energy, a stupor (mania attonita). In other instances, there are detached and violent explosions, with a total disregard for the safety of the patient himself or those about him.

If a person suffering from melancholia is still able to think, his mind is filled with the most depressing images. He broods over his own unworthiness, and his self-accusations often lead to rejection of food and attempts at suicide. He becomes possessed with the idea that he is pursued, and the overclouded mind pictures to itself the most frightful dangers and troubles which are about to overtake him. The dread ripens finally into a fixed conviction, and the so-called "illusions" become a deeply-rooted and ruling power in the otherwise deserted world of thought.

We cannot leave this strange—I might say specific—product of psychical disturbance, the development of hallucination, without further comment. It shows how even the intellectual life may fall a prey to genuine neurosis, and in the same manner as the general run of neuroses already indicated on pp. 156, 157. Hallucination is a group of impressions, which is accompanied by especially strong emotions, and in a measure, is caused by them, and on this account is longer retained *i. e.*, is more frequently repeated. Now in proportion as the desire is repeated on the part of the individual to realize the visionary idea, or he is fearful and anxious lest it come true, the brain learns to adapt itself to the diseased exercise of these impressions, so that they recur finally with the greatest ease and almost without external incitation. The excited brain may be compared to soil in which the delusion has taken firm root, and become fixed like an arrow in the flesh, lacking organic connection with the other reasoning processes of the person, an element as foreign to the individuality as if belonging to some one else. Yet, if we set aside all the dreadful adjuncts which our fancy applies to lunacy, we find nothing but a simple neurosis, and that a delusion is nearest in kin to neuralgia.

The groups of symptoms already considered presuppose an anatomical condition of the brain in which the exercise of its functions is advanced or hindered, but never completely arrested. An effectual arrestation of the activity of the cerebral cortex, a psychical paralysis, only occurs after certain changes have set in, which, though slight in themselves, are diffuse, insidious and irrevocable, and result in atrophy of the cerebral centre. They develop equally in the brain of an acute psychosis or of other cerebral disturbances, or they appear in conjunction with a persistent or often re-appearing hyperæmia, as in alcoholism.

What is commonly called weak mindedness or idiocy is a deterioration and ultimate deadening of energy in all the departments of intellectual life, and forms the cardinal symptom of psychical paralysis. Memory usually suffers first. This produces breaks in the chain of impressions, and destroys the logical sequence of the reasoning process. The warmth and tenderness of the emotional nature is lost; a repellant indifference in morals and æsthetics takes their place. Desires and ambitions, however temperate they may have been, being no longer controlled by the will, force themselves to the surface of the impoverished mind and produce vacillations of the most ludicrous and disconnected sort. If a hallucination has once been cherished, it is apt to survive for a time the general wreck, although it is no longer able to greatly transport or excite the person.

NEURO-VEGETAL DISTURBANCES.

It is, *par excellence*, an animal regulation that even the nutritive processes are in a certain degree subject to the authority of the nervous system. Assimilation is, indeed, one of the fundamental conditions of living matter. It can, independent of all nervous authority, accomplish much that is grand and beautiful, as the vegetable kingdom constantly teaches. There are even diseased conditions in the organism, which are nothing more than an uncontrolled assimilation of fresh vitality by that already existing. This assimilation which rejects the regulation of the nervous system is expressed in tumors. In general, however, both the blood supply of the parts and the tissue changes in their parenchyma cells are subservient to the orders of the nervous system; inasmuch as the latter fixes the quantitative values of both, according to the varying needs of the parts and the resources at the disposal of the general organism.

(*a*) ANGIO-NEUROSES.

We learned on p. 17 how the blood supply of the body is regulated by that ingenious apparatus, constructed of nerves and ganglia, designed to dilate and contract the blood vessels. It is, unfortunately, so constituted as to be easily deranged by all sorts of pathological causes, whereupon we have hyperæmias and anæmias, which are entirely disproportionate to the needs of the body, and form instead the basis or concomitants of a special group of disturbances, known as angio-neuroses. The chain of causal phenomena—as far as it can be distinguished—aims at an irritation or paralysis of the sympathetic. Occasional lesions of this nerve in the cervical region—in particular, gunshot wounds—have furnished excellent material for analysis and diligent study on the part of our neuro-pathologists and ophthalmologists. Paralysis, and also irritation of the cervical sympathetic, provoke highly characteristic groups of symptoms, which are seen in a non-traumatic and as yet etiologically unexplained angio-neurosis, known as migraine (hemicrania). By this term we understand an intermittent pain on one side of the head, which attacks certain individuals periodically, from puberty up to extreme old age. During the paroxysm the face is usually pale and contracted, the eye on the painful side small and inflamed, the pupil dilated, the temporal artery tense and hard. In short, there is a painful tetanus in the cervical region of the sympathetic nerve, with vasomotor paralysis and paralysis of the iris. Later, the symptoms of irritation recede and make room for those of paralysis of the sympathetic. The latter are present from the first in rare cases of hemicrania. Marked congestion of the entire side of the head is accompanied by contraction of the pupil, and an exceedingly characteristic slight droop of the upper lid (ptosis), with or without increased secretion of sweat.

Angina pectoris is another irritation of the sympathetic. It is accompanied with an accelerated pulse, contracted peripheral arteries, icy coldness and pallor of the extremities, and a sensation of excruciating pain, shooting from the substernal region into the left arm. This pain appears to be occasioned by dilatation of the arch of the aorta, due to the recoil of the blood and the subsequent stretching and distortion of the adjacent nerve plexuses.

Basedow's disease is now also reckoned as an angio-neurosis, though not as a spasm, but as a paralysis of the cervical sympathetic. A prolonged period of palpitation of the heart, either with or without cardiac hypertrophy, will be succeeded by a swelling of the thyroid gland, and soon after by a singular protrusion of the eyeballs. The pulse reaches 140 or even 200 beats per minute. This disease arises in a few days. The strong pulsation of the thyroid arteries, the loud blowing sounds heard over them, the turgescence of the tumor, rising and falling in accord with the intensity of the heart's action, all convince us that this is due solely to a dilated condition of the numerous tributary vessels of the thyroid gland. The thyroid and the ophthalmic arteries are, as we know, the two most valuable safety-valves against congestion of the brain, which may account for the fact of their being conjointly implicated in this remarkable angio-neurosis, which certainly does not implicate the entire cervical sympathetic. The more diffused the etiological reflexes, the less apparent is the participation of the sympathetic. Other criteria are then needed to establish the "nervous nature" of a hyperæmia or anæmia; such are, the rapid appearing and disappearing, the symmetry of the phenomena, the presence of a neuralgia, the dependence upon a contemporary disorder in another part of the body, which is especially to be construed as a reflex hyperæmia or anæmia.

(b) TROPHO-NEUROSES.

In considering the dependence of cellular assimilation upon the nervous system, we have repeatedly indicated the value of motor innervation in nourishing all those parenchyma cells, which, like the muscular fibres, are in their function pre-eminently assigned to the care of the nervous system. Not alone the need of certain substances which are necessary to restore their working capacities, but also the power to take up these substances from the blood, are increased through its action. Undoubtedly we have to do with certain chemical affinities which are satisfied by the taking up of a little albumen, a comparative large amount of fat, and still more oxygen, in loose chemical combination.

It is, perhaps, allowable to assume a similar restorative influence of centrifugal innervation in the non-active muscles, but chiefly in all the less active cells of our organism. I surmise that there are in the latter certain fibres of the sympathetic which have the signification of trophic nerve-fibres. Farther than this we cannot for the present advance, nor is there any support for the supposition of a hunger in the cells, whose demands are conveyed to the central nervous system by sensitive nerves. It is at present of more consequence to attribute the disordered condition of the tissues to the accumulated products of excretion and exhaustion, and to look for relief in the rapid rinsing of the tissues with arterial blood, brought about by reflex action. This theory would also require sensitive nerve fibres, which, on account of their assistance to nutrition, we might also call trophic. We shall be inclined to dispute the identity of these sensitive trophic nerves with the connective tissue nerves described on p. 17, but must not forget that the irritation of the *sensitive* nerves which execute the animal functions is also able to produce hyperæmias. We must, accordingly, ascribe trophic functions to these latter as well, although not in the same degree as those we ascribed before to the animal *motor* nerves.

From these premises we may conclude:—

(1) That, in view of our imperfect knowledge of trophic nerves, strictly speaking, and the difficulty of defining their territory, it is not possible or allowable to pronounce upon independent tropho-neuroses with any degree of precision.

(2) That we may look for tropho-neuroses in all prolonged disturbances of the sensory-motor apparatus.

(3) That no radical differences appear as regards the quality of the disturbances, but they all have something to do with a certain plus or minus of the factors of nutrition which are subject to nervous control.

These expectations are confirmed by actual knowledge. Those longest known and most intelligible to us are the nutritive disturbances, which appear concomitantly in all the elementary forms of sensory-motor disturbances, provided that the latter are of some duration. Reference may here be made to the descriptions in Paralysis; trophic disturbances were also mentioned under anæsthesia, as well as under neuralgia and convulsions.

The disturbances themselves always follow the same course. Simple atrophy of the chief cells of the diseased part either may or may not be—according to the seat of disease—associated with a permanent dilatation of the local blood vessels. As this dilatation is not the result of a temporary inhibition, but of a permanent muscular paralysis, it gradually assumes a more stationary character. It becomes the starting point for a progressive hypertrophy of the connective tissues, such as may be seen in any prolonged venous hyperæmia. There is also a singular display of non-resistance in the attitude of the imperfectly innervated parts towards external irritations. This incapacity for resistance is seen in various degrees of intensity, from a certain "marked inflammability" up to "gangrene." I explain this as follows:—

The original disease has impaired the capacity of the central organ for the reception of the centripetal accessions, so that the peripheral parts are unable to surrender their customary quota of excitation to the central nervous system, and are forced involuntarily to react with their whole strength upon themselves. All tropho-neuroses, however, are composed of the three above-named factors and their results, as the following consideration will show.

Beginning with the "concomitant tropho-neuroses," we accord the first place to the atrophy of inactivity of the muscles. We have already noted the appearance of the same, after section of the peripheral nerves, and studied the results and nature of the vasomotor paralysis, which is induced by simultaneous separation of the vasomotor nerves (p. 248). Vascular paralysis usually is absent when the muscular paralysis originates, let us say, in the spinal marrow, and not in a mechanical injury of the different nerves. This is the case in spinal paralysis of children, and probably also in progressive atrophy of the voluntary muscles, which commonly begins with emaciation of the muscles of the thumb, and also in saturnine paralysis. When the immobility of the muscles is compulsory and non-nervous, as in pathological rigidity of certain joints, the muscular fibre withstands the inaction-atrophy for a long time. Its final disappearance is associated with a new formation of fatty tissues, which may be a sign of the continuance of such nutritive processes, at least, as are not essentially muscular, being due perhaps to the agency of the sympathetic. Similar effects are visible in artificial fattening, and in that mysterious atrophy of the muscular system which, occurring chiefly in the lower extremities of half-grown boys, has been named, on account of the prolific interstitial formation of fat, Pseudo-Hypertrophia Lipomatosa.

In addition to these processes in the muscles themselves, there occur in peripheral paralysis certain changes in the skin, which we can only judge from the standpoint of diminished nutrition. The skin often becomes thin, smooth and glossy, especially about the fingers (glossy fingers). The epidermis is not properly attached to the surface of the papillary layer, and scales off easily, or forms vesicles, which contain a serous fluid. The nails grow thick and become curved; often, indeed, separate wholly from the matrix. The hair drops out, etc. The deeper parts, such as the bones and joints, tend to atrophy, while the loose connective tissue begins, under the auspices of the vascular paralysis, to proliferate, threatening the paralyzed limb with general cirrhosis.

The feeble resistance which the paralyzed parts oppose to external lesions is most surprising. Trifling injuries and insignificant chemical and thermal irritants of various kinds produce at once tedious ulcerations. Gangrene (Decubitus paralyticus) is easily acquired and progress rapidly.

As previously stated, I ascribe this latter series of phenomena to the simultaneous paralysis of sensation, which is never lacking in peripheral paralyses. This view is supported by the fact that just this paralysis is especially conspicuous in isolated sections of sensitive nerves. Thus, in rabbits, the section of the ophthalmic branch of the trigeminal nerve produces in the corresponding eye a predisposition towards inflammation, which leads inevitably to ulceration of the cornea, conjunctiva, etc., unless the eye be shielded from external irritants. Section of both pneumogastric nerves is likewise followed by a condition of inflammability in the lung, whence develops rapidly a pneumonia, due to the irritation of the liquids of the mouth, which are unhindered from flowing into the bronchi.

Convulsions and hyperæsthesia may at times also lead to trophical disturbances, but this is in rare cases, where they appear as persistent affections.

The more "independent tropho-neuroses" include any number of atrophies, inflammations, and gangrenous processes. Their whole aspect intimates the participation of the nervous system, although it cannot as yet be satisfactorily proved that they originate in any definite local alterations of the same. Among simple atrophies we may specify those which attack one-half of the face and extremities; those causing sudden whitening of the hair, from fright and anxiety; those causing loss of hair in patches in what is called the area Celsi, and the scattered white patches in chorea minor.

The most perplexing of all are certain inflammations of the skin which coincide to all appearances with affections of sensitive nerves, particularly herpes zoster. Violent itching accompanies the appearance upon the skin, over the course of certain sensitive nerves, of a group of pearl-sized vesicles. Their arrangement marks very distinctly the course of the nerve—for example, that of an intercostal nerve. After a few days they dry up and heal over. Von Bärensprung and von Recklinghausen have discovered in this disease an inflammatory redness of the corresponding intercostal nerves and of the intervertebral ganglion, and this very nearly establishes the participation of the sensitive nerves in the formation of these vesicles. "Psoriasis cutanea," which is marked by the presence of numerous red and slightly swollen patches and abundant epidermic products, also hints at a nervous origin, by the symmetry of the exanthema which often breaks out on the back. It may pass for a statement subject to many limitations, when I ascribe these neurogenous inflammations to the confluence of two etiological influences, each of which would of itself be insufficient to achieve the same result. These are (1) an angio-neurosis, or, at least, a tendency towards vascular dilatation, due to the local derangement of certain sensitive centres; (2) an accumulation, as in the case of trigeminal ophthalmia, of the usually ineffectual irritants of the skin, which, on account of a local affection, cannot be discharged, and hence produce a much more powerful local effect.

To the latter agency we may refer all cases of "neurotic gangrene," whose whole expression and diffusion are suggestive of decubitus paralyticus, water cancer (c. aquaticus, Noma), *mal perforant du pied*, symmetrical gangrene of the face, and leprous necrosis, where the insufficient centripetal removal of peripheral irritation is especially conspicuous in the anæsthesia produced by leprous neuritis, which accompanies it.

IV. SPECIAL PART.

The *species morbi* is determined by the cause of disease, on which depends the point of attack—and I might almost say—the entire plan of attack of a disease. The cause of disease regulates the order and the manner in which the organs shall be attacked; whether, and at what time fever shall set in, as well as the intensity and particular type of the same; and the degree of injury to the heart and sensorium. The cause of disease, in short, includes everything by which we distinguish one disease from another. There is no other distinction but that of cause, which furnishes those peculiarities of diseases, by which they can be readily classified into major and minor varieties.

It is, of course, understood that such a classification is only concerned with the actual and genuine causes of disease, excluding all that is casual and irregular. We can conceive of an etiological division of diseases which would be governed by the vehicle through which the disease is conveyed to us. In such a case we would have nutritive diseases, infectious diseases, climatic diseases, diseases due to certain vocations, etc. This system, although etiological, is purely artificial, and could not, for a moment, be seriously entertained. The following pages are devoted almost exclusively to the question of food, clothing, atmosphere and infection. Natural groups of diseases are only formed when we adopt as the standard of division the independent agency of the cause of disease as well as its quality and natural history existence.

Thus we have five chief classes, to which there is at present added a sixth, Idiopathic, *i. e.*, diseased conditions whose causes are as yet unknown.

(1) Traumatic diseases; (2) Parasitic disease; (3) Diseases due to defective nutrition and growth; (4) Diseases of over-exertion; (5) Diseases of premature senility.

It not unfrequently happens that several distinct diseases occur in one individual. In such cases clinical analysis is not content merely to notice the various concurrent etiological phenomena, but it makes them of first importance in diagnosis, prognosis and therapeutics. Thus it is evident that medical instinct has long since accustomed itself to perceive in any given illness a plurality of diseases. Such a patient represents to us, not, as he imagines, one disease, but several diseases, whose symptoms either co-exist independently, or interfere with each other, and furnish products of amalgamation.

I. TRAUMATIC DISEASES.

Trauma, in its broadest sense, is any external attack which forcibly alters the physical or chemical composition of a part or the whole of the body. Hence we distinguish mechanical, chemical, electrical traumata, and traumata due to the extremes of heat or cold.

(a) MECHANICAL TRAUMA.

In order to comprehend the attitude of the body towards the various mechanical assaults to which it is exposed, we must first of all concede that, in structure and texture, it is so ingeniously contrived as to offer the greatest possible resistance to mechanical agencies. The brittle and sensitive bones are generally enveloped in a thick sheath of soft elastic substances, and the skin is of such decided elasticity and firmness that it resists the pressure of a blunt surface by an incredible amount of stretching, even allowing brief but extensive displacements of the subcutaneous parts without itself becoming lacerated. But everything has its limit, and there are a series of mechanical traumata which effect a permanent breach of continuity; such are incisions, bites and lacerations, blows, knocks, stings, contusions and falls.

"Solution of continuity" is the first and general result of every mechanical trauma. This is usually well marked when the parts are really cut with a sharp instrument, or in a genuine fracture of the bones. There are bruises and contusions which produce solutions in continuity in the more delicate structural parts, where the pathological condition is not at all perceptible immediately after the injury. In such instances the depth of the lesion inflicted can only be judged by the irrevocable loss of function (commotio cerebri) or by the gangrene which at once sets in (subcutaneous contusions, as in kicks from a horse). Apart from these, we must consider, in a fresh wound: the amount of blood lost or still escaping; the possibility of air or fat entering the blood paths; the loss or destruction of tissue; the entrance of foreign substances into the wound; and, finally, the quality of the injured parts, which determines on the one hand the value of the functional disturbance, on the other the local probabilities of recovery.

The reunion of the divided parts, their restitution as a scar, the closing up of the bodily parenchyma exposed by the wound—in short, the healing of the lesion—is not so much the deliberate intention of the recuperative powers of nature as it is the result of an inflammatory process, which has been induced by the mechanical irritation of the parts. A hyperæmia of the remaining intact blood vessels leads to a serocellular exudation, which is directed from all quarters towards the injured spot. Here the exudate reaches those portions of the tissues whose nutrition has been threatened by the traumatic lesions which they have suffered. In favorable cases, we have to do with but a thin tissue stratum, which, when the parts are properly and promptly approximated, can be nourished by the aid of the exudate, until a sufficient number of new formed vessels, together with a moderate supply of connective tissue, reunite the edges of the wound (union by first intention). In less favorable cases, both large and small shreds of tissue undergo necrosis, and must, together with all other foreign matters, be loosened and removed before the edges can reunite. The cleansing and healing up of the wound by second intention is accomplished by granulation tissue, which establishes a layer of pus at the junction of the healthy and necrosed parts, separating the two, but soon leading to cicatrization. The epithelial covering of the surface is derived from the surrounding epithelial borders.

Disturbances in these processes are mainly due to the deposition in the wound of a cleft fungus, Billroth's *cocco-bacteria septica*. Since we have learned from Lister how to frustrate the poisonous influence of this fungus, exerted upon the blood and juices of the body, wounds complicated with septicæmia, pyæmia, diphtheria, and erysipelas are exceptional; in residences and towns they no longer occur epidemically. A more careful discussion of this subject will be found under the head of infectious diseases.

Thrombosis and embolism are favorite elements of pyæmia, to which they impart a metastatic character. They appear, however, at times independently, in traumatic inflammations.

We must not omit to mention trismus and tetanus, of which we have already spoken, as important and dangerous complications even of small and cicatrized wounds.

(b) CHEMICAL TRAUMA.

Our body is likewise protected against the inroads of chemical injuries. The horny layer of the epidermis, with its wonderful impermeability and great power of resistance, is certainly the best possible protection against the most powerful acids and alkalies. But there is a limit to everything, and the protective power of the horny layer of the epidermis is limited both by time and space. It can only withstand a brief contact with the more powerful chemical reagents, and the protective power of the horny layer does not extend beyond its territory. Beyond the territory of the teeth and the entrance to the nares the case is different. Chemical processes take place in the stomach and the intestinal canal; solid bodies undergo decomposition and liquefaction, and are able and even compelled to pass into the body through convenient channels. The mucous membrane of the stomach and intestines is so constructed as to facilitate such an entrance. The sense of taste usually gives warning of the reception of injurious ingesta, but if it fail to do so, and the warning pass unheeded, there is nothing to prevent the dangerous substances from eventually penetrating into the blood and from thence into the entire body, in the same manner as food and drink. Even the squamous epithelium of the mouth and œsophagus are more vulnerable to chemicals than the epidermis, and beyond the cardia the epithelium affords absolutely no protection.

The organism's system of defence against pernicious gases is still weaker. The mouth can, at least, be kept closed when necessary, but if we would not suffocate, we must inhale pernicious gases. We have yet, to be sure, the sense of smell as a sentinel, but this sense has become so badly contaminated by the advance of culture, by cohabitation and division of labor, that the individual of to-day regards his nose as a generally useless and, in view of ceaseless catarrhs, troublesome organ. Thus we inhale, *nolens volens*, every noxious gas which associates itself with the indispensable oxygen. Not all of the particles of dust which pass into the respiratory tract adhere to the moist walls of the same and are again expelled into the outer air by the motion of the cilia lining the cylindrical epithelium. Some of them penetrate as far as the wall of the alveoli and pass into the lymph vessels and glands of the lungs. Here they obstruct the absorbent system of the organ, if they do not go further and produce chronic inflammation and suppuration (Anthracosis, Siderosis, etc). The pathogenetic microphytes follow the same path, although they appear to pass more directly into the blood; their subsequent operation evinces, at any rate, that very few have remained any length of time in the lung.

But to return to chemical trauma. It is based upon the fact that the normal chemical structure of the bodily parts is either permanently or temporarily destroyed by the influence of some fluid or gaseous substance, which already possesses unsatisfied chemical affinities, or develops the same at the moment of attack. The slightest degree of chemical action may be said to exist when the chemical continuity of the part attacked is merely threatened, which results in a firmer union of its molecular structure; in other words, when the chemical irritation rouses the physiological action of the involved bodily parts (exciting influence). When this irritation oversteps a certain limit of time and intensity, the heightened action develops into the opposite extreme, that of paralysis (indirect benumbing influence). Occasionally the attack is so powerful that the phenomenon of heightened activity does not appear at all (direct benumbing). The first stages of a process of a more lasting chemical metamorphosis now begin. As only a portion of the molecular structure is at first involved, assimilation is able, with the aid of the injured parts and their gradual restoration, to repair the damage. In the later stages we find an irrevocable change in the entire molecular structure, which entails a definite exclusion of the part from the organic whole. The latter may take place immediately (necrosis, mortification, caustic action), or so spread that the actual advent of death, *i. e.*, the separation, is merely a question of time.

In reviewing the great number and diversity of the chemical agencies here concerned, and also the widely differing chemical contexture of the body, the inference is natural that these dissimilarities might prove a closer affinity between certain chemical agencies and certain tissues and organs of the body. This inference is found to be correct, for we see that when a chemical body is brought into contact at the same time and in the same form with all the organs and tissues of the body, a selection generally takes place, by means of which some organs and tissues exhibit a decided preference for the chemical body. All degrees of chemical combinations may be present at this particular point, while, perhaps, other organs and tissues take no active part. Such a case is, however, only supposable when the chemical body has really been absorbed through the channels already mentioned, when, after passing through the stomach, intestines or lung it reaches the blood, and is diffused by the same throughout the body. That many chemical bodies have already entirely or in part satisfied their free affinities is proved by the ordinary fate of the very strongest mineral acids, which immediately enter into such close union with the membranes of the organs of deglutition and the stomach that nothing remains for resorption.

Finally, the significance of the chemical attack in relation to the remaining organism is determined exactly: (1) by the physiological importance of the organ attacked; (2) by the extent of the change undergone. Inasmuch as both of these are regulated by the quality of the incorporated chemical body, and the manner of its incorporation, and both of these factors are usually evident, we are enabled, in most cases, to predict with reasonable certainty the result of the incorporation. Thus we arrive at the great and important subject of the science of poisons, and at the same time of that of chemical remedies. The foregoing reflections have fully prepared us to investigate the countless chemically-operative substances furnished us by nature, in all their varied effects, either as remedies or poisons.

For practical purposes, we are in the habit of separating poisons from remedies, and since pathology deals properly only with the intoxications, we should be justified in following the above division. But it is plainly a more scientific method to consider individually each chemical body, and after a careful analysis of its constituents, formation, or origin, to state where and how it approaches the human body, and the local results developed in consequence; also, whether and under what circumstances it is received into the blood, and what are the chosen seats of its chemical activity. Lastly, we shall consider the varying degrees of its influence, and always determine in what quantity it may be incorporated as a remedy, and in what amount as a poison.

(c) THERMAL TRAUMA.

(1) *Increase of Bodily Temperature.*

In treating the subject of fever, we had frequent occasion to mention the heat-regulating apparatus, that interesting mechanism whose design is to protect the animal body against the injurious consequences of the extreme variations in temperature to which our atmosphere is exposed at every point of the earth's surface. We regarded it as an undivided whole, whose action upon the entire or a part of the body is regulated by the perception of a greater or smaller, general or local loss of heat.

A general checking of the escape of heat is most effectually accomplished by an unusual elevation of the external temperature. This is resisted by the heat-regulating apparatus, first of all, by an increased fullness in the blood vessels of the skin, and later, by the secretion of sweat and its evaporation. The process is assisted instinctively on our part by cessation from physical labor and by wearing thin clothing. These means are, however, insufficient when the outer temperature greatly exceeds that of the body, when evaporation is checked by a calm and very moist atmosphere, or when the bodily temperature is abnormally raised by violent muscular activity. Under such circumstances day-laborers, pedestrians, or marching soldiers may become overheated and suffer sunstroke (Insolatio) when the temperature is not over 30° or 36° C. (86° to 96.8° F.) The rapid increase of the blood heat to 40° C., or 44° C. (104° F. to 111.2° F.), brings about an over-irritation of the central nervous system, which is ushered in by a warning phase of irritation. The latter is expressed by a loss of appetite and nausea, followed by hallucinations and mental disturbances with suicidal impulses. The attack itself is marked by a sudden loss of consciousness. The sufferer falls down insensible, the pulse, which, in the prodromal stage was full and hard, is raised to 140 or 160 feeble and scarcely perceptible beats.

The imperfect contractions of the heart occasion general cyanosis, which is found, especially after death, well marked in the brain and lungs. Death ensues from pulmonary œdema. The temperature frequently continues to rise after death—often an entire degree. Decomposition sets in very soon. An astonishing number of colorless blood corpuscles are found in the varnish-colored blood.

The local retention of heat produces at first the same results as the general. There is a local hyperæmia accompanied by intense redness of the skin and secretion of sweat. When, however, the impeded escape is substituted by an unavoidable accession of heat, exceeding all physiological limits, we obtain those local affections of the skin and underlying parts known as burns. In this case the accession of heat appears as an inflammatory irritant. We distinguish three degrees of burns, according as the inflammatory irritant produces a permanent redness of the skin, vesication, or callosities. The local effects of these higher grades of thermal trauma do not differ from the corrosive effects of chemical bodies and present the same objective points to medical diagnosis. This is especially true of cases where the burn involves a large portion of the surface of the skin. If a third or more of the skin be burnt or destroyed by caustics, there follows an inevitable although gradual cooling off of the blood, which, at 32° C. (89.6° F.), or 30° C. (86° F.) is fatal to life. No increased production and no economizing of heat, however ingenious, can compensate for the extraordinary loss which occurs through the hyperæmic portions of the bodily surface which have been robbed of the protecting epidermis.

2. *Decrease of Bodily Temperature.*

Here, also, we find both a general and a local escape of heat. We are, in the main, well protected against the decrease of the normal heat of the body produced by the lowering of the outer temperature. Slight variations of temperature are equalized by the activity of the heat-regulating apparatus; the higher degrees of cold are averted by warm clothing, which answers every purpose.

The influence of a periodical, moderate fall in external temperature is extremely beneficial to the body. In order to diminish the escape of heat, the muscular fibres and arteries of the skin contract, and the blood is thus forced toward the central organs. The blood supply of the heart, lungs, brain and liver, becomes increased, and they become capable of increased activity. The heart beats more rapidly, the respirations are more frequent and deeper. The blood being loaded with oxygen, the well-fed brain experiences a wonderful sense of vigor and freshness. A repetition of this condition at proper intervals furnishes a powerful impetus to the entire nutritive system. A reserve supply of fat is stored up, and the functions of the brain are strengthened; we have, in short, all the curative effects produced by the well known cold water and fresh air cures.

Let, however, this general withdrawal of heat overstep a certain limit, and there follows over-irritation and weakening of the functions of the central nervous system, in particular of the spinal marrow, which appears singularly sensitive to excessive cold.

The acme of the changes is reached in death by freezing, when neither the heat-regulating apparatus nor additional clothing have been able to maintain the requisite temperature of the blood. The diminished excitability of the central nervous system is apparent in the enfeebled heartbeats and respiration, as well as in the feeling of exhaustion which rapidly increases and urges the unfortunate victim to seek relief in sleep. The degree of exhaustion is greater, the greater the preceding excitation. The latter is due to the forcing back of·the blood from the surface to the brain, and conspicuously to the use of alcohol, which in itself reduces the temperature of the blood, so that everything combines to explain the well-known fact that death by freezing very frequently overtakes drunkards.

The most palpable effect of a local withdrawal of heat is the freezing of individual parts of the body. Although we are able to sufficiently shield the greater part of the body from the effect of a very low temperature, it is impossible to protect all portions equally well. We must see, hear, breathe and use our hands and feet, in spite of the cold. Thus it happens that, in rigorous weather, our noses, ears, fingers and toes are liable to be frozen.

The next result of the local withdrawal of heat is a contraction of all the smooth muscular fibres of the skin, of the *media vasorum*, and the erector papillæ muscles. The skin becomes pale and shriveled, the fingers and toes white and cold as marble. It is assumed that irritation from cold incites at once muscular contraction. This contraction is as purposeless as the contraction of the same structure in intermittent fevers. It would be plainly much more practical to allow the blood to flow through the gaping blood vessels of the threatened territory in a full and rapid stream, replacing in this manner the previous loss of heat. Fortunately, there is, in most cases, an almost immediate over-irritation and relaxation of the muscular fibres, by means of which the desired condition accomplishes itself. Furthermore, there is a tickling sensation in the parts as they grow cold, which often becomes so painful that we are led to employ mechanical irritation, such as pressing, rubbing and stamping. This induces an arterial hyperæmia which speedily terminates the athermic irritation.

Freezing does not occur until the over-irritation and counter-irritation already mentioned are withdrawn, or until, in spite of the abundant supply of warm blood, the cooling off of the parts continues until a pitch is reached where a permanent molecular alteration of the tissues is established. The nature of this alteration is unknown. To designate it as *vita minor* is a simple confession of ignorance. It is expressed in various disease-pictures, whose complete unity and individuality are not apparent until the effect of the cold has passed away, and the frozen part begins to return to its normal condition.

A permanent redness of the skin, combined with an often almost insufferable itching, constitutes the lowest stage of freezing. The next stage is presented by chilblains, *i. e.*, sharply-circumscribed, roundish swellings, of a bluish-red color and a flabby consistency, which are also associated with an annoying sensation of itching, or even of violent pain.

A weakened power of resistance, a certain sacrifice of the elasticity and contractility of all the firm cutaneous parts, and especially a diminution in blood pressure, are present in chilblains and in the hyperæmia due to cold. This lack of resistance is conspicuously shown toward irritations from cold, which, although slight, and of short duration, produce a disproportionate exhaustion, and at the same time an extensive and permanent dilatation of the blood vessels and swelling of the parenchyma. The frozen members usually remain in a quiescent state during the summer, but at the first approach of cold weather, begin to swell and be painful. The extreme stage of freezing constitutes necrosis. The frosted parts are removed by inflammation and suppuration, if this result has not been previously attained by timely amputation.

Diseases of Exposure.

A particular kind of local withdrawal of heat furnishes the *raison d'être* for what are called diseases of exposure. These include hyperæmic, sub-inflammatory, and inflammatory conditions which are marked by "regional" occurrence and by a "periodic-typical" course, the latter being, of course variously obscured by irregularities, complications, and quantitative excess of individual symptoms. The connection between these diseases and cold is established by the nervous system. A molecular change in the sensitive nerve-ends of the region affected by cold is transmitted (in a manner as yet unknown) to the central nervous system, and thence to the seat of disease, where it appears in the shape of an alteration of the vascular wall with the results already enumerated.

If we desire to observe the process of taking cold step by step, we must consider the condition of the skin at the time of taking cold as the starting point.

We all know that we take cold most easily after being overheated. When the temperature of the blood has been raised by violent and continued muscular exertion, like running, marching, dancing, calisthenics, and the blood, in order to cool more rapidly, seeks the surface of the body and produces a strong hyperæmia of the skin, there is immediate danger of taking cold. The skin is then more irritable and much more sensitive to cold than normally. This is equally true of those superficial parts which, from other causes, possess an abnormally large blood supply, secrete much sweat, etc., *i.e.*, the parts which have been rendered susceptible by an excess of clothing.

Diseases resulting from exposure are most frequent in the temperate zone. They are of much rarer occurrence both among the naked or half-clothed natives of the torrid zone, and among the Esquimaux who wear a uniform covering of skins throughout the year. We know of no other way to attach our clothing than upon our shoulders and around our hips. At these points, consequently, there is an unavoidable accumulation of thick and heavy folds, so that the lumbar and deltoid regions are most warmly and constantly covered. The temperature is always higher here than that of the skin, perspiration is more frequent and profuse, and as there is usually admirable protection against cold, there is, in consequence, unusual susceptibility to the same. As with the regions of the shoulder and hip, so with the feet, which we shield from wet and injuries by thick and impermeable leather soles. The same applies in a measure to all portions of the body which we are in the habit of covering. They are more or less over-sensitive to cold.

Seeking to locate this heightened susceptibility to cold, and addressing ourselves first only to those structural parts which exhibit most plainly the phenomena of irritability, viz.—the nerves and muscles—we find, in the muscles, a disproportionately strong contraction answering to a moderate withdrawal of heat; in the sensitive nerve ends a strong and rapid advance of molecular change, which, when presented to our consciousness as a sensation of chilliness, demands that we should exert ourselves to prevent the local loss of heat. This can only be a physical change in the nerve ends, a transition of the molecule from a strong to a weak thermal activity, preparatory to complete rigidity.

A moderate sensation of cold is, however, unfortunately, so pleasant that even sensible people require many severe lessons before they learn to adopt the proper measures against taking cold, preferring to entirely ignore cold as a cause of disease, rather than submit to the requirements of our trying climate. It is remarkable that in sleep the central nervous system rarely, if ever, disregards the warning of the cutaneous nerves, when threatened by cold, or fails to acknowledge them by suitable reflex activity. Uncovered arms and knees are promptly thrust under cover, as may be seen nightly with sleeping children. In this respect we are more reasonable in sleep than when awake, when we cannot deny ourselves harmful enjoyment. There are, of course, besides the pleasurable sensation of cold, other causes which lead us to disregard the danger from exposure. Such are, great mental pre-occupation, or a *force majeure* which prevents the perception or avoidance of the danger.

The best means for averting cold is, without doubt, the proper protection of those parts of the body which are exposed to its influence. The precautions used against freezing are found to be equally efficacious here, namely, the mechanical treatment of rubbing, kneading, massage, etc. By thus establishing "counter-irritation," *i. e.*, an irritation-hyperæmia, the effects produced by the loss of heat are neutralized by the abundant addition of warm blood.

If the withdrawal of heat is not checked, there is danger

that the contraction of the cutaneous blood vessels, and the relative exclusion of warm blood attendant thereon, should co-operate with the external withdrawal of heat to produce a numbed condition of the terminal nerves. This I consider the immediate provocation to the diseases produced by cold. The subject includes much that is peculiar. The withdrawal of heat is, as a rule, neither powerful nor of profound effect. An almost imperceptible breeze will soonest give cold. The most superficial cutaneous layers, or, indeed, only the nerve ends, appear alone to be acted upon. The sensitive nerve-ends of the papillary layer terminate, as we know, in different papillæ from those of the terminal capillary vessels, so that the isolated action of cold upon the tactile corpuscles is not improbable. The epithelial nerves are also to be considered. Hence, after taking cold, there is a sense of numbness and formication in the skin, apart from the slight and almost regularly-recurring chill, which proceeds from the affected part. But the perception of these finer grades of sensitiveness which mark a cold, require so attentive a central nervous system that the generality of patients " do not know how they caught cold."

Deserving of special notice is the danger to cold arising from the fact that the typically sensitive portions of the skin are liable to perspire easily, so that the clothing becomes saturated with perspiration. Wet clothes are good conductors of heat, consequently, when the outer air reaches them and they become cold, they extract the heat from the surface of the skin in so marked a degree that only the most violent physical exercise can counteract their effect. And when, besides the inner moisture and the outer cold, the body is subjected to soaking rain, we may with great likelihood look forward to a fit of sickness.

We must reluctantly concede that there still exists a gap in our exact knowledge of the relations of exposure to the diseases resulting from exposure. Although the fact of the connection admits of no doubt, it is, notwithstanding, difficult of definition. In the foregoing discussion we have found little which is characteristic of the process of taking cold above any other local withdrawal of heat. I have tried to establish the probability of the isolated action of cold upon the sensitive nerve-ends, the numbness of the tactile corpuscles, or even of the epithelial nerves, as characteristics, of the process of taking cold. I desire to emphasize the consequent discord in the centripetal irritations, which, proceeding from the skin, as well as from the other bodily organs, are incessantly communicated to the central nervous system. These irritations determine the measure and distribution of the continuous active participation of the central nervous system, which is consummated within the tonus of the vascular and bodily muscular structure. This might point to a local " attack of irritation," which would induce a local "inhibition of muscular innervation." The direct paralysis of individual or groups of muscles, from cold, would chiefly support such a conclusion. I doubt, however, whether that painful affection, usually called muscular rheumatism, can be ranked under this head. At any rate, it exhibits a combination of vaso-motor and neuro-muscular paralysis. In most cases, the vaso-motor paralysis constitutes the starting point of the entire disease resulting from exposure.

The regions of the arterial vascular system are continuous with the organs of the body, but in especial are they intimately connected with the mucous and other membranes which are organically circumscribed and simple in their functions. Local hyperæmia, brought about not so much by a vaso-motor inhibition as by a kind of reflex paralysis of the central source of power, is what generates the process of taking cold. This hyperæmia attacks the heart, joints, nasal cavity, isthmus of the fauces, pharynx, larynx, trachea, bronchi, small intestines, bladder, lungs, pleura, eyes, ears, etc. It is associated with a certain inclination to concentrate the blood supply in the direction of free surfaces. This localization is aided by the weight of the blood, which operates in inflammations of the lungs. There are other irritants which tend partly to localize, partly to increase the rheumatic hyperæmia. Among these we must enumerate physiological exertion, which makes some organs especially sensitive at the moment of exposure to cold. We know that articular rheumatism is often the result of violent and prolonged bodily exertion, over-heating in dancing, for example, which likewise leads to rheumatic endo-, myo- and pericarditis. People who have suffered much from diseases resulting from exposure generally possess a *locus minoris resistentiæ*. The mucous membrane of the respiratory tract, especially the nasal mucous membrane, is most frequently attacked.

There still remains an important point for pathology to

ascertain, viz., to what circumstance is it due that these diseases are not content to establish an hyperæmia, however strong it may be, but proceed to inflammation and exudation. It is possible that there are two factors at work.

First of all, we have not a simple fluxion, but a neuroparalytic filling of the blood vessels, which is aided by a permanent change in the nervous system. But so soon as any, even an arterial hyperæmia assumes a more permanent character, the blood which fills the hyperæmic part develops by its own gravity a gradual retardation of the circulation, with increased lateral pressure. This is conspicuous in proportion to the dilatability of the capillary walls of the part and their nearness to the surface, it being less noticeable in those whose situation is deeper. Thus we have a partial explanation of the already-mentioned tendency of rheumatic hyperæmia to concentrate on the surface, and to cause the filtration of the liquid constituents of the blood from the peripheral capillaries. Just at this point the second inflammatory factor exerts a powerful influence. This factor is the implantation of lower organisms. These are not usually capable of withstanding the normal forces at work in the production of the animal tissue change which are prejudicial to their welfare; but, when once introduced into a region where a sluggish interchange of blood is followed by a still more sluggish tissue interchange, they find a congenial soil in which to settle and proliferate. They are not necessarily specific pathogenetic microphytes. As a rule, they are merely the usual fungi of decomposition, which are taken in with the food and respiration, and are in part deposited upon the mucous membrane, and in part carried by the blood to the different vascular regions of the body, reaching thereby the parts affected with rheumatic hyperæmia. There can be no doubt but that the local process assumes thereby an acutely inflammatory, purulent, or even putrid character. In its newly-acquired character, metastates of the primary inflammation are possible. But we must constantly bear in mind that the implantation of microphytes is in these instances a secondary matter, which would not justify us in classifying rheumatism as an infectious disease.

As even the most hasty portrayal of all diseases resulting from cold would exceed the limits of this work, I must content myself with a brief summary of the same.

I. Local inflammations of the mucous membranes, to which are applied the terms simple and catarrhal. The most common are: catarrh, coryza, catarrhal tracheo-bronchitis and catarrhal laryngitis. Rarer are catarrhs of the conjunctiva and the external auditory meatus. Catarrhal tonsillitis and pharyngitis are very frequent; they are often associated with catarrh of the Eustachian tubes.

II. Inflammations of glandular organs, principally the sporadic form of croupous pneumonia and acute nephritis.

III. Inflammations of the motory apparatus; arthritis and rheumatic myositis.

IV. Inflammations of the heart; endocarditis, myocarditis, rheumatic pericarditis.

V. Non-specific sero-fibrinous inflammations of the pleura.

(d) ELECTRICAL TRAUMA.

In the preceding traumata we have been able to name certain contrivances by which the organism has been in a measure ingeniously protected. Against electrical traumata there is no such protection. On the contrary, the close connection between electric movement and the excited state of the active nerves prepares an easy entrance for electricity into the body. If electrical manifestations were more frequent in the natural world, we should more frequently meet with diseased conditions attributable to the same. This is, however, not the case, for, with the exception of lightning, no electricity is dangerous, although much has been said, especially among the laity, about magnetism as a cause of disease. Electro-magnetism has become a valuable factor in equalizing pathological disturbances in the nervous system and thereby in all the organs of the body. Both the constant and interrupted electrical currents are employed, chiefly in order to preserve the excitability of the nerves and exercise their terminal apparatus, by assisting the impaired or obstructed innervation, until the diseased obstruction shall be removed.

II. PARASITIC AND INFECTIOUS DISEASES.

The diseases resulting from mechanical injuries, from heat and cold, and from chemical injuries, must be distinguished from those which are communicated to us by our fellow-creatures, just as inanimate nature is distinguished from animate nature. By the latter I do not allude to battle and bloodshed, nor to the attacks of wild beasts to which men are sometimes exposed and which partake more of the nature of mechanico-chemical traumata, but of the fatal operation of those beings which have chosen the human body for habitation and subsistence, and lead in and upon man—as it is expressed—a parasitic existence. There are many animals and plants whose nature forces them to this mode of subsistence; others, again, which only feed upon the juices of the human body in the absence of other food.

All these plants and animals approach us from without. They fly, jump and crawl upon us, are inhaled with the air, acquired from clothing and utensils, and are rubbed in and inoculated in a thousand and one different ways. Any free surface of the body affords them a foothold. Often it is the skin or the mucous membranes; in many cases it is the inner surface of the respiratory apparatus or that of the stomach and intestines.

As soon as a deposition (invasion) is effected, the peculiar (specific) life of the invader asserts itself. The neighboring cells and juices must furnish nourishment, and are either decomposed, dissolved, or consumed as a whole. The body reacts, and inflammations of various kinds set in. But the affection remains purely external, so long as the parasites confine themselves to the surface, so long as they remain *epizoa* and *epiphyta*, in the restricted sense of the terms.

It is quite different, however, when they or their progeny forsake the seat of their original deposition, in order to penetrate into and infect the body. The smaller animal parasites, like the trichinæ, effect this by the vigorous activity of their movements, especially when their bodily structure is such as to favor their entrance into the body. The vegetable parasites, being generally deprived of the power of voluntary motion, depend primarily upon their small size for their chances of infection. Fungi of the size of the common mould varieties send out their mycelia as far as to the deepest layers of the loose epithelium, but are very rarely able to effect an entrance into the bodily parenchyma proper. Germ-fungi of the size of the *torula cerevisiæ* and the *mycoderma aceti* are also unable to enter. Only the most minute—the cleft-fungi (*Schizomycetæ*)—are small enough to penetrate into the blood and lymphatic vessels, through the interstices of the bodily texture. Their smallness often borders upon the imperceptible.

The cleft-fungi are, notwithstanding, not invariably devoid of individual motion. The earliest known and most frequent variety of decomposition-bacilli were named vibrios (quivering animalcules), because the tiny bacilli, moving rapidly to and fro in the putrescent fluid, executed rotary and forward movements, which, to the first observers, resembled the uneasy ferreting movements of the infusorial animalcules. In stagnant water we perceive microbes darting with lightning speed across the line of vision, and upon evaporating and coloring the sediment with methyl-violet, we find the microbes to be provided with short, thread-like feelers, which serve them, in their rapid passage, as a "screw." It is possible that other schizomycetes and their germs possess a similar mobility, which facilitates their entrance into the bodily parenchyma. When the invaders have once reached the blood, no further assistance is required to diffuse them with it throughout the body and complete the work of infection.

With the achievement of this latter step, the fight for life between man and the parasites is transferred from the surface to the interior of the body. We feel little concern in regard to the epizoa and epiphyta, knowing that at the worst they can be removed with comparative ease and safety, and rendered innocuous, but with the entozoa and entophyta it is a more serious matter.

The entozoa, it is true, upon migrating into the blood, are easily observed. Some of them (Filaria sanguinis and Distomum hæmatobium) choose the blood for a permanent abiding place. Others use it as a convenient channel through which to gain a more congenial locality for further development. Such, principally, are the tænia embryos, which develop into Echinococcus hepatis or Cysticercus cellulosæ. The trichinæ embryos appear to reach the muscles, not by way of the blood, but directly through the tissues. All these entozoa produce at the point of implantation inflammatory processes, which, although in themselves of a simple non-specific sort, may, upon occasion, give rise to serious lesions of a local and general nature, and even terminate in death.

Of a much more complicated character are the results due to the immigration of cleft-fungi, viz., Infectious diseases.

The very entrance of these unwelcome guests is liable to inflict severe injury upon the channels of entrance. Here we find surface colonies, where the colonists multiply to many times their original number, before the first assault is directed towards the interior. This is the signal for the outbreak of inflammations at the first faint attack, and in local lymph paths and glands—inflammations which bear a markedly "specific" imprint.

The character of a specific inflammation has been considered in the general division of this work. It includes hyperæmia, exudation, but chiefly inflammatory irritation, regulated and controlled by a living virus, which declares its species by many well-defined, often-repeated, and obvious characteristics.

The majority of the "invading" specific inflammations are marked by the intervention of some sort of tissue necrosis, either as in diphtheria, as a preliminary to further changes, or, as in tuberculosis, where the completed products of inflammation undergo necrosis. This tissue necrosis is the exclusive product of the microphytes. It reveals, so to speak, the tendency of their vital activity and gives us a clue to other specific inflammatory phenomena. The slight inclination of certain tuberculous, syphilitic, leprous and other products of inflammation towards organization, their arrest as partly formed granulation tissue, and also the striking individual formation of separate cells into an "epithelioid" structure,—all may be chargeable to the parasites, which weaken the vital energy and the relations to the organism at large. The recent discovery of tubercle- and lepra-bacilli in these very epithelioid cells appears to confirm this hypothesis. So much is certain, that these cells invariably represent the acme of the specific process and are, if necrosis ensue, most fittingly perpetuated in the same.

Just beyond these cells, or, in their absence, immediately adjoining the necrotic process, there arises a qualitative, non-specific, reactive inflammation. This is not rarely of a salutary character, if it succeeds in disarming the poisonous visitors by encapsulation, or throws them off by suppuration together with the specific products of inflammation, thus protecting the threatened body from the general infection.

If the reception of the microphytes becomes an accomplished fact, we may expect, first of all, a condition of fever, which, according to previous definitions (*Vide* Fever and its Cause), we shall understand either as a direct, fermentative increase of temperature, or as one attributable to the irritated nervous system. To attain this end, a large amount of active virus is, of course, required. Consequently, when there has been no previous proliferation of the parasites at the point of the first superficial implantation, when only one, or at most a limited number of the diseased germs have passed directly into the blood, a certain space of time must necessarily elapse before the few become, by continued division, sufficiently prolific to effect an irritation of the central nervous system, or, to establish zymotic processes of any magnitude. This period of "proliferation of the schizophytes in the blood" is called the stage of incubation. It is not probable that the proliferation occurs in the blood while in motion. The swelling of the spleen in most infectious diseases intimates, on the contrary, that the growth is especially successful there, where the blood flow is retarded almost to stasis. From this or some equivalent focus, there ensues a flooding of the entire body with the microphytes, which being single, continuous or repeated, determines whether the infectious disease in question shall be accompanied by single, continuous, or repeated paroxysms of fever.

Hereupon comes a new localization of the poison. The cleft-fungi are undoubtedly carried past all the organs of the body. In a treatise* which has failed to attract attention I explained why the arteries, and, particularly, the arterial capillaries, are likely to be first chosen by the wandering cleft-fungi as their new point of settlement (*Vide* specific inflammation, embolism, etc., General Part). This is not, however, a satisfactory explanation of the phenomena of localization. We are reminded of the intoxications when we see that certain fungi select certain organs. Since the natural organs of secretion, the kidneys, intestinal canal, skin or lungs are affected, it leads one to think that it is an attempt on the part of these organs to reject the unusual *materies peccans*. It would doubtless be more correct to infer a co-operation of the local vascular apparatus with the conditions of growth imposed by the chemical contexture of the parenchyma, and from this standpoint alone to judge of the localization of diseases of the secretory organs. For

*On Vasculitis Specifica, a contribution in honor of the Three Hundredth Anniversary of the University of Wurzburg.—*Leipzig.*

experience teaches us that this attempt at secretion is of very little account, as the body must either dispose of these entoparasites by consuming, i. e., oxydizing them, or be consumed by them in return.

The specific processes of inflammation evoked by these secondary localizations are most manifold and characteristic. They proceed, as already stated, invariably from the blood vessels, and with great partiality from the terminal arteries, around which the inflammatory products are first deposited (Specific Endo- and Peri-Vasculitis). From here they advance into the parenchyma, whereupon the same metamorphoses take place which we have already studied in the invading inflammations. We meet with the same tubercle cells in the primary seats of inflammation in the phthisical lung, as in the miliary tubercles which usurp the small arterial ends in resorption tuberculosis. As in tuberculosis, so we find in all other infectious diseases. Nothing is more calculated to demonstrate the unity of these diseases under a uniform pathological irritation than this typical recurrence of the specific products of disease at all the centres of localization.

I have not the requisite space to describe here the further changes undergone by the microphytes after their deposition in the blood. This pertains to pathological anatomy and histology, to which branches I must repeatedly refer the reader. I shall, however, take occasion to return to the subject of the abode and diffusion of the pathogenetic schizophytes outside of the human body, and of the ways and means in which infection may be communicated.

(a) ANIMAL PARASITES.

Arthropoda.

Acarus Scabiei (Itch mite). Body rounded, 0.2 to 0.4 mm. in diameter, possessing long bristles, and short spines pointing backward; eight legs, short and conical, four of which project forward, and are provided with stalked suckers. Between the latter, a short head, with apparatus for biting and sucking.

It inhabits canals made by itself, in the upper layers of the epidermis, whence it occasionally descends into the corium in search of food. The female deposits in these canals, eggs, from which the six-legged larvæ are very rapidly developed. These wander over the cuticle seeking a home of their own, until, after repeatedly casting their skin, they become sexual animals.

The first deposition of the acarus is generally made in the thin skin between the fingers and toes, as well as on the flexor surfaces of the arms and legs. Later, the whole skin may become involved. An annoying itching causes severe scratching, which results in inflammation of the corium. Red papules and watery vesicles form, and these, after being scratched open, are covered again with a brownish scab. The entire skin becomes, finally, reddened and thickened, and an abundant epidermal exfoliation takes place.

Acarus folliculorum (Comedone mite). Slender body, 0.2 mm. in length, four pair of short feet on the anterior portion of the body. Harmless tenants of sebaceous glands (Comedones), especially of the nose.

Pediculis capitis, p. pubis, p. vestimentorum (head-louse, crab-louse, body-louse); *cimex lectularius* (beet-bug); and *pulex irritans* (common flea), need only be mentioned.

Pentastomum denticulatum, a still unexplained arachnid, found now and then, in a calcified condition, in the liver.

Nematodes.

Parasitic nematodes, like all round worms, have a long, cylindrical, unarticulated body, which resembles a contractile tube, within which are situated the digestive tract and genital organs, which are furnished with a mouth, anus, and also a sexual opening.

Ascaris lumbricoides. The male is about 25 cm. long, the female, 40 cm. Bodies round, like earth worms, but yellowish-white in color. The ovaries contain numerous rather long and very thick-shelled ova, 50 to 60 μ. in diameter. The latter are found in the fæces of man, but their development is obscure, as is also the manner in which the young ascarides find a new home.

The round worm lives in the small intestines, but rarely occasions any serious disturbances, except, perhaps, when it travels through the ductus choledochus into the liver, and produces abscesses.

Oxyuris vermicularis (Thread worm). Female, 10 mm. in length; male, 4 mm. Long and thin, like threads. Eggs, oblong, flattened on one side. Thousands of them exist in the intestines, whence their nocturnal journeyings often bring them to the verge of the anus. The excessive irritation thus produced disturbs the sleep of children (the oxyuris is rarely found in adults), and leads to abuse of the genital organs and to masturbation.

Trichocephalus dispar. Female, 4–5 cm. long; has a straight, involuted, thick body, containing the ova, which are oblong and provided, above and below, with small nodules. The male is spiral. Both male and female have flagellated, attenuated, anterior extremities. These harmless parasites are sparsely distributed throughout the small intestines.

Strongylus duodenalis (Dochmius, Anchylostomum). Body 1 to 1.5 cm. in length, round, expanded in the centre, head distinct and furnished with four strong teeth. The male terminates posteriorly in a funnel-shaped, loose pouch; the female is sharply pointed. In the tropics it is a frequent inhabitant of the duodenum. It bites into the mucous membrane, sucks itself full of blood, and, like the leech, leaves a bleeding and wounded spot behind. The Egyptian chlorosis and the much discussed beriberi disease of the Sunda Islands appear to be due to this worm.

Eustrongylus gigas. 1 m. long and 12 mm. in diameter; blood-red. Observed in the pelvis of the kidney. More common in animals than in man.

Anguillula stercoralis. Thread-like worms 1 mm. in length. Myriads of them live in the large and small intestines, occasioning diarrhœa, wasting anæmia, and stubborn stomatitis. Cochin China.

Trichina spiralis. The smallest but most dangerous of European round worms. Male attains at most 1.5 mm. in length; female 3 mm. Owing to their smallness and transparency, hard to distinguish with the naked eye. The body is round, pointed anteriorly, truncated posteriorly. Adjoining the oral cavity is the beginning of the intestinal tract, which is provided with a series of large gland-cells. In the female, the highly-developed genital apparatus occupies the remaining space in the body. It not only contains eggs in all stages of development, but also the matured embryos, which are discharged from the genital pores, situated in the centre of the body. A single female can mature as many as 400 young. The process takes place in the small intestines of the pig, mouse, and, unfortunately, also of man. The trichina embryos advance from the intestinal lumen through the intestinal wall, and between the layers of the mesentery into the connective tissue of the body, and thence into the muscular structures, where they temporarily reside. The muscles along the anterior surface of the spinal column, the diaphragm, scaleni, and muscles of the tongue and larynx are chiefly chosen, but no muscles are safe from their incursions.

The muscle-trichina penetrates into the interior of a muscular fasciculus and feeds upon the contractile substance. After it has grown to a length of 1 mm. the so-called "encapsulation" of the worm ensues. It rolls itself spirally together and remains without change of place or position for years at a time. In the meantime the muscular fasciculus is completely destroyed. Two capsules are formed: an inner one belonging to the animal proper, and an outer connective-tissue capsule, richly provided with blood vessels. The former is homogeneous, transparent and reasonably dense. After it becomes calcified the trichinæ are readily seen with the naked eye in a freshly prepared section, while at other times a careful microscopical examination is required. The outer capsule supplies the animal with an abundant blood interchange, so that its life is preserved even in the calcified investment.

A further stage of development comes when the meat is eaten in a raw or half-cooked condition. Pork in the latter condition is especially dangerous to eat, and the flesh of rats for swine. The gastric juice in the stomach eventually dissolves the calcified capsule and liberates the trichinæ, which in a few days arrive at a sexual state. Thus begins anew the cystic development before described.

Very soon after eating meat infected with trichinæ a violent pain is felt in the intestines, and painful intestinal catarrhs set in, which are like those of cholera. Then comes the migration, accompanied by fever, pain in the muscles, and paralyses which, if they attack the laryngeal and respiratory muscles, are liable to be immediately fatal. The danger is greatest about the fifth week after the fatal meat has been partaken of. The lethal result is indicated by increasing weakness of respiration, cyanosis, anasarca, and lastly, pulmonary œdema.

Filaria medinensis. Guinea worm. A thread-like worm, of the thickness of a violin string, and reaching a meter in length. Found exclusively in the tropics, especially in

Guinea. Causes painful abscess of the skin, chiefly on the leg and heel. It was known to Galen.

Filaria sanguinis hominis. Smallest animal parasite which infests the human body. Only 0.35 mm. long, and 0.006 mm. in diameter. Lives in great numbers in the blood, from whence it settles in the kidneys and produces hæmaturia. Only found in the tropics (Egypt, India, Bahia, Gaudeloupe).

Trematodes.

All flat worms have a flat, leaf-like, unarticulated body, and are provided with a single opening which serves both as mouth and anus, and which leads into a short, bifurcated intestinal canal. This opening is found on the pointed anterior portion of the body, at the bottom of a sucker; close at hand is the genital pore, and back of that is a still larger, abdominal sucker.

Distomum hepaticum. A broad, brown, flat body, 2.8 cm. long, 1.2 cm. broad, with a short wide disk (head). The coiled convolutions of the female genital apparatus form a dark blue spot behind the abdominal sucker. The ovaries are situated on the sides of the body, between them the seminal canals. The distomum hepaticum has both male and female organs of generation.

It occurs in a sexually mature condition in many of the mammalia, in the biliary ducts of the liver, and causes, in sheep, what is known as "liver rot." Rarely found in the human body.

Time will not permit a detailed description of the interesting metamorphoses of the distomum hepaticum, by means of which the "generation changes" in these animals have been discovered (Cercaria, nursing conditions, etc.)

Distomum lanceolatum. Distinguished from the large liver distomum by its small size and its narrow, lance-shaped body. In other respects it is synonymous, both in place and manner of living. Leuckhart once found forty-seven specimens of the distomum lanceolatum in the gall-bladder of a shepherd girl.

Distomum hæmatobium. Here we must distinguish between male and female. The male, 1.2–1.4 cm. long, has an oblate body, hollowed out like a gutter-pipe, in which cavity the perfectly cylindrical body of the female has often been found reposing.

The distomum hæmatobium is a pest to the Upper Egyptians and Abyssinians. They pass apparently from the intestines into the blood, from whence they deposit their eggs in the mucous membranes of the urinary apparatus and the intestinal tract. The ulcerations produced at these points by the development of the embryos are responsible for the frequency of kidney and calculous diseases in Egypt.

Cestodes.

The cestodes are flat, tape-like, intestinal parasites, of a white color, consisting of a short-necked tapeworm head (Scolex), and a long chain of tapeworm segments. The head, smaller than a pin's head, is provided with suckers.

The neck is a fine thread, to which the first narrow segments are attached. Further on, the segments become distinct, broad, and flat, and finally develop to ten times the width of the head and to a corresponding length, after which the mature tapeworm segments (proglottides) appear as elongated plates in the shape of a melon seed, and are broken off and discharged with the fæces. During this time there has been developed in each segment of the tapeworm, both a male and a female genital apparatus, the latter of which is crowded with eggs at the time of discharge. With the exception of two fine "water vessels" situated at the sides of the worms, there are no internal organs visible. Nutrition is supplied by osmosis directly from without, which is made possible by the flattened shape of the segments. The whole color of the tapeworm is due to spherical particles of limestone, distributed throughout the entire bodily parenchyma. It is maintained that the tapeworm is able to execute movements on a large scale, to curl itself up, for instance; I have personally observed that the freshly-discharged proglottides exhibit, while still warm, a peculiar quick motion.

In most tapeworms there is a complex metamorphosis connected with generation, inasmuch as the embryos upon emerging from the eggs, instead of remaining in the intestinal canal of the new host, perforate the intestinal wall and enter the connective tissue and the blood. Having located themselves in a favorable spot, they develop, first of all, into the cysticercus or the "bladder worm" of the Finlander. This cysticercus may remain for some years or may finally perish;

if, however, it in any way, while living, reaches the alimentary canal of the particular class of animal which it infests in its mature condition, it becomes attached by the head, the vesicle falls off, and then a succession of segments form, constituting the tapeworm.

Tænia solium and Cysticercus cellulosæ. Tænia solium inhabits the small intestines of man. The cubiform head, of the size of a pin's head, is furnished with four prominent suckers. In front of them is the rostellum, a slightly prominent conical snout, surrounded by a double row of curved hooks. These hooks appear capable of being elevated out of and inserted into corresponding grooves in the surrounding parenchyma. That portion of the head opposite the rostellum is occupied by the neck of the scolex. The scolex matures oblong links or segments, each of which encloses a part of the preceding one. The ovaries form clustering appendages of a central canal, which terminates in a small projection at the side of the body. The aperture of the much smaller masculine genital apparatus is also found at this point. It is marked by a baggy sac, the cirrus, which is regarded as the copulative organ.

The eggs, which are almost round, have thick, radiatingly-striated shells. Nature has ordained that they should be received into the stomach and intestines of swine by the ingestion of human fæces. Here the shell is dissolved and the embryo released. Migration begins at once and the parasite penetrates into the porous connective tissue, and reaches, often in a roundabout way, the very spots which best favor its development into a cysticercus. Such localities are the connective tissue of the muscles, the pia mater cerebri, the vitreous body of the eye. The embryo—thus far a simple mass of protoplasm furnished with six hooks—is now converted into a vesicle filled with a clear liquid, and attains in two or three months' time the size of a pea. In this shape the worm is found, by the hundred and thousand, in "measly" pork.

Such a vesicle is easily moved from its position. A white spot is then visible, from which, upon gentle pressure, a genuine tapeworm head may be squeezed out. This has been concealed in a corresponding, pouch-like contraction of the vesicle wall, upon the surface of which it has been formed, in a manner as yet unexplained.

It has been proved by numerous experiments that the tænia solium is taken into the small intestines of man by the consumption of "measly" pork. The injuries inflicted by these tænias are often overrated, but it appears that they may give rise to irregularities of digestion, inclination to diarrhœa, etc., and in delicate and sensitive organisms moreover, to nervous symptoms amounting to slight convulsions.

Of more serious moment is the appearance of the cysticercus cellulosæ in man. It is difficult to say how the tapeworm eggs are transmitted from the fæces to the mouth. It may be by inhalation of the dried particles. It is not a frequent visitor, but when it does appear its deposition in the eye threatens that member with dimness of the lens, with iritis and choroiditis, or with total loss of the organ; its deposition in the pia mater of the brain and in the ventricles brings on cerebral disturbances and lepto-meningitis. If the cysticerci are seated superficially in the muscles, they may occasionally be felt under the skin, thus furnishing criteria for diagnosis.

Tænia medio-cannellata. It bears a general resemblance to tænia solium, with the following differences: Its length and breadth are usually greater; head larger, 2.5 mm. in diameter; it has neither rostellum nor hooks, but its four suckers are very prominent and powerful. The ripe proglottides are long and very full of eggs. Proglottides, in order to develop, must find their way into the intestines of cattle, from which point the embryos wander out into the muscles and internal organs. Beef thus affected infests man, when consumed by him as food.

Tænia medio-cannellata is indigenous to every part of the globe, while tænia solium is rare in southern countries. The pathological conditions produced by both are identical.

Tænia echinococcus. This smallest of all known tænias lives in the intestinal canal of the dog. It is a tapeworm consisting of only four links and scarcely a half centimeter in length. Half of this length is occupied by the fourth sexually mature link. The head is a perfect tapeworm scolex, with suckers and a rostellum surrounded by hooks. Experience has proved that the intimate association of dogs with men may lead to an infection of the latter by the tapeworm eggs. The embryos, becoming released in the intestine of man (as well as in those of other warm-blooded animals), pass immediately through the intestinal wall into the blood vessels and connective tissue. Through the vena porta they gain access to their favorite abode, the liver. They may also be found in the loose sub-serous connective tissue of the peritoneum; in the sub-mucous connective tissue of the urinary ducts; in the lungs; and, in fact, occasionally, in almost any of the bodily organs.

There now ensues the development of the embryo into the well-known echinococcus cyst, whose enormous size is quite disproportionate to that of the original tænia. The steady accumulation of a clear fluid internally keeps pace with the growth of its cuticle, which becomes a millimeter in thickness, and is of the consistency and milk-white color of coagulated albumen. It is finely laminated, and contains here and there spaces filled with granular parenchyma, while its entire inner surface is furnished with a thin parenchymatous layer. From the parenchyma islets in *the interior* of the cuticle, a new vesicular formation can take place simply by a continuous accumulation of fluid and the formation of a cuticular layer. The secondary or daughter-cysts force themselves into the interior of the mother-cyst. Dozens of these daughter cysts are often found inside of the mother cyst. They range in size from a pea to a hen's egg, and the mother cyst in which they are enclosed attains occasionally the size of a child's head. New scolices, as a rule, are only developed inside of the daughter cyst. They arise by threes or fours on the inner surface of certain stalked protoplasmic capsules, large numbers of which hang down from the wall. Were it not for the thickness of the cyst wall, which limits the whole process of growth to the interior, these protoplasmic projections would probably form just such open pouches outwards, as occurs with cysticercus cellulosæ. As it is, the echinococci scolices have little prospect of development. Unless something unforeseen occurs, the whole cyst dies *in loco*, and, in a favorable case, is also buried *in loco*, *i. e.*, infiltrated with salts of lime.

In less favorable cases the cysts, upon reaching the size of a hen's egg, produce all sorts of inflammatory reactions in their neighborhood. A connective tissue capsule always forms around the cyst. But this is not all. A trauma of the hepatic region occasions a suppurative "abscess-forming" inflammation, which may discharge itself externally. It can only be thrown off from the lungs by means of a similar inflammation; more easily, as it seems, by way of the urinary passages. The echinococcus-cysts have, furthermore, the effect of tumors upon the neighboring organs, and of thrombi and emboli upon the lumen of the blood vessels which they inhabit.

There is a species of echinococcus in cattle, where the daughter cyst grows outward instead of inward. It is possible that it is the same species which in man is designated as echinococcus multilocularis. Here we find in the liver a spot as large as a goose-egg converted into a tough, callous mass of connective tissue, permeated with numbers of echinococcus cysts as small as a pin's head. Within this focus is found, as a product of impaired nutrition, a "centre of softening," which the physician pronounces an abscess of the liver, from which it differs little in clinical importance.

Bothriocephalus latus. The full grown tapeworm measures 5-8 mm. The thread-like neck bears the head, which is a club-shaped or obtuse swelling 2.5 mm. long, 1 mm. wide, with two long grooved suckers ($βοθρίον$). The segments of the worm measure more laterally than longitudinally, but the last proglottides are somewhat quadrangular. The sexual pore is situated in the middle on the surface, and is surrounded by the puckered-up, brownish-colored uterus, with which it forms a raised hump. It is found in the western cantons of Switzerland and in the northeast of Europe.

Infusoria.

We may reckon with the parasitic infusoria which are found in the intestinal and vaginal mucous membrane—cercomanas intestinalis, trichomanas vaginalis—some protozoa which are occasionally met with in the liver and muscles. They do not occasion any particular injury by their presence. The one-celled infusoria are termed "psorospermia," and colonies of them in closed membranous investments 0.5-1 mm. in length, are called psorospermia cylinders.

(*b*) VEGETABLE PARASITES.

Mould Fungi.

Aspergillus glaucus. The greenish mould which grows on walls is composed of an elongated, cross-partitioned, loose mycelium, which sends out thick, perpendicular, thread-like offshoots. When the latter attain a length of .5 mm., their extremities become club-shaped. From the latter radiated projections, the so-called sterygmata arise, from which chains of ten or more spherical spores are given off.

If these spores are injected into the blood of a squirrel, they lodge in the most dissimilar organs, among others, in the brain and kidneys, where, encouraged, as it seems, by the high temperature, they develop rapidly into a fibrous mycelium. Local inflammations set in, which, if excessive, become dangerous, and even fatal.

A non-artificial *mycosis aspergillina* has not yet been observed. The spores of aspergillus niger, penicillium glaucum, mucor mucedo, the most common of the mould fungi, do not germinate in the bodily parenchyma. They have, however, occasionally been found in the external auditory canal.

Achorion Schönleinii. The spores are deposited in the oily moisture, which surrounds the cast-off epithelium, enveloping the roots of the hairs. They grow here into thin, jointed threads, which are only slightly ramified, and which send out from short, alternating lateral shoots short chains of obovate spores. When water is added, the latter spring away from each other, and develop at the same time into round, yellowish globules, which again proceed to germinate. When deprived of nourishment, the cells of the mycelium threads form dark green, permanent spores, each containing two nuclei.

The deposition of the achorion schönleinii produces "scald head (tinea favosa). The whole head is often covered with yellow," pea-sized scabs, in flakes and discs. The skin is attenuated under each scab, but soon recovers upon the extermination of the fungus, which is easily accomplished.

Trichophyton tonsurans. A parasite of the true hair shaft, whose spores are fixed at the point where the hair emerges from the skin, and which proliferate from here directly into the interior of the hair. Having formed long chains of fungus cells, they force the hair cells apart and at length produce a loss of continuity. The hair falls out as soon as the diseased spot in the shaft has grown about 2mm. above the surface of the skin. Bald spots, *i. e.*, where there are only a few broken off hairs, mark the deposition of this fungus (herpes tonsurans). It is easily eradicated by destroying the fungus.

Microsporon furfur forms in the lower epidermal layers a mycelium composed of unarticulated threads, which mature within them numbers of round spores. Certain pale brown, roundish spots .5–5 cm. in diameter, are thus formed (pityriasis versicolor).

The breast, back and upper portions of the arms are the favorite seats of the microsporon furfur.

Oidium albicans forms a mycelium consisting of rather thick and succulent filaments, which are constricted, four-sided, and rounded off at the point of contact. These filaments contain the glistening spores.

This fungus is found in certain yellowish-white, circumscribed and easily detached depositions in the mouth and pharynx, as well as in the œsophagus of nursing children, or even of adults exhausted by a long illness. The depositions contain, besides the fungi, portions of cast-off pavement epithelium and of food, chiefly wheat bread (known in medical terminology as Thrush or Aphthæ.)

Yeast Fungi.

Sarcina ventriculi. In chronic stomach troubles, where the contents of the stomach display abnormal processes of fermentation and decomposition, we find at times a lower order of parasites, which consist of minute cubical cells. The fact that these are always in groups of four, and resemble a cubiform, cross-like constricted peddler's pack, has given rise to the name of sarcina. Appears to belong to the yeast fungi.

Cleft Fungi.

The Schizophytes are the smallest plants, indeed the very smallest living creatures. Some of the pathogenetic schizophytes are inconceivably minute, but there are a number which may be recognized with an ordinary microscope, and made distinct by using the proper staining fluids and good illumination, so that even now, where we are as yet upon the threshhold of the science of microphytic diseases, we can command much definite information in regard to the natural history of the pathogenetic schizophytes.

All cleft fungi are in structure globular, rod-shaped, or spiral, being composed of a colorless homogeneous substance, whose refractive powers vary widely in the different species. Many of them, when suspended in water, show a lively individual mobility, and when the remaining conditions are furnished, *i. e.*, suitable food and temperature, apply themselves without delay to the main end of their being, to propagation by simple cleavage (σχίςις). This supposes a moderate growth by internal apposition to have already taken place. As soon as the granules attain a certain circumference, and the rods a certain length, they separate in the middle.

Every fungus is enveloped in a juice-layer or sheath of its own, whose consistency is regulated by the amount of surrounding water, which, accordingly, either checks or encourages any possible activity of the fungi as well as the displacements necessary to their growth. If the schizophytes settle upon surfaces, which, although moist, are not liquid, the mucous or gelatinous consistency of the sheath above mentioned prevents the cleft-fungi from separating from each other, although they continue to proliferate within themselves; the sheath represents a common covering for the entire progeny of a parasite, and as proliferation by division continues, there arise of necessity large colonies, which have been called by F. Cohn, *zooglœa* aggregations. The latter are round, or roundish in shape, and become so large that they are even visible to the naked eye. They are most perfectly developed in the semi-solid nutritive gelatines, which are now, according to Koch's formulæ, most frequently employed in cultivating the individual species of schizophytes. So varied are they in form and color, according to the kind of schizomycetes sown, and yet so characteristic of each particular kind, that it is far easier to determine the species from these colonies than from the shape of the individual bodies.

The color of the schizophyte colonies is exclusively in the investment juices of the fungi. The latter is often of a dazzling yellow, blue or red color, but the fungus itself is seen upon close examination to be quite colorless, a proof, moreover, that important physiological differences may co-exist with the somewhat overrated homogeneity of schizophytes.

Whenever the conditions necessary to the growth of the schizophytes are not fully satisfied, there arises a modified development, which, in the higher plant world, is known as the formation of spores and ova. The rods, instead of growing longer, gather protoplasm at one or more points, which points resemble roundish, shining balls; each of these balls, enveloped by a thick, self-prepared capsule, represents a germ, which only awaits the return of suitable conditions of growth —water, food, temperature, etc.—to again expand into a rod and resume the process of division.

Many of these germs, especially those bearing flagella, contribute, by their own mobility in water, somewhat towards the selection of a new abode. Most of them become so extremely light after dessication that the slightest breath of air, even the *courant ascendant* of every warm human body, suffices to lift and carry them away. Thus it is that the schizophytes represent one of the constant elements of dust, and that unusual precautions must be taken to entirely rid a place from them. It is only after prolonged rains that the atmosphere is quite free from schizophytes and then only for a short time.

Pasteur urges a division of the entire tribe of schizophytes into those requiring air and those not requiring air. The latter separate the oxygen which they require for their growth from the combined gases of the soil upon which they feed. They are, accordingly, well adapted to assist in the decomposition of organic bodies, and represent the great group of decomposition fungi in the broadest sense of the word. The others, which cannot live unless surrounded by pure oxygen, are, in consequence, more restricted as to their abode. As a general thing, they can only, like the mould fungi, exist upon the damp surfaces of some fostering soil, and are, on the whole, of less importance. Unfortunately, however, the presence of "free oxygen in the blood" affords them an entrance into the body, and the schizophytes requiring air become thus one of our most dangerous foes.

Many pathogenetic schizophytes reside at present exclusively in the human body. Still we cannot assume that this has always been the case, but must rather concede the possibility of Darwin's theory, according to which the gradual accommodation of the schizophytes to the human body has, by a local specializing process, effected an alteration in their vital qualities. The possibility that such a process of acclimation and transformation might still take place is suggested by the occasional outbreak of entirely new infectious diseases. It is not only improbable, but also unnecessary, to assume that every new chain of individual sicknesses, every so-called epidemic, requires a new acclimation and transformation. The very development of the countless, permanent spores in only one case of disease furnishes countless germs, the very fewest of which only need to find a sheltered dwelling-place, in order to create, at the proper time, a new epidemic.

The manner of acclimation is a much-disputed point in the

study of fungi. According to Buchner, Nägeli's pupil, artificial culture has proved that a certain hay fungus, resembling outwardly the schizophyte of anthrax, will not, when taken freshly from the hay, vegetate in blood which has been inoculated with it. But cultivate the fungus first in cold, then in warm, albuminous solutions, and it soon attains a capacity fully equal to that of the common fungus occurring in anthrax. These results, if universally recognized, would furnish a fair representation of the manner of breeding. In the meantime, they are supported by investigations into the general and historical course of some infectious diseases, which almost indicate that the fungus under consideration must have first settled in certain mucous or purulent products upon some point of the bodily parenchyma before it sought and found a way into the interior. The apparently sudden outbreak of devastating plagues, like cholera, syphilis or diphtheria, is best explained by supposing that a fungus growing as an epiphyte has suddenly gained the power of growing as an endophyte, thus creating an apparently new infection.

The acclimation of the fungus in the body is fortunately counterbalanced by the acclimation of the body to the fungus. The vegetation of the body learns to resist the invading fungus growth. This power has been gained in hard but successful struggles against great numbers of dangerous adversaries, as well as in the slighter exertions required to overcome the incorporation of less formidable foes, which are by nature weaker, or have become so by artificial means. How this is accomplished, and in what tissue change the immunity resides, by which the naturally or artificially inoculated body defies the plague, is unknown. We cannot yet unravel the mystery. We only know that the course of many infectious diseases is thereby mitigated or entirely checked. And what is true of the individual is also true of the entire race and its relations to plagues and national diseases. National diseases have also an ascendant and descendant stage of intensity, in proportion as the race learns to accommodate itself to the vegetation of the respective schizomycetes. Partly because the poison is taken up in small quantities, which by degrees are spread more and more over the surface of the earth, and becomes thereby more and more diluted; and partly by inheritance, viz., syphilis, tuberculosis, leprosy, the poison is finally communicated to constantly increasing numbers of people, and produces in them a relative immunity against renewed infection.

But we must conclude here, in order not to rob the consideration of the individual schizophytes of its legitimate material. The above suffices to show how easily the so-called fungus theory may be introduced into the domain of infectious diseases, and also to justify myself if I unreservedly support the same.

As we are at liberty to select any particular vital quality of the pathogenetic schizophyte as a basis for the division of the same, we shall not hesitate to proceed from the already well established standpoint concerning the theory of miasm and contagion. Hence according to the substratum (soil?) in which the pathogenetic microphyte gains those qualities which prepare it to invade and infect man,* we divide them into:—

1. Microphytes which live and feed outside the body, particularly in soil which is damp, exposed to the air, and filled with decayed organic matter, and from which they can be readily inhaled and reach the blood of man. Here they proliferate, and produce a feverish condition in the entire body, but do not appear in the excretions of the patient, as germ-producing spores. The microphytes are, consequently, restricted to certain localities, which, although sometimes of considerable extent, are only dangerous, *i. e.*, productive of endemics to those who live in them or frequent them. Miasmatic microphytes.

The chief representative of the diseases due to miasmatic microphytes is malaria, in all its forms, viz., the simple intermittent, the anomalous and irregular intermittent, the pernicious, remittent and protracted swamp fever, and the malarial cachexia. The malarial fungus has not yet been identified. Klebs and Tommasi have directed attention to a bacillus procured in the notorious malarial districts near Rome.

2. Microphytes, which, like the miasmatic microphytes, require a soil outside of the body, in order to produce those

---

* Only those microphytes will be considered which have been definitely pronounced to be the exclusive cause of a well known infectious disease. To establish this rule, from which I shall make but few exceptions, careful culture experiments must be made, and the typical recurrence of all symptoms of disease must result, when the material thus obtained is carefully inoculated.

forms of vegetation which are able to infect man and produce a characteristic disease. They possess, however, germinating spores, which pass into the fæces and emanations of the patient, and are themselves capable of impregnating another soil outside of the body, where they then ripen into infectious shapes. The vegetation of these microphytes is, as we see, more and more transferred to the human body, with a proportionate emancipation from the external soil. The microphyte thus becomes transportable, and the disease assumes less of an endemic and more of an epidemic character, although its epidemic diffusion is still confined to certain localities, such as dwellings and places of business. Such are miasmatic-contagious microphytes. Among the diseases produced by this order of microphyte, dysentery approaches most nearly to the purely miasmatic forms. After that yellow fever, cholera and typhoid fever. A few points have been gained regarding the vegetable originator of the latter disease, from Eberth, who observed a medium-sized bacillus in a specific medullary infiltration of typhoid mesenteric glands. The cause of the slow advance in this department of science is found in the danger to life accompanying all such experiments.

3. Microphytes which have partially or entirely freed themselves from an external soil, in order to take up their habitation the more exclusively in the animal, *i. e.*, human body. Here they multiply, and in the course of a characteristic infectious illness, produce offspring, which being transplanted into a healthy and receptive body, are at once prolific and pathogenetic. Contagious microphytes.

The diseases due to contagious microphytes may be separated into four subdivisions.

(*a*) The first contains contagions whose free development requires the furthering influences of certain telluric, atmospheric, and other less well-known changes. To this class belong some of the historical epidemics, an example of which is the English "sweating fever." Also dengue fever, influenza, hay fever, cerebro-spinal meningitis, spotted and relapsing fever. In relapsing fever, we meet with a more generally known pathogenetic microphyte.

Spirillum Obermeieri. Exceedingly thin, spiral filaments, 0.15–0.2 mm. in length, with a rapid rotary and progressive motion, found in each drop of blood withdrawn and examined during an attack of fever. Under a magnifying power of 400, the microscope shows in almost each slide one or more specimens. The parasite disappears from the blood at the crisis of the fever, which is usually accompanied by excessive sweating.

All attempts at artificial culture have as yet been fruitless. Vaccination with blood drawn during relapsing fever has been of marked success, as has been proved especially by Münch, by auto-inoculations. The transportation of the microphyte in ordinary infection has thus far not so much as been conjectured.

(b) The second group of contagious diseases introduces us to poisons whose breeding places are in the bodies of animals rather than men, and which are, in consequence, designated as zoönoses. They can only be introduced into the human body by inoculation (bites, stings, etc.), and produce a diseased condition, which, although differing from the corresponding animal disease, is sufficiently typical to establish the identity of the poison. This group, whose main representatives are anthrax, glanders, hydrophobia and mouth and foot pestilences, contain the most familiar pathogenetic microphytes.

Bacillus Anthracis. Anthrax fungus. A good-sized, somewhat firm and perfectly immovable little rod, found in great numbers in the blood of cattle, sheep, stags, etc., suffering from anthrax. These little rods are bred in a temperature of at least 19° C. (66.2 F.), increase rapidly by division, and grow into long filaments, which repeatedly subdivide, producing finally, as a "permanent spore," a very glossy globular structure, one or two of which are found in each rod.

When inoculated into a small surface wound, the anthrax poison produces violent circumscribed dermatitis, accompanied by necrosis and a blackish scab, which stands out sharply from the reddened and œdematous skin (malignant pustule, charbon). When introduced with food, this poison enters the blood and gives rise to intestinal ulceration, fever, severe cerebral symptoms and hemorrhage, which generally produce death.

The poisonous nature of the anthrax bacillus may be diminished by subjecting it to a temperature of 53° C. (125.6° F.), and in various other ways. It may then be utilized for preventive inoculation. This inoculation, however, only protects gregarious animals against inoculated anthrax, not from the anthrax which attacks the body through the intestinal canal. Still, we may look forward to more successful preventive inoculations with a poison whose virulence is thus reduced. The above measure was first suggested by Buchner and practically applied by Pasteur.

Actinomyces. Radiated fungus. A micrococcus, which, in a favoring soil forms balls as large or larger than a poppyseed, from which grow many fine, unarticulated, dichotomous ramifying filaments. Glossy, spherical swellings of considerable size then appear at the ends of these filaments, displaying longitudinal cleavage, and a constriction of the smaller pieces at their sharp ends. The entire "granule" is bright yellow to brown in color.

Portions of these fungi are taken in through the mouth, and enter the body chiefly through carious tooth cavities. Fistulas of the gums, and submaxillary abscesses are formed, in the pus of which the yellow granules of the actinomyces are seen. The fungus, which now follows the blood vessels and lymphatics, produces abscesses wherever it settles. The lungs, retro-peritoneum, mediastinum and the subcutaneous connective tissue are favorite seats of such abscesses, which are similar to those occurring in chronic pyæmia.

Actinomyces occurs frequently in cattle, rarely in man.

(c) The third group treats of contagions which, although chiefly affecting man, are upon occasion transmitted to certain classes of animals, that is to say, may be transmitted to them by inoculation. The disease in animals shows certain typical features different from that occurring in man, just as in the previous group the disease in man differed typically from that in the animal. We consider here the accidental wound fevers —erysipelas, septicæmia, pyæmia, diphtheria—and the most serious of all infectious diseases, tuberculosis.

Micrococcus Erysipelæ. A small, round granule, which grows in links, and has no individual mobility. Found in the connective tissue of the skin; has been cultivated by Fehleisen in infusions of beef, peptones and gelatine. Produces, when inoculated, an inflammation of the skin, which is migratory and accompanied by high remittent fever. Adjoining a healthy spot there may be a zone moderately infiltrated with micrococci, which, in its turn is followed by a zone infiltrated with small cells, in which the micrococci are no longer visible. The infiltration of the micrococci and the inflammatory exudation progress most rapidly in the superficial lymphatic plexuses of the skin.

The microphytes of diphtheria, septicæmia and pyæmia have not as yet been individually propagated. The experiments already made establish, however, that there are many different species of decomposition microphytes, some of which evoke septic conditions in one class of animals, some in another. Thus it is probable that certain species of decomposition-fungi are dangerous to the human body. There may be one variety which selects granulating wounds and mucous membranes upon which to produce diphtheritic inflammation; another which, without local inflammation, passes directly from a fresh wound into the blood and creates a sudden, fatal septicæmia. Still a third whose invasion is marked by phlegmonous inflammation, purulent infiltrations, thrombosis, embolism, metastatic abscesses, and violent remittent fever (pyæmia).

Bacillus Kochii. Tubercle bacillus. Next to the bacillus of leprosy the smallest of all known bacilli. Characterized by a peculiar investment, which can be dissolved by strong alcoholic solutions. This explains the difficulty of so coloring the bacillus (with the coloring matters at our disposal) as to make it accessible to microscopical diagnosis. It also affords a possible explanation of the great tenacity and diffusion of this bacillus, which thrives in every region known to man. It becomes mingled with the dust of the atmosphere, chiefly from the spittle of consumptives which has been dried by the sun and air. This naturally occurs more frequently in streets than in dwelling houses, where the spittle is deposited in cuspidors and handkerchiefs. Thus a certain universality is ensured to the tubercle fungus, by which it inhabits all the abodes of man, chiefly, of course, the uncleanly ones.

The tubercle bacillus is partial to the moist inner surface of the respiratory organs, although the deposition is not effected with equal ease in every case and at every point. The majority of people are non-receptive as regards this deposition, and, when receptive, display many different degrees of susceptibility. In some a catarrhal condition of the bronchial mucous membrane seems to pave the way for the deposition; in many others, the catarrh must be regarded as the first result of the deposition. There are, moreover, local favoring conditions without which no deposition can be made. It is only in the apex of the lung—where respirations are less perceptible and the ventilation is poor—that the settlement is made (at least in adults) while the remaining portions of the lung are temporarily ignored. Only particular points, such as those points where the smallest bronchioles merge into the respiratory parenchyma, admit of the first engrafting, etc.

What then follows after the tubercle bacillus has gained a firm footing in the apex of the lung is recorded in the pathological anatomy of phthisis tuberculosa. I cannot again enter into the oft-repeated details of this process. I will merely give the outline of the elementary histological process, *i. e.*, of the specific tuberculous inflammation, produced by the bacillus tuberculosus. The first definite product produced by it is a cellular deposition in the form of nodes, ridges and other irregular-shaped but circumscribed intumescentiæ in the connective tissue. The minutely nodular miliary shape of this first product of tuberculous inflammation is especially frequent, and so typical that for a long time the miliary tubercle was regarded as the exclusive product of tuberculosis. As a first aid to diagnosis the miliary tubercle will always be eminently useful, although it cannot be allowed to usurp the monopoly as a specific product.

In an analysis of a miliary or non-miliary, recent, tuberculous centre of inflammation, we cannot overlook a typical dissimilarity of internal arrangement. The centre or axis of the globular, or rather more retiform structure, is composed of large epithelioid cells, having a powerfully-refractive, finely granular protoplasm, and numerous smooth nuclei frequently arranged in pairs. Further investigation shows almost always in the centre of these large cells some specimens of the genuine giant-cell with numerous peripherally situated nuclei containing nucleoli. Externally the epithelioid cells are surrounded by a broad zone of common exudate cells. Only in the latter are intact blood vessels still to be found, while further in they are completely obliterated, and cannot even be filled by powerful injections.

The bacillus Kochii is most apt to be found in the giant-cells already mentioned. The finely-granular protoplasm of the latter contains, as a rule, several of these delicate bacilli, distributed apparently without any particular system. Bacilli are likewise found in the free spaces between the epithelioid cells, some singly, others in groups. The general impression gained is that the invasion and growth of the bacillus has produced (1) a circumscribed inflammation with cellular exudate, (2) a peculiar enlargement of the nearest exudate cells into epithelioid structures, (3) the growth of some into giant-cells. It seems probable that the formation of the giant-cells is especially due to the "introduction of bacilli into the cell body."

We are thus, in a measure, authorized to charge to the account of the bacillus Kochii all the characteristic features of tuberculous inflammation, from its initiation up to its acme, and are furthermore strengthened in this view by the peculiar sort of retrograde metamorphosis which takes place in the tuberculous inflammatory products. This is "cheesy necrosis," which at one time was esteemed as pathognomonic of tuberculosis as the miliary tubercle.

Cheesy degeneration yields, like diphtheria, a firm, yellowish-white product, which, in its later stages, after the processes of softening and dissolution have converted the original firm substance into a rather crumbling or greasy consistency, bears a striking resemblance to certain varieties of cheese.

The incipient cheesy degeneration is apparent to the naked eye as a white cloudiness of the otherwise more transparent, gray, inflammatory product. Histological investigation reveals a metamorphosis of the cells into opaque, granular, stiff and indistinctly-outlined flakes, in which the application of ordinary coloring agents fails to disclose a nucleus.

A section frequently shows fibrous cleavage of the entire substance. These fibres are grouped in a circular manner around certain points within the cheesy centre, which I regard as an unsuccessful attempt towards the formation of granulation tissue. The whole is, however, so closely compressed and even in the thinnest sections so opaque, that it is useless to attempt a more minute examination.

A period of inactivity sets in when cheesy degeneration is complete, after which further chemico-physical metamorphoses are consummated, which are known as "softening of the cheesy centre." The coagulated albuminous bodies become, as it were, digested, and would gradually dissolve, like the large, cheesy nodules of the brain, into a clear, greenish-yellow liquid, were this process not usually forestalled by a rupture externally of the centre of softening, and the discharge of the partly-decomposed matter. These partly-decomposed, crumbling, pulpy masses are, assuredly, very similar to cheese, but, nevertheless, are not particularly characteristic, since similar products result from the drying-up of pus contained in abscesses.

The lung is the favorite seat of Koch's bacillus. We find here, as a result of the tuberculous inflammation, cheesy change and softening—that first a single lobule is affected; later, however, the process spreads, so that, finally, entire lobes of the lung die and are cast off. The name Phthisis is, accordingly, most suitable.

The disease is propagated in various ways from its starting point in the lung. The spittle of consumptives, being full of bacilli, constantly infects new portions of the mucous tract, spreading along the surface and operating most powerfully upon spots into which it is rubbed and pressed with a certain mechanical force, or where the epithelial protection is less perfect. Thus, in the passage through the larynx, the edges of the true vocal cords, the vocal processes and the folds of the posterior rim of the glottis, are favorite seats of tuberculous ulceration. Swallowed spittle occasions tuberculous ulceration of the lymphatic glands in the small and large intestines, the result being the so-called intestinal consumption. The nose, tongue, pharynx and stomach may in this way be infected, although this is rare.

Another manner in which the poison and the tuberculous inflammation may be diffused is through the lymph paths of the lung. The tubercle fungus causes here a specific lymphangitis, which to the naked eye resembles an eruption of many closely aggregated miliary tubercles. Tuberculosis is conveyed through the lymph paths to the bronchial lymphatics on the one side, and to the surface of the pleura on the other. The lymphatic glands swell and undergo cheesy degeneration; the phenomena in the pleura are more complicated.

There are cases where the eruption of miliary tubercles gives rise to a circumscribed inflammation and agglutination of the two pleura. Such a permanent contact is wont to produce an infection of the costal pleura as well. The adhering parts, when separated by the knife, show an equal extent of both surfaces covered with miliary tubercles, and even a few nodes in the adjacent efferent lymphatics.

In other instances the pleurisy itself attains greater intensity and diffusion. Consumptives are, as we know, much inclined to pleurisy. Both adhesive and purulent forms are observed, but it is at present difficult to decide in what degree the tubercle fungus is active as a causative agent in the pleurisy of consumptives, and in what degree the collateral hyperæmia of the pleural blood vessels, which is a necessary result of the internal disturbances of the lung, is concerned.

The bacilli may also penetrate into the blood vessels of the lung and thus into the blood vessels of the entire body. It is not alone in the pulmonary veins that their depositions are found; the eruption of miliary tubercles throughout the whole body testify to the widespread infection. The disseminated tubercles are especially abundant in the liver, serous membranes and choroid coat of the eye. Still there are many reasons why we should not associate general miliary tuberculosis too intimately with pulmonary consumption. It by no means runs a regular course. There are, on the contrary, numbers of cases where pulmonary tuberculosis is not productive of tuberculosis of the bronchial lymphatic glands, and still more numerous instances where it terminates in a cheesy degeneration of the lymphatic glands, and where general infection does not occur because of the obstruction of the blood lymphatics. Let us not forget that the usual picture of tuberculous inflammation shows the specific products surrounded by a circle of young granulation tissue which contains blood vessels, and might upon occasion be utilized to separate the cheesy masses. This separation may be brought about by suppuration and discharge, or by encapsulation and toleration of the dead parts. In any event it intimates the possible emancipation of the organism from the invading microphytes, and allows us in many cases to regard consumption of the lungs as a local and therefore curable disease.

Nevertheless, it can hardly be doubted that consumption of the lungs produces a decided change in the whole organism, which, among other things, is seen in the predisposition towards the disease found in the progeny of consumptives. In this sense tuberculosis may be called an hereditary disease. What it is that is transmitted from parent to child no one has as yet determined.

The morbid tendency of individuals with inherited "scrofulous" diathesis is noticeable in their attitude towards inflammatory irritants. Very trifling inflammatory causes, which are easily overcome by a healthy man, produce in them a lasting impression. Poor blood and a weak-walled vascular system are effective allies. Scrofulous inflammations begin, consequently, as a rule, with a hyperæmia, in the first rush of which the veins and capillaries are excessively dilated. Its further course does not correspond to this stormy commencement. The blood current is retarded in the relaxed and therefore dilated blood vessels. In following the course with the naked eye, as may be done in the conjunctiva, we note, indeed, an accumulation of blood in the blood vessels, accompanied by convolutions of the smallest veins, etc., but the blood interchange is sluggish, and the blood, in consequence, is dark, with a bluish tinge. Now follows the exudation, or rather the equivalent of such. There is no rapid outwandering of colorless blood corpuscles from the vessels, no rapid and abundant secretion or suppuration. A cellular exudate is furnished, it is true, but the exudatory current is weak. The cells scarcely advance beyond the limits of the blood vessels. They remain in the perivascular connective tissue, producing thus a parenchymatous infiltrate, which, at best, disappears but slowly. The superficial secretions are semi-fluid and dry up rapidly.

Such inflammations threaten principally the outer skin, mucous membranes, and joints of scrofulous persons, those points, in fine, which are most frequently subjected to trifling irritations of a mechanical or chemical nature. Investigation has not, as yet, been able to establish whether Koch's bacillus is concerned in the origin of these inflammations. It has, however, been proved that it exists in the secondary products of inflammation, which have always been considered as the most important, if not the pathognomonic products of scrofula. These are the scrofulous swellings of the lymphatic glands.

Even before the discovery of the bacillus, the hyperplastic, cheesy degenerations, which are so often found in scrofula in the lymphatic glands of the neck, and occasionally in other regions, were regarded as tuberculous inflammations. The positive certainty which we now possess serves as an important key to the understanding of numerous other tuberculous phenomena.

It is possible, and, indeed, often occurs, that the cheesy glands become either permanently encapsulated or are thrown off by periadenitic suppuration, so that the organism is preserved from the pernicious influence of the poison contained in these glands. On the other hand, it is plain that the body is in danger of infection with tubercle bacilli and of an outbreak of the so-called acute miliary tuberculosis. Thus it is that the latter extremely dangerous general disease, which, after weeks of violent fever, results in death, is oftener met with in persons of a scrofulous diathesis than in non-scrofulous consumptives. There is, to be sure, a frequent commingling of the phenomena of scrofula and of localized tuberculosis (phthisis), chiefly in cases where the seat of a tubercular phthisis is found, not in the lung, but in the bones, brain, kidneys, testicle, uro-genital mucous membranes, etc.

The manner in which these varieties are introduced is as yet unknown. Many points in the foregoing description will doubtless be subjected in future to more careful study, and brought into more correct relations to the whole. No one can be more ready than myself to acknowledge the provisory nature of these statements.

Tuberculosis is also transmissible to animals. In cattle it appears as murrain. Rabbits and guinea pigs may be rendered tuberculous by inoculation with the tuberculous products of man. In from four to six weeks the inoculated tuberculosis develops into a fatal disease. Sections show the different organs filled with small-celled, yellowish-white tubercles and infiltrations in the act of undergoing cheesy change.

(*d*) The last group of contagious diseases is the exclusive property of the human race. The respective microphytes appear to disdain any other soil, and require for propagation a direct transmission from man to man. They are transmitted in smallpox, scarlet fever and measles, by inspiration, in syphilis by vaccination, in hooping-cough and other contagious catarrhs (gonorrhœa) by the catarrhal secretion reaching the mucous membranes of healthy individuals. Leprosy must be classed by itself.

The poison of scarlet fever reaches the human organism by inspiration. An inflammatory irritation of the isthmus faucium and pharynx, which is often very severe, seems to point to the local effect of the fungus. This is followed by its reception into the blood, and after a period of incubation, lasting from from four to seven days, by very high fever and rapid pulse. A diffuse but intense redness breaks out on the skin, with which is associated a premature loss of the horny layer of the epidermis. This is the most infectious period. It appears, therefore, that the fungi, having been deposited in the skin, are freed with the desquamative process. The rather frequent accompaniment of renal inflammation indicates an attempt of this organ to secrete the poison. One attack usually provides against a second.

The poison of measles is also breathed in. In about thirteen days after reaching the blood it produces moderately high fever, whose defervescence is marked by a characteristic eruption. First the neck and temples, then the breast and entire body, are covered with red spots, which are often slightly raised, and feel like nodes. Some days later desquamation ensues, at which time the danger of infection is greatest, which would indicate a scattering of the poison from the cuticle. In exceptional cases there is marked inflammatory irritation of the channels of entrance, the mucous membrane of the nose and the bronchial tubes. The first attack does not always afford protection against a second. Some persons have had measles three times.

What we now regard as the smallpox microphyte is a peculiar elongated microphyte found in the smallpox pustule. Whether this supposition be correct or not, remains to be established by future—and we trust not far distant—research.

The poison of smallpox is communicated by inhalation of infected air. After ten to thirteen days a chill initiates the fever, and three days later a cutaneous eruption makes its appearance, with a scarcely perceptible subsidence of the fever. The anatomical characteristics of this eruption are discussed at length in my Manual of Pathological Anatomy. Bright red spots, appearing first on the head, then on the other portions of the body, are superseded on the fifth day after the chill by raised nodules, on the sixth by vesicles filled with a clear liquid (the smallpox lymph). Each vesicle is subdivided into compartments, because the exudate does not remove the cells of the epidermis *in toto*, but scatters them into layers and lamellæ. On the ninth day the vesicle is replaced by a pustule, and to the clear liquid is added numbers of out-wandered pus corpuscles. The straw-colored pustule with its dark red halo presents a most characteristic appearance. About the twelfth day the pustules begin to burst and dry up. This process is accompanied by excessive itching, which tempts the patient to scratch himself and thus deepen the scars which subsequently form at the seats of this purely superficial pus secretion.

The intensity and extent of this eruption determines in part the risk to the life of the patient. The more extended the ulceration (variola confluens), the stronger the alteration in the vascular wall (variola hæmorrhagica), the more serious the prognosis. Complications and secondary affections of the nervous system, eyes, lungs, etc., must also be considered.

The immunity afforded by an attack of smallpox is most complete and can, fortunately, be obtained by inoculation with cowpox (vaccine), so that those who have been inoculated with cow-virus are either entirely exempt from genuine smallpox or experience it in a mild form.

In spite of the most clever investigations, we have not been able to establish the vegetable origin of syphilis. It seems to be a slowly-vegetating microphyte, firmly attached to its native soil, with some portion of which it can alone be transferred, *i. e.*, inoculated into, another person. This transpires most frequently through the intimate contact of the sexual organs in coition. The insignificant lesions of the skin thus caused afford an entrance to the syphilitic poison. A slight redness at the point of entrance, which shows itself within the first few days, and then disappears, is generally overlooked. The poison, however, increases slowly, at the inoculated spot, whence it spreads, and is carried by the lymphatics, first of all, into the next lymphatic glands. It is probable that even at this juncture certain particles of poison pass from the lymphatic glands into the blood. Still, the greater part remains temporarily at the vaccinated spot and in the adjacent lymphatic glands. After the space of about twenty-eight days, it produces a powerful irritation of the tissues, resulting in a small-celled, firm and thick infiltration of the connective tissue around the point of inoculation, the so-called initial sclerosis, and a similar swelling and induration of the local lymphatic glands. The sclerosis develops into the hard or Hunterian chancre; the swollen inguinal glands remain thus for a long time without advancing to further development (indolent bubo).

Four weeks having again elapsed, the infection of the general organism has advanced sufficiently to demand more extensive reaction against the poison. Side by side with the often very decided eruptive fever, we find surface inflammations of the cuticle and mucous membranes. Every variety of exanthema has been observed on the syphilitic skin. There are erythematous, papular, pustular, squamous syphilides; the hair frequently falls out.

In proportion as the disease runs an uninterrupted course, the deeper are the parts implicated in the specific processes of inflammation; first of all the eye (Iritis syphilitica) and the testicle, then the brain, osseous system, liver, and other organs.

. Secondary syphilis produces a peculiar variety of tissue, known, on account of its soft, elastic consistency, as gumma. It is at first reddish and vascular, afterwards whitish, and forms round nodes, which average the size of a pea, and are closely aggregated in groups. The microscope shows good-sized, closely-aggregated granulation cells, which are undergoing in places fatty degeneration. These gummata are found, not only in the deeper-seated organs mentioned, but also in the skin and mucous membranes. Here they are located in the connective tissue, and form nodular swellings, which afterwards soften and are discharged, occasioning widespread destruction.

The syphilitic virus must be destroyed in the body, for it cannot be eliminated. In no place can it overstep the epithelial boundary of the body, either from within outwards, or from without inwards. This is manifested in certain features relating to the hereditary transmission of the disease. The semen of a syphilitic man, the ovum of a syphilitic mother, transmits syphilis to their posterity. When, however, syphilis has been acquired by the mother towards the end of pregnancy, the disease is not transmitted to the child. It would seem to be impossible for the poison to pass through the double capillary wall and also the thick epithelial layer of the placental cells.

Therapeutists are also forced to acknowledge this factor. Luckily we possess in mercury a remedy which is admirably adapted to render the syphilitic virus in the organic juices innocuous.

Microphyton Gonococcus. The purulent secretion of urethritis and elythritis gonorrhoica, when treated with proper staining fluids, reveals a remarkable fact, viz., that a portion of its pus corpuscles contain, in addition to the nucleus, a group of good-sized micrococci, ranging in number from 4–20. The same are also found in the free secretion mingled with the pus corpuscles.

It thus appears that in gonorrhœa, gonococci are carried to the healthy mucous membrane; that they proliferate rapidly in a few days' time and penetrate through the investing epithelium into the deeper layers of the mucous membrane. Having in this manner reached the vascular and nervous parenchyma of the mucous membrane, they produce an inflammation, and the gonococci are taken up into the parenchyma of the colorless blood corpuscles. They thus pursue their way, some of them reaching the surface in company with the purulent secretion, some penetrating through the lymph-paths into the interior of the body. Now, although this secretion brings about a rejection of the poison from the body, there is danger that the process of resorption may infect the general organism. There was formerly much talk of gonorrhœal metastases; at present those statements require revision.

Bacillus Lepræ. Although the artificial culture of the bacillus lepræ has not yet been successful, nor has its pathogenous nature been proved by inoculation; it does not seem to me to admit of a doubt that the bacillus discovered by Armauer Hansen is the vegetable originator of leprosy, or elephantiasis græcorum.

In leprosy we are confronted by a disease whose character has been greatly altered in the course of centuries. A thousand years ago it was the plague of Europe and the countries bordering on the Mediterranean. The slightest touch was contagion, and it was necessary to separate lepers from the rest of the world, and keep them, until their death, in lazarettos. Now it is confined to a few territories, chiefly on the coasts of Norway, Sweden, Italy and Asia. It is not that the disease itself is less frightful and deforming in its effects than at the period of its greatest diffusion, but that it is no longer equally contagious. The cases are carefully noted and may be counted, in which there is evidence of contagion. Only the hereditary transmission of leprosy is held to-day to be possible, and, in most cases probable. It, furthermore, appears that the nature of the bacillus is changed, just as similar gradations have been observed in the quality of syphilitic virus.

Leprosy is pre-eminently a cutaneous disease. Red and

swollen blotches first appear on the least protected and most exposed surfaces of the body. Later there appears a small-celled infiltration in the shape of nodes and boils, which first attack the most prominent points—the nose, superciliary ridges, auricle, chin, malar processes, lips and knuckles. It is evident that the bacillus lepræ is concerned with the external injuries, and has effected a settlement there. Delicate sections of leprous skin show countless, short, tiny bacilli, which are the smallest known pathogenetic bacilli. They lie in groups in the larger cells of the leprous nodes, and are likewise found together with the cells in the tissues.

The peripheral nervous system is, next to the skin, the favorite seat of leprosy. Knotty and cord-like infiltrations of the nerve sheaths cause an insensibility of the skin (lepra anæsthetica), and a tendency to partial gangrene, such as we have seen in tropho-neuroses.

This short sketch will not permit of a more extended description of the phenomena of leprosy. My aim has merely been to furnish the reader with a sufficiently clear justification of my plan of etiological division of diseases.

III. DEFECTIVE DEVELOPMENT AND GROWTH. DISEASES OF EVOLUTION.

Preliminary Remarks.

Although there is no doubt that disturbances of development and growth must be regarded as a special group in our etiologically-based division of diseases, we encounter difficulties when we attempt to point out those symptoms which may be regarded as universally characteristic. We can only say that the diseases of this group are frequently traceable to circumstances and conditions of the parental organisms whence the diseased bodies descended, and that we have to do with congenital, or rather, with inherited diseases.

This "hereditary" nature of a disease is manifested in various ways, but most clearly in cases where a defect of the father or mother is repeated identically in the child.

It is highly probable that in some disposition of the minutest and most imperceptible elements of the ovum and spermatic fluid there exists the idea of the whole, which, under certain conditions appears as a local and individual plan of development. In fecundation, when the ovum and the spermatic fluid are brought into contact with each other, both bring with them the same generic plan of development, although the individual characteristics of each are different, and in fact often widely divergent. I will not allude here to the peculiarities of race, to the conformation of the cranium and face, to the color of the skin, and the peculiar growth of the hair, but merely call attention to the large number of actual pathological appearances, which give an individual stamp to the generic plan of development, as existing both in the ovum and in the spermatic fluid. The most varied diseases of organs, acquired as well as inherited, produce in the generic development of both male and female germinal material, modifications which exert an influence upon the development of the children. Such inherited diseases may be: an hydrocephalic brain, a phthisical lung, tumors and defects of all kinds; also the lack or excess of susceptibility in certain organs towards physiological irritation, which must depend upon a certain anatomical quality of the same. In general we must regard the modifications produced by the diseased condition of the parents as local weaknesses, more seldom as actual paralyses of the principle of development, which have given rise to corresponding weak spots, *i. e.*, gaps, in the individual plan of development.

If both father and mother should chance to have the same weak spot, as often happens in marriages between near relations, the danger is apparent that the development of the child in this particular locality will be very defective. This is substantiated by the well known deterioration of the children of such unions.

On the other hand, the weak spots in one parent may be neutralized by corresponding vigor in the other, and a perfectly healthy child may be born of two partially diseased parents.

Inherited diseases show, however, that this is not a mere matter of addition or substraction. On the contrary, the child selects—as in the configuration of the face, nose, eyes, mouth—one organ from the father, another from the mother, and receives into the bargain the weak spots, which are, of course, often modified by the opposed plans of development.

It is much more difficult to understand why perfectly healthy parents should give birth to children who are afflicted successively with the same defect. As most of these cases are malformed, *i. e.*, plus or minus certain members, we are led to the conclusion that the combined individual plans of development have exerted a harmful influence upon the generic plan.

It often occurs that inherited deformities are absent from one or two generations, but re-appear in the third. In such cases it is astonishing to note the enormous tenacity with which the protoplasm retains and is able to repeat a series of processes which it has once experienced. I am, however, unable to agree with those who characterize certain human anomalies as monkey skulls, monkey hair, monkey thumbs, monkey shanks, and thus trace the impression of the protoplasm backwards into the Darwin age of human development.

Before proceeding to individual consideration we must somewhat limit our territory of disease. It is necessary to exclude on the one hand inherited infectious diseases, especially hereditary syphilis, where the child receives from his parents a certain principal of syphilitic poison, from which it generally in a short space of time derives abundant interest; on the other hand, congenital but not inherited pathological conditions, which arise from intra-uterine diseases of organs, especially traumatic and embolic inflammations. Unfortunately, this latter group cannot, on account of insufficient criteria, be separated from true defects in growth, and must, therefore, be considered conjointly. We distinguish them according to the period of time in which the disturbance of development manifests itself:—

(1) Defective arrangement of the blastoderm.
(2) Defects of intra-uterine development.
(3) Defects of extra-uterine development, or during growth.

1. DEFECTIVE ARRANGEMENT OF THE BLASTODERM.

(*Monstrosities.*)

We have now to consider that first appearance of the primitive trace in the area pellucida of the germinal vesicle, which denotes the commencement of fœtal development. If there be but one primitive trace it is difficult to see how its deposition can effect a disturbance in development. It is quite another thing when there are two embryos in the same area pellucida. Twins are occasionally found in the same chorion, which proves that they must have been developed from one egg. It seems at least possible that two primitive traces can be disposed in the area pellucida in such a manner as to prevent mutual disturbances in the development of the two embryos. Still it is also possible that this favorable result can only be attained in an unusually large area pellucida, for we learn from observation of numerous monstrosities that in all the various dispositions of two embryos in the same area pellucida there is occasionally a fusing together of the embryos, and *eo ipso* a corresponding disturbance in development. Basing upon the fact that every primitive trace is as a radius to the surrounding border of the area opaca, let us consider one primitive trace as remaining stationary, while the other revolves around in the area opaca; thus, we shall obtain in turn the different pictures of deformities.

It is most commonly the case that both embryonic implantations are opposed to each other in the same meridian, head to head. In this position, fusions (Pagationes) between the embryos in the median line occur. These fusions vary in locality and in the time of their occurrence, thus inducing different grades of disturbance of development.

The more the ova are left to themselves the more independent do they become of each other, hence twins are often found attached to each other only at a certain point; for instance, by the brain (Cephalopages), by the buttocks (Pygopages), by the sternum (Xiphopages), or by the umbilicus (Omphalopages). Had the formative material of the area been a little more abundant true twins might possibly have been born. In the so-called "janus formation" we encounter a grave disturbance of development. Here are two distinct bodies joined together by an enormous head with two faces. In these cases, without doubt, there, was a union of the two axes (chordæ dorsales) at their anterior extremity, at the so-called sellæ turcicæ, so that there was no opportunity for the union of the corresponding halves of the head. There was, however, nothing to prevent the left half of the head of one embryo from uniting with the right half of the head of the other, to form a joint face. All double faces in janus formations are composed partly of one, partly of the other fœtus. A preponderating side in one of these common faces is probably due to an inexact approximation of the axes, leading to such a diminution in the size of one of the faces that, as a rule, only the ears remain (Synotus).

Thoracodidymus is a monstrosity in which twins are united by the thorax.

Gastro- and hypogastrodidymus are monstrosities in which twins are united by the abdomen.

Should, however, the second primitive trace, instead of being diametrically opposed, assume a more diagonal position, there result lateral fusions. In both diprosopus and janus monsters the embryonic axes meet at their anterior extremity. Hence we have in diprosopus also two distinct bodies and one enormous head, but the two faces arranged side by side. The two ears nearest each other are often absent, the two nearest eyes converge often into a single eye of considerable size. A perfectly symmetrical one-sided fusion, mesodidymus, is said to be found in fishes, the right half of the body of one being very slightly connected with the left half of the body of the other. This fusion has never been observed in man. On the other hand, we very often find remarkable duplications of the upper part of the body (Anadidymus), in which a single lower extremity supports two separate heads (Dicephalus) or two distinct trunks (Dicormus). All possible intermediary forms can be considered under the latter head. Their origin can only be traced to the fact that the corresponding primitive traces lay head to head and close to each other, while their pedal extremities lengthened towards the same point on the radius of the area pellucida. The two lines then united—in proportion to their original approximation—to form a single primitive trace.

A special group of double formations results when, as it not rarely occurs, one of the two embryos attains full development, while the other is more and more stunted in its growth. The former go by the name of autosites, the latter parasites. They are also called *fœtus in fœtu.*

It is well known that even in completely developed twins, one may be comparatively robust, while the other is small and weakly. It is a mistaken idea to consider the smallest twin the youngest, and to explain it on the ground of a second impregnation.

Many remarkable things occur when unequal twins are united to form a double monster. Epicome is that variety in which the head of the autosite is surmounted by another head, placed vertex to vertex. This is evidently a stunted symphyocephalus. Epignathus is a double monster in which an incomplete fœtus is rooted, by its blood vessels, in the palate of one more complete. Heterodidymus is a living autosite to which is affixed, as a parasite, a small doll-like twin, attached to the thorax. Notomeles and pygomeles monsters are parasites which have a single extremity attached between the shoulder blades, or to the sacrum of the autosite.

All the monsters heretofore enumerated are classified as fœtus in fœtu *per implantationem*, in contradistinction to fœtus in fœtu *per inclusionem*. In the latter the parasite not only takes root in the autosite, but is entirely enclosed by the latter, *i. e.*, they have one skin in common. The most important members of this class are found in the inborn tumors of the spinal column and throat. In the former an extensive tumor, often as large as a man's head, is situated in front of the spinal column, completely covered by the skin. Its bulk is made up chiefly of a melanotic, sarcomatous tissue, but contains also portions of fœtal bodies, especially limbs, and occasionally flat bones or jaw-like structures with teeth. Again, a tumor is found arising from the end of the spinal column in the region of the sella turcica, to which it is attached by the pedicle. Extending from the throat, it emerges in shapeless masses from the mouth. The bulk of this tumor is also made up of all sorts of sarcomatous tissue. Occasionally we see, intermingled with individual masses, incomplete arms and legs, or a face, which is recognized as such by two pigmentary spots corresponding to eyes, and an opening for the mouth.

2. DEFECTS OF INTRA-UTERINE DEVELOPMENT.
(Defective Formation.)

The manner in which the body is formed, both in its collective shape and in its individual parts, is a favorite subject for modern research. Any one with an imagination at all vivid can view a process of uninterrupted development, and watch the leaf-shaped embryo until, after manifold transformations, it assumes the form of a definite living being. It is not my intention to depict here, even in a hasty manner, that series of shifting changes which succeed each other until the curving edges of the leaf unite and form an entity. The great number of monsters and inborn monstrosities of individual organs testify to the equally large number of disturbances to which the typical process of evolution is subject, disturbances originating in a defective constitution and formative activity of the germ, or produced by disease and unfavorable local conditions.

To defective formative activity is referable first of all the incomplete closure of the different bodily cavities—the cleft formation, in the broad sense of the word. The so-called diverticulum of Meckel, of the small intestines, is the first intimation of delayed closure of the navel; this is followed by congenital umbilical hernia and an escape of all or the greater part of the intestines from the abdominal cavity. Further down we have defects in the anterior wall of the bladder (exstrophy), in which there is a deficiency in the anterior parietes of the abdomen, extending up to the umbilicus, with an equal absence of the pubic symphysis. Hiatus sterni is a longitudinal cleavage of the sternum, which may be increased by muscular action, but is entirely covered by the skin.

Single and double hare-lip are congenital deformities of the face, in which the sides of the lip fail to unite. Fistula colli congenita is a deformity in the neighborhood of the ear and neck. The former are due to defective union between the horizontal plates of the superior maxillary, the inter-maxillary, and the palate bones. These malformations range from a slight cleft in the upper lip—usually on the left side—up to large double-sided fissures, which not only cleave the lips up to the orbit, but also the hard and soft palate. Congenital fissures of the neck, extending frequently up to the ear, are the result of a defect in the corresponding fœtal parts.

Normal closure is particularly apt to be lacking in the cerebro-spinal cavities. The defective formation here is referable rather to a premature dropsical condition of the brain and spinal cord (internal hydrocephalus) than to a defective *nisus formativus*. Congenital hydrocephalus is the mildest appearance of the former. If the hydrocephalus appear at a time when the brain and spinal marrow are still composed of vesicles, the vesicles burst, and the implantation seats of the brain and spinal cord disappear. Anencephalia and amylia are the results. There is not the slightest effort made towards the formation of a skull or spinal column. There is a striking similarity in the faces and bodies of all anencephali (frog's head). The absence of the nervous system induces a cessation of all individual development.

If, in the process of further development, the hydrocephalic accumulation of water localizes itself at a particular spot, there results local cleft formation of the skull and spinal marrow, known as encephalocele and spina bifida. In every instance the development or non-development of the enveloping bones and skin is in proportion to the development of the brain.

A continuous pressure exerted upon the fœtus in utero from without can only be recognized as a factor of disturbance when there is a lack of liquor amnii, whose special function it appears to be to counteract the effects of pressure. Geminus papyraceus is the most palpable illustration of such a condition. Here we find, in a uterus whose interior is almost wholly occupied by a well-developed twin, a second one which has been literally forced to the wall, and which comes into the world as a small, compressed corpse. The so-called "heartless monstrosities" are examples of stunted twins. In them not only the heart, but often the head is lacking (Acephalus), or the head and the trunk (Acormus). Sometimes, indeed, there is nothing more than a shapeless mass of tissue covered with skin (Anidæus).

A slight pressure on the fœtus causes "a diminution in size" of certain parts of the body. Hence we have the undersized brain and skull (Microcephalus), and an arrested development of those layers and plates which adjoin each other in the median line of the body, causing defects of smell and sight. Occasionally the middle portions of the skull anteriorly are absent, and also the upper part of the face. In the latter, both eyes unite in a single monstrous cyclopian orb (Cyclops). Here likewise belong the syrens, a variety of monsters which have the lower extremities joined together. Congenital dislocations and club foot are probably both due to impeded normal evolution.

The last group of intra-uterine malformations, and one especially interesting to physicians, concerns extremely ingenious but complicated metamorphoses by which are formed (1) the central rudiments of the blood vessels leading into the heart and large vessels, (2) the indifferent rudiments of the uro-genital apparatus which subsequently terminate in the permanent male or female genito-urinary organs, and (3) the separate excretory passages for the intestines, bladder and genital apparatus.

If the primary position of the heart be toward the right, not only is the apex of the heart inclined to the right, but a complete change of the asymmetrical bodily organs is brought about, so that the liver and spleen lie on the left side, the aorta is on the right, the vena cava is on the left (situs viscerum inversus). Again, the so-called isthmus of the aorta, between the subclavia and the ductus arteriosus Botalli, proves to be a somewhat uncertain provision, as it is occasionally defectively developed, and the blood is thus forced to traverse the collaterally-dilated branches of the internal mammary, the transversus colli, the scapular and other arteries of the trunk, in order to reach the branches given off by the descending aorta. In cases where there is an early inflammatory stenosis of the right conus arteriosus and pulmonary valves, the retarded formation of the intra-ventricular and auricular walls is of a very salutary effect. The blood, which cannot after birth reach the lung in the ordinary way, flows through the patulous foramen ovale in the interauricular wall, and through the permanent gap in the interventricular wall, in order to reach the left heart and aorta, and thereby eventually the lungs, through the ductus arteriosus Botalli. The history of cyanopathy shows this to be but a scanty compensation, yet it prolongs life for a time at least.

The most ordinary anomalies of the genital apparatus are those connected with the ducts of Müller and the uterus. Such are the uterus bicornis, in which the Müllerian ducts begin at the orificium internum to unite into a simple canal; the uterus bipartivus, in which, although the ducts unite and form a single body, the cavity is divided by a partition-wall; the uterus unicornis where only one of the Müllerian ducts reach maturity; lastly, the uterus defectivus, where both ducts fail to develop.

Hermaphroditismus is another example of defective, one-sided development of the genital organs. It is, generally speaking, more apparent in the external genital organs than in the internal ones, for we find, upon subjecting the genital glands to microscopic examination, that we have really a male before us. The first indication of hermaphrodeity is afforded by a small slit in the urethra, pointing backwards. The orifice of the urethra is then transferred to the base of the penis, the latter assumes the shape of a clitoris, and its foreskin is reflected in folds on both sides. As the penis becomes more and more like the clitoris, these folds resemble the labia minora. Advancing inward, we find that the utriculus prostaticus has developed into a structure of considerable length, extending by its fundus beyond the stunted prostate; we see the ligamenta rotunda and lata, in which latter the genital glands are enclosed. We observe, instead of a single scrotum, two folds of skin reflected to the right and left. They may be compared to the labia majora. These folds are, as a rule, empty, but there have been instances where one testicle has descended. Hermaphrodeity is generally better developed on one side than on the other. A perfectly distinct hermaphrodite, in which both ovaries and testicles are present, has been observed but once, at least, in man. In this instance, the external organs of generation resembled those of a man.

The separate orifices pertaining to the rectum, the urethra, and in the female to the vagina, are formed, as is well known, about the fourth week of fœtal existence, by a seasonable division of the "cloaca" belonging to the orifices. Should, however, the respective partition walls fail, in women, to move down into their place, the "cloaca" persists. This defect is most serious when the anterior wall of the bladder is absent.

Simple atresia of the anus is far more common. In it the lower end of the gut does not quite extend through the buttocks.

3. DEFECTIVE EXTRA-UTERINE DEVELOPMENT.

The subject which we have now to consider is a difficult one. It concerns the inherited weaknesses of certain organs or systems of the body, in which there is at birth no tangible abnormality, but which develop in after life pathological disturbances either of function or form.

All the organs of the body, as we know, do not increase equally in size during the period of extra-uterine development. In fact, the irregularities observed in intra-uterine development are continued in extra-uterine life. The growth of the organs may be compared to a race in which first one, then another of the organs takes the lead. The best developed at birth are the brain and liver. After the air has penetrated the lungs, and the process of digestion has been established, the lungs and intestines take the lead. Soon the child learns to stand and walk, and make a general use of the musculo-motor apparatus. Accordingly, we observe between the end of the first and the end of the fifth year a powerful growth of the bones, muscles, and corresponding nerves. A similar stage is that between the ages of fifteen and twenty, during which the body attains full development. At these periods the blood and blood-vessels—particularly the heart—are far behind in the race. When we consider that the development of the genital apparatus at puberty, and the psychical excitations resulting therefrom, require an unusual supply of blood, we can readily understand why this period of growth should be regarded as particularly critical.

At this time of disproportion in the rate of growth of organs, we often have the first indication of inherited weaknesses. Inherited nervous troubles appear in the recurrence of neuroses descending from parents or grandparents, though with the limitation that most of them appear vicariously, one for another, or may be replaced by groups of symptoms which are less sharply defined, and even by tangible anatomical changes in the brain and spinal cord. Under this head stand epilepsy, psychosis, hysteria, idiocy, and chorea major, with retarded development of the brain, and even hydrocephalus. To be also noted is insufficiency of the sphincter muscles, causing lagophthalmia, incontinence of urine, spermatorrhœa, and that "foolish dropping down of the lower lip," mentioned by Shakespeare in one of his dramas; also, defects of accommodation, color blindness, etc. In short, be the nervous system affected where it may, the great capacity of this tissue is evident in its power to record impressions and transmit them to later generations.

Some of the tumors also arise at this period of rapid bodily growth. I have already (p. 41) indicated my views regarding the participation, or rather non-participation, of the nervous system in the origin of tumors. It must be borne in mind that the periods of rapid growth in organs are equally the periods of greatest irritability. This is seen most distinctly in certain inflammatory and sub-inflammatory conditions of the osseous system. It is true that we are at present unable to assign a definite cause for rachitis (rickets), that, we might almost say, inflammatory disturbance in the growth of bones. But, be the cause an hereditary transmission of disease (syphilis), or an individual disturbance of tissue change, every one must, I think, admit that it must be a continuous one, since it affects the system at the two periods of rapid growth already mentioned, viz., in the first year of extra-uterine life, and at the time of puberty. (Early and late rickets.) We also know very little in regard to the etiology of cretinism, whose results are opposed to those of rickets, in that it hinders the transformation of cartilage into bone, and arrests the development of the skull and skeleton. It is well known that inherited tuberculosis chiefly attacks the growing bones, and that more than one-half of all cases of caries fungosa (tuberculosis of bones) are restricted to youth.

The very anatomical changes which accompany the growth of bones develop insensibly on the one hand into inflammation, on the other, into formation of tumors. Examples of this are: periostitis, ostitis ossificans, rarefying myelitis, also the numerous ecchondroses, exostoses, periostoses, and hyperostoses. To be brief, the temporary weakness in the continuity of the organs, which is caused by the powerful growth of the osseous system, not only makes them susceptible to external irritation, but, associating itself with local weakness already existing in the individual plan of development, conducts in the former to inflammatory, in the latter to onkological excesses of growth. I have mentioned the osseous system in particular merely to illustrate the most important theories regarding diseases of growth, and must leave it to the reader to seek analogous instances in other organs.

I have alluded briefly to an important group of local excesses in growth, viz., tumors. Their origin was discussed in detail in the General Part; I shall, accordingly, limit myself to the statement that in many tumors we can assign no better cause for their origin than a possible inherited weakness in the relationship between a local group of cells and the organic unit of the body—in the first instance, probably the nervous system—to which disturbance the remainder of the recognized predisposing causes may lead. Inflammatory conditions, scars, etc., are to be included among these; also the senile involution of the whole organism, which favors the local emancipation of such tissues as are already of a more independent growth, especially the epithelial, and thus, either alone or more frequently in connection with chronic inflammatory irritants, gives rise to cancerous growths. See also page 251.

IV. DISEASES DUE TO OVER-EXERTION.

Every active organ becomes, in the course of time, fatigued, and requires rest to fit it for renewed activity. If this rest is not afforded, if the organ is forced by continuous, even though physiological irritation to "over-exertion," it will, although in a measure responding to the summons, do so at the risk of incurring serious harm, not only to itself, but to the entire body.

We mentioned (pp. 17 and 18), the means at the command of the organism for supporting and preserving its organs when extra demands for work are made upon them. The hyperæmia produced in such cases not only furnishes a more abundant supply of nutritive material by which to replace that consumed, but it affords more oxygen to aid the work, and a working organ is a consuming organ. Here, as elsewhere, the destruction progresses more rapidly than the restoration. Accordingly, the organ must, from time to time, have rest, in order that nutrition may keep pace with consumption. Now, if no rest is afforded the organ, and the nervous system continues its demands for extra work and establishes an active hyperæmia, it is plain that a double danger must result. First, the protoplasm of the active cells may be too much drawn upon, the organ become worn out, even partially atrophied, and so exhausted as to require a prolonged period of rest before it can regain its normal condition. Second, the excessively protracted active hyperæmia harbors in itself a danger. The longer the duration of an arterial hyperæmia, the slower and more incomplete its disappearance. The cause of this appears to be in a certain relaxation in the walls of veins especially, after they have remained for some time in a condition of passive dilatation. If the return to normal is indefinitely postponed, the active hyperæmia becomes an independent condition of disease, forming the basis for further changes of an inflammatory nature.

Over-work, and the diseases resulting therefrom, occur chiefly in the organs of sensation and motion. It is here that the reckless use of the enormous stock of elasticity which is lodged in the central nervous system produces a renewed and sufficient excitation, even in the exhausted and therefore less excitable terminal apparatus. It is true that over-use also occurs in organs presiding over nutrition and generation, but careful consideration shows that it is then an unreasonable use of "free will," which produces in the above-named systems an excessive and harmful activity, by calling into play powerful and unnecessary physiological irritants.

Although it must be admitted that over-work constitutes an independent cause of disease, still its effects are rarely seen in distinct and well-defined pictures of disease; on the contrary, they frequently present to the physician kaleidoscopic images, in which over-exertion constantly recurs as the prominent motive.

The attacks of the great majority of insane people are due to a functional irritation of the cortical substance of the cerebrum. Although a congenital, inherited, or acquired weakness and incapacity for resistance may be found in the diseased brain, yet the *status presens* is an excessive activity of the cortical cells, which has produced an equally excessive and proportionally "lasting hyperæmia." This tenacity of the hyperæmia develops a *circulus vitiosus*. The hyperæmic cortical substance of the brain is in itself active. The hyperæmia is closely united to functional excess, and a patient may consider himself fortunate if his skillful physician is able, by the most powerful remedies, to break up the circulus vitiosus.

The over-exercise of the sexual organs, especially in sexual intercourse, and similar sexual excitations, leads more frequently than is supposed to true diseases of this kind There are many diseases which are observed only, or at least preponderatingly, in men. Nature has implanted in man, side by side with a limited degree of sexual capacity, that boundless passion by which the race is propagated. It thus happens that men demand too much of their organs of generation, and must, of course, suffer the consequences. I am *a priori* inclined to attribute all diseases of the nervous system which are peculiar to men to sexual excesses, knowing full well that it will never be possible for me or any other physician to properly estimate the significance of this etiological factor.

Short-sightedness is sometimes regarded as a result of over-use. In the majority of cases, it is hereditary, although many near-sighted persons attribute the defect to over-exerting their eyes in reading small print, and working with insufficient light. Bad school desks, *i. e.*, with the seat at some distance from the desk, tables which are too high or too low, compelling children to focus from a short distance, are especially to blame. Long-continued strain upon the apparatus of accommodation is of itself not sufficient to lengthen the visual axes, but this is done when it is combined with the tension which accompanies strong convergence of the visual axes, in which the bulb of the eye is lengthened and the sclerotic extended by the pressure of the muscles of the eyeball. Moreover, by the bending forward of the head congestion ensues, which favors softening of the latter membrane. As all of these things occur in certain degrees, even when the eyes are used in moderation, myopia is a good example of the "using up" of an organ by over-use.

V. DISEASES OF INVOLUTION.

The ordinary course of nature provides for all creatures an easy death by a gradual retrogressive growth (involutio) of all their organs. The full physical development is reached in the thirtieth year, and involution begins between the fiftieth and sixtieth. The formation of blood abates, the monthly discharge of the female ceases, and nature becomes more economical with its blood. It is no longer able to assist several organs simultaneously with an active hyperæmia; on the contrary, when the stomach demands additional blood, the brain must dispense with it, and *vice versa*. The continued determination of large quantities of blood, as required in sexual intercourse, becomes rarer and more imperfect. As the blood diminishes in quantity there is also a diminution in the directly dependent juices of the tissues, called turgor vitalis. The skin grows flabby and shrivelled, the iron strength of the powerfully contracted muscle relaxes, and even the cushion of fat, whose augmented size for a time conceals the increasing atrophy of the parts, is itself soft and flabby, and but a pitiful caricature of the classically full and rounded outlines of youth.

All the organs and tissues become successively involved in this general deterioration of nutrition. Not all organs, however, claim an equal amount of nutriment from the blood; there are some which require a constant and very abundant blood supply, while others are able to dispense almost altogether with the blood supply. The former—the heart and liver—begin at once to give evidence of diminished nutrition by a certain atrophy of their cells, while all the connective tissue parts, membranes, tendons, ligaments, sheaths, etc., remain unchanged in bulk. All the other bodily organs are ranged between these two extremes. Next in order to the liver are the lungs, then the osseous system, the muscles, the nervous system, and finally, the epithelial structures.

It is not my intention to intimate by the foregoing observations that all senility is referable to defective blood formation. I desire, on the contrary, to emphasize the fact that every organ of the body possesses a certain individual durability, which is determined by the development of the person in question and the factors contributing thereto (p. 41)—a durability, to my thinking, to which the organ is as it were adjusted. Individual differences of this sort are most marked in the blood vessels, higher organs of sense, and genital glands, in which the appearance of certain forms of premature involution cannot be explained by immoderate physiological use. For natural exercise, non-exercise and immoderate exercise of an organ during a person's lifetime, all exert a determining influence upon the vitality of the organ. This influence is manifested primarily upon its growth and nutrition, as discussed at length on pp. 16, 17; the surplus gained by a moderate amount of active hypertrophy may be properly regarded as so much capital for the use of the organ in its advancing years. The lungs, muscles, and also the larynx are especially capable of being permanently strengthened by methodical exercise. Non-exercise, on the other hand, no less than excessive employment, leads to premature incapacity, and, at last, to atrophy of the organ concerned. Such occurrences are not surprising at the present time, when a division of labor is becoming more and more universal, and when many persons are obliged during the entire day to repeat again and again at stated intervals the same automatical labor.

It is scarcely necessary to state that the pathological changes which are undergone by an organ also greatly influence its vitality and usefulness. Such, pre-eminently, are chronic inflammatory conditions, especially those due to intoxicating liquors.

The above is a sufficiently complete summary of the causes of normal or premature senectus (senility). Whether such senility is or is not "pathological" in character, remains a debatable point. One peculiar feature of tissues as they grow old, and one which must be construed, not only as a cause, but also as an effective disease is "senile tissue-proliferation." The epithelium and osseous tissues as well as (with restrictions) the tissues of the inner coat of arteries, are subjected to senile proliferation. The chief diseases of extreme old age in this department are many varieties of epithelial carcinoma, arthritis deformans, chronic endarteritis.

The fact that these tissues should, upon the first signal of general involution, at once commence to increase by cell division, and fall a prey to an unlimited degenerative growth, is one of the strangest paradoxes in pathology, and one whose explanation can only be vaguely conjectured.

A very ingenious theory is that offered by Thiersch, who attributes to the epithelial structure a sort of perverted growth due to diminished resistance, which is brought about by the diminished turgor vitalis in the blood vessels and connective tissue. As the epithelium proliferates normally by division on the side nearest the connective tissue, there would be nothing astonishing in a continued aggregation and deposition on this side, in other words, an advance of the epithelial limits towards the interior; the only difference being that, normally, the point offering the least resistance to this demand for space is found on the exterior, instead of on the interior. If this arrangement were, as Thiersch presumes, reversed in advancing age, there would be danger of the epithelium proliferating into the connective tissue, i. e., producing carcinomatous degeneration.

Two other etiological considerations are still deserving of attention, as throwing light upon the local circumscribed appearance of cancer. First, the usually distinct subinflammatory condition of the diseased territory, which by an abundant cell-infiltration produces a softening and breaking down of the firm connective tissue fibres, and a subsequent diminution in the power of resistance which the territory is able to oppose to the incursions of the proliferating epithelium. Second, the relatively great independence which distinguishes the growth of the epithelium. The epithelium never yields entirely to the universal cessation of growth, which sets in, in all non-epithelial organs, between the ages of twenty and thirty. The losses sustained by the shedding of the older cells are continually repaired by the formation of young cells. The measure of this growth is probably subject to the control of the nervous system. We have already (p. 41) accorded to the nervous system an important influence in the supervision of the normal limits of growth, and the latest discoveries regarding the "nerve terminations in the epithelium" authorize us to assume a similar supervision in the case of epithelial growth. The measure of this authority is, however, undoubtedly of an extremely vacillating nature. The nervous relation may be fundamentally weak, and even at certain points hampered with hereditary defects. It is not improbable that by the intervention of still other etiological features—especially an inflammatory loosening of the epithelial connective tissue boundaries—this restraining influence of the nervous system might be weakened and suspended. I must acknowledge that these speculations have something visionary about them, yet I know not how else to consider these matters which daily intrude themselves upon our notice, and I cannot overcome the desire to discuss them in this general manner.

The skin is principally subject to senile carcinoma; after that, the stomach, intestines, uterus, prostate gland, etc.

An exhaustive survey of the *malum senile articulorum* proves it to be a tendency towards peripheral hyperplasia which involves the entire osseous system of the body. Cartilaginous excrescences are found, not merely on the edges of the articular cartilage, where they give rise to the characteristic disfigurations of arthritis deformans, but also under the perichondrium of the costal cartilages, and even of the tracheal annular cartilage. The changes in question are most frequent in the costal cartilages, and they offer convenient subjects for microscopical investigation. I have chosen a sufficiently thin section of a good-sized costal cartilage with which to illustrate the nature of the histological changes.

In surveying the entire section with a low magnifying power, we perceive it to be divided by certain pretty broad lines into six or seven territories. A large round central area is bounded by several small oval areas. In the asbestos-like border lines of division we find the matrix of the cartilage split into fibres and undergoing a process of softening and liquefaction, while the matrix in the areas is of a homogeneous, strongly-transparent constituency. Certain portions of the cartilaginous tissue are suffering from distributed nutrition, which we regard as a primary factor of the change, and one directly due to senility. With this disturbance of nutrition there is associated in the most surprising manner a second circumstance; the cartilaginous cells are without exception in the act of proliferating by division. As a result, we see in the direction of the perichondrium flattened and even conical protrusions consisting wholly of cellular, almost embryonic cartilaginous tissue, and furnishing the real cause of the striking external deformity of the cartilage. It is still noticeable that the central cartilage cells, especially those within the domain of the softened cartilage, have also proliferated by division. A single cell has become an immense round nest of cells; from 10–20 daughter-cells are still retained within the capsule of the mother-cell, affording thus a striking demonstration of the productivity of a single, and even worn-out cartilage cell.

How, we ask, does the cell acquire such power? In the malum senile articulorum, where exactly the same histological motive is found, an inflammatory irritation has been surmised, as a solution for the difficulty. Hence the name, arthritis deformans. In my opinion, we should attribute this senile tissue proliferation to a removal of the nervous control over the assimilation of the cells. We may conceive how, with the suspension of the nutritive relations existing between the cartilage and blood, there should be a decline in the formative limitations imposed by the nervous system, and, in consequence, one last rise in assimilation, that elementary principle of cell-life. The fact that no cartilage nerves have as yet been discovered, is not, I think, sufficient ground for denying the nervous susceptibility of the cartilage tissue. The fact also that cases of arthritis deformans have been cured by the use of the constant current is certainly not unfavorable to my view.

One of the most difficult points we have to settle is the relation which arthritis deformans bears to atheroma of the arteries. There is no doubt that we have here a genuine, though it may be weak and gradual, inflammation. Köster has established a hyperæmia of the vasa vasorum, and a cellular infiltration of the surrounding parts, corresponding to the sclerotic plates of the intima. I have subjected these observations to the most careful scrutiny, and have been able to verify the greater part of them. But what is the cause of this chronic inflammation, and why is it that it is found—aside from the syphilitic endarteritis of the cerebral arteries—only in old and middle aged persons? There must, of necessity, be some connecting link in the etiology of this disease with the natural or pathologically-induced wasting of the arterial system, and this, if I mistake not, is found in the mechanical expansion of the blood vessels. The artery is built and arranged for certain moderate degrees of dilatation. It likewise accommodates itself to occasional greater demands, after which it returns, to all appearances, to normal. But is it not possible that prolonged or violent attacks of fever, that increased activity of the heart resulting from alcoholic excesses, from violent emotion, muscular exertion, etc., should, after frequent repetitions and even temporary over-dilatation of the blood vessels, produce, finally, a permanent cumulative effect? And in what would this effect consist? First of all, assuredly, in a general dilatation of the arterial system, such as is found in all old persons; after that in a strong mechanical irritation of those portions of the vascular system which are attached in such a manner to neighboring parts as to prevent them from dilating when an excessive dilatation is demanded. Such points are, principally, the origin of the various arteries arising from the aorta, viz., intercostal, bronchial, mesenteric and renal arteries, and, in especial, the large vessels arising from the arch of the aorta. In addition, we have the preponderating expansion of those points where there is most friction from the increased blood current, in the curves and ramifications of a blood vessel. The immediate effect of mechanical irritation of all these points is a permanent hyperæmia of the vasa vasorum; the secondary result is a hyperplasia of the intima. The entire disease bears a general resemblance to those diseases which characterize old age.

CONCLUSION.

In the foregoing sketch I have endeavored to classify the Natural Species of Diseases, according to their principal and sub-divisions. This might be construed as an attempt on my part to add another to the long list of pathological systems of disease which are recorded in the history of our science. Nothing, however, can be further from my purpose than to treat, as is the manner of those systems, each particular case of disease as a unit, and to "systematize" the immense number and variety of individual cases. In our special pathology most of these cases of disease unite in themselves several of the natural disease units, which proceed from the unity of a definite cause of disease and the uniformity of its operations upon the organism. I have brought these natural disease units, varieties, or species, into a new relation, which I call special pathology in the strictest sense of the word, and which I regard as the true province of scientific medicine.

For twenty years we have been watching the birth and development of this new pathology. I have merely attempted to make it somewhat more intelligible, and while guarding on the one hand against the inroads of specialistic and casuistic pathology, to emancipate it on the other from the enveloping forms of general pathology.

INDEX.

	PAGE
ABSCESS, defined	27
—— metastatic	72
Actinomyces	224
Albuminuria	140
Anæmias, essential	128
Anæmia, pernicious	129
—— pseudo-leucæmic	129
—— splenic	129
Anæsthesia	159
Analgesia	160
Angina pectoris	180
—— tonsillaris—quinsy	35
Angioma	51
Angio-neuroses	179
Animal disturbances	159
Arthropoda	206
Asthma	137
Ataxia	173
Atrophy of fatigue	18
—— of inaction	18
—— simple	95
BASEDOW'S disease	180
Blood-corpuscle formation, disturbances in	127
Blood-formation, disturbances in	121
Blood-plates of Bizzozero	64
Blood-purification, disturbances in	133
CACHEXIA	82
Calcification	100
Carcinoma	49
Catalepsy	167
Catarrhs, desquamative, blennorrhœa, seborrhœa	33, 201
Cestodes	211

	PAGE
Chill	76
Chlorosis	128
Cholæmia	133, 148
Chondroma	50
Chorea	167
Cicatrization	29
Circulation, collateral	102
——— derangements of	101
——— general, derangements of	112
Cleft fungi	217
Cloudy swelling	31
Coagulation-necrosis	31
Coma	85
Convulsions	161
——— reflex	163
Cyanosis	118
Cysts, dermoid	54
——— retention	50
——— softening	96
DEATH from heart failure	114
——— signs of	114
Decubitus paralyticus	183
Degeneration, amyloid	83
——— cheesy	227
——— colloid	99
——— fatty	94
——— mucoid	98
Delirium	85
Delusions	178
Development and growth, defective	236
Development, extrauterine, defective	245
——— intrauterine defective	241
Diabetes insipidus	139
——— mellitus	148
Diabrosis	109
Diarrhœa	125
Diapedesis	107
Diathesis, scrofulous	229
——— uric acid	145

INDEX.

	PAGE
Dieresis	108
Disease, Addison's	133
——— definition of	9
——— division of	186
——— due to overwork	247
——— local outbreak of	13
——— of involution	250
——— paralytic and infectious	205
——— physiological extension of	91
——— the anatomical distribution of	57
——— traumatic	187
Dropsy, cardiac	119
——— renal	142
Dyspnœa	135

ECLAMPSIA	86
Emboli	66
——— lodgment of, predisposition of certain organs	70
Embolism	68
——— the consequences of	71
Enchondrosis	49
Endothelioma	51
Epilepsy	165
Epithelioma	52
Eutrophia	18
Exostosis	49
Exudate	119
Exudation, inflammatory	22

FEVER	73
——— relation of microphytes to	206
Fibroma	50
Frenzy	176
Freezing	194

GANGRENE	111
Gastrectasis	122
Glandular hypertrophies	49
Glychæmia	143
Gout	146
Granulation	29

INDEX.

	PAGE
HALLUCINATION	177
Heart's action, (sudden decrease or) failure in	117
Hematoma	111
Hemorrhage	106
Herpes zoster	184
Heteroplasms, archiplastic	52
—— paraplastic	50
Hydræmia	140
Hyperæmia, active	16
—— arterial	18
—— collateral	103
—— venous	104
Hyperæsthesia	157
Hypercinesia	161
Hyperplasia	86
Hypertrophy	18
—— inflammatory	37, 47
Hypnotism	167
Hypocinesia	168
ICTERUS	148
—— gravis	150
Idiocy	178
Illusions	177
Inflammation	20
—— catarrhal	33, 201
—— chronic interstitial	36
—— croupous	34
—— diphtheritic	31
—— parenchymatous	30
—— pus formation	26
—— special varieties of	30
—— specific	38, 215
Infusoria	215
Insolatio	192
Ischæmia	102
KIDNEYS, derangement in the function of	138
LEPROSY	235
Leucæmia	130

	PAGE
Lipoma	50
Livores mortis	115

MANIA ... 178

Marasmus	126
Melanæmia	130
Melancholia	177
Melanosis	131
Metastasis	58
Micrococcus	224
Migraine	179
Monstrosities	238
Motor neuroses	164
Mould fungi	215
Myxoma	50

NECROBIOSIS ... 94

Necrosis	93
Nematodes	207
Nervous system, irritation of	84
Neuralgia	158
Neuro-vegetal disturbances	179
Nutrition, defective	126
——— disturbances of	92
——— local principles of	18

ŒDEMA ... 103

Osteoma	51

PAIN ... 87

Papilloma	49
Paralysis	168
——— cerebral	174
——— peripheral	169
——— reflex	174
——— spinal	172
Parasites, animal	206
——— vegetable	215
Pathology, general, introduction and classification of	16
——— special	186

	PAGE
Phlogosis	20
Polypi, mucous, of scalp	50
Psoriasis cutanea	184
Psychical irritation	175
—— paralysis	178

RESPIRATION, disturbances of	134
—— Cheyne-Stokes	137
Rigor mortis	94

SARCOMA	51
Shock	89
Smallpox	232
Suffocation	138
Symptoms, deuteropathic groups of	57
—— protopathic groups of	13
Syphilis	233

TERATOMA	46
Tetanus	89
Thrombi, migrating	69
Thrombosis in heart and arteries	67
—— in veins	61
Trauma, chemical	189
—— electrical	201
—— mechanical	187
—— thermal	192
Trematodes	210
Trismus	89
Tropho-neuroses	181
Tuberculosis	226
Tumors, benign and malignant	54
—— definition and general etiology of	40
—— general anatomy and nomenclature of	42
—— heteroplastic	50
—— hyperplastic	49

ULCERATION and ulcer	85
Uræmia	138
Urinary gravel and calculi	147
Urobilinuria	152

	PAGE
VEGETATIVE disturbances	91
Verruca	49
Vomiting	128
YEAST fungi	217

CATALOGUE No. 7.

A CATALOGUE

OF

BOOKS FOR STUDENTS;

INCLUDING A FULL LIST OF

The ? Quiz-Compends?

AND MANY OF

THE MOST PROMINENT

Students' Manuals and Text-Books

PUBLISHED BY

P. BLAKISTON, SON & CO.,

Medical Booksellers, Importers and Publishers,

No. 1012 WALNUT STREET,

PHILADELPHIA.

⁎⁎⁎ For sale by all Booksellers, or any book will be sent by mail, postpaid, upon receipt of price. Catalogues of books on all branches of Medicine, Dentistry, Pharmacy, etc., supplied upon application.

THE ?QUIZ-COMPENDS?

A NEW SERIES OF COMPENDS FOR STUDENTS.

For Use in the Quiz Class and when
Preparing for Examinations.

Price of Each, Bound in Cloth, $1.00 Interleaved, $1.25.

Based on the most popular text-books, and on the lectures of prominent professors, they form a most complete set of manuals, containing information nowhere else collected in such a condensed, practical shape. The authors have had large experience as quiz masters and attachés of colleges, with exceptional opportunities for noting the most recent advances and methods. The arrangement of the subjects, illustrations, types, etc., are all of the most improved form, and the size of the books is such that they may be easily carried in the pocket.

No. 1. ANATOMY. (Illustrated.)
THIRD REVISED EDITION.

A Compend of Human Anatomy. By SAMUEL O. L. POTTER, M.A., M.D., U. S. Army. With 63 Illustrations.

"The work is reliable and complete, and just what the student needs in reviewing the subject for his examinations."—*The Physician and Surgeon's Investigator*, Buffalo, N. Y.

"To those desiring to post themselves hurriedly for examination, this little book will be useful in refreshing the memory."—*New Orleans Medical and Surgical Journal.*

"The arrangement is well calculated to facilitate accurate memorizing, and the illustrations are clear and good."—*North Carolina Medical Journal.*

Nos. 2 and 3. PRACTICE.

A Compend of the Practice of Medicine, especially adapted to the use of Students. By DAN'L E. HUGHES, M.D., Demonstrator of Clinical Medicine in Jefferson Medical College, Philadelphia. In two parts.

PART I.—Continued, Eruptive, and Periodical Fevers, Diseases of the Stomach, Intestines, Peritoneum, Biliary Passages, Liver, Kidneys, etc., and General Diseases, etc.

PART II.—Diseases of the Respiratory System, Circulatory System, and Nervous System; Diseases of the Blood, etc.

∗∗* These little books can be regarded as a full set of notes upon the Practice of Medicine, containing the

Synonyms, Definitions, Causes, Symptoms, Prognosis, Diagnosis, Treatment, etc., of each disease, and including a number of new prescriptions. They have been compiled from the lectures of prominent Professors, and reference has been made to the latest writings of Professors FLINT, DA COSTA, REYNOLDS, BARTHOLOW, ROBERTS and others.

"It is brief and concise, and at the same time possesses an accuracy not generally found in compends."—*Jas. M. French, M.D., Ass't to the Prof. of Practice, Medical College of Ohio, Cincinnati.*

"The book seems very concise, yet very comprehensive. . . . An unusually superior book."—*Dr. E. T. Bruen, Demonstrator of Clinical Medicine, University of Pennsylvania.*

"I have used it considerably in connection with my branches in the Quiz-class of the University of La."—*J. H. Bemiss, New Orleans.*

"Dr. Hughes has prepared a very useful little book, and I shall take pleasure in advising my class to use it."—*Dr. George W. Hall, Professor of Practice, St. Louis College of Physicians and Surgeons.*

No. 4. PHYSIOLOGY.

A Compend of Human Physiology, adapted to the use of Students. By ALBERT P. BRUBAKER, M.D., Demonstrator of Physiology in Jefferson Medical College, Philadelphia.

"Dr. Brubaker deserves the hearty thanks of medical students for his *Compend of Physiology.* He has arranged the fundamental and practical principles of the science in a peculiarly inviting and accessible manner. I have already introduced the work to my class."—*Maurice N. Miller, M.D., Instructor in Practical Histology, formerly Demonstrator of Physiology, University City of New York.*

"'Quiz-Compend' No. 4 is fully up to the high standard established by its predecessors of the same series."—*Medical Bulletin, Philadelphia.*

"I can recommend it as a valuable aid to the student."—*C. N. Ellinwood, M.D., Professor of Physiology, Cooper Medical College, San Francisco.*

"This is a well written little book."—*London Lancet.*

No. 5. OBSTETRICS.

A Compend of Obstetrics. For Physicians and Students. By HENRY G. LANDIS, M.D., Professor of Obstetrics and Diseases of Women, in Starling Medical College, Columbus. Illustrated.

"We have no doubt that many students will find in it a most valuable aid in preparing for examination."—*The American Journal of Obstetrics.*

"It is complete, accurate and scientific. The very best book of its kind I have seen."—*J. S. Knox, M.D., Lecturer on Obstetrics, Rush Medical College, Chicago.*

Price of each Book, Cloth, $1.00. Interleaved for Notes, $1.25.

"I have been teaching in this department for many years, and am free to say that this will be the best assistant I ever had. It is accurate and comprehensive, but brief and pointed."—*Prof. P. D. Yost, St. Louis.*

No. 6. MATERIA MEDICA. Revised Ed.

A Compend on Materia Medica and Therapeutics, with especial reference to the Physiological Actions of Drugs. For the use of Medical, Dental, and Pharmaceutical Students and Practitioners. Based on the New Revision (Sixth) of the U. S. Pharmacopœia, and including many unofficinal remedies. By SAMUEL O. L. POTTER, M.A., M.D., U. S. Army.

"I have examined the little volume carefully, and find it just such a book as I require in my private Quiz, and shall certainly recommend it to my classes. Your Compends are all popular here in Washington."—*John E. Brackett, M.D., Professor of Materia Medica and Therapeutics, Howard Medical College, Washington.*

"Part of a series of small but valuable text-books. . . . While the work is, owing to its therapeutic contents, more useful to the medical student, the pharmaceutical student may derive much useful information from it."—*N. Y. Pharmaceutical Record.*

No. 7. CHEMISTRY. Revised Ed.

A Compend of Chemistry. By G. MASON WARD, M.D., Demonstrator of Chemistry in Jefferson Medical College, Philadelphia. Including Table of Elements and various Analytical Tables.

"Brief, but excellent. . . . It will doubtless prove an admirable aid to the student, by fixing these facts in his memory. It is worthy the study of both medical and pharmaceutical students in this branch."—*Pharmaceutical Record, New York.*

No. 8. VISCERAL ANATOMY.

A Compend of Visceral Anatomy. By SAMUEL O. L. POTTER, M.A., M.D., U. S. Army. With 40 Illustrations.

*** This is the only Compend that contains full descriptions of the viscera, and will, together with No. 1 of this series, form the only *complete Compend* of Anatomy published.

No. 9. SURGERY. Illustrated.

A Compend of Surgery; including Fractures, Wounds, Dislocations, Sprains, Amputations and other operations, Inflammation, Suppuration, Ulcers, Syphilis, Tumors, Shock, etc. Diseases of the Spine, Ear, Eye, Bladder, Testicles, Anus, and other Surgical Diseases. By ORVILLE HORWITZ, A.M., M.D., with 43 Illustrations.

Price of Each, Cloth, $1.00. Interleaved for Notes, $1.25.

THE ?QUIZ-COMPENDS?

No. 10. ORGANIC CHEMISTRY.
JUST PUBLISHED.

A Compend of Organic Chemistry, including Medical Chemistry, Urine Analysis, and the Analysis of Water, and Food, etc. By HENRY LEFFMANN, M.D., Professor of Clinical Chemistry and Hygiene in the Philadelphia Polyclinic; Professor of Chemistry, Pennsylvania College of Dental Surgery; Member of the N. Y. Medico-Legal Society. Cloth. $1.00.
Interleaved, for the addition of Notes, $1.25.

Nature of Organic Bodies. Transformations under various conditions. Organic Synthesis. Homologous and Isomeric Bodies. Empirical and Rational formulæ. Classification of organic bodies. Hydrocarbon. Derivatives of Hydrocarbons, Alcohols and Ethers. Benzenes and Turpenes. Fat Acids, Oils and Fats, Sugars, Glucosides. Cyanogen Compounds Amines and Amides. Alkaloids. Ptomaines. Animal Chemistry. Nutrition and Assimilation. Food, Water and Air. Urinary Analysis. Index.

The Essentials of Pathology.
BY D. TOD GILLIAM, M.D.,
Professor of Physiology in Starling Medical College, Columbus, O.
With 47 Illustrations. 12mo. Cloth. Price $2.00.

₊ The object of this book is to unfold to the beginner the fundamentals of pathology in a plain, practical way, and by bringing them within easy comprehension to increase his interest in the study of the subject. Though it will not altogether supplant larger works, it will be found to impart clear-cut conceptions of the generally accepted doctrines of the day, and to prevent confusion in the mind of the student.

A POCKET-BOOK OF
PHYSICAL DIAGNOSIS
OF THE
Diseases of the Heart and Lungs.
A MANUAL FOR STUDENTS AND PHYSICIANS.
BY DR. EDWARD T. BRUEN,
Demonstrator of Clinical Medicine in the University of Pennsylvania, Assistant Physician to the University Hospital, etc.
Second Edition, Revised. With new Illustrations. 12mo. $1.50.

₊ The subject is treated in a plain, practical manner, avoiding questions of historical or theoretical interest, and without laying special claim to originality of matter, the author has made a book that presents the somewhat difficult points of Physical Diagnosis clearly and distinctly.

STUDENTS' MANUALS.

TYSON, ON THE URINE. A Practical Guide to the Examination of Urine. For Physicians and Students. By JAMES TYSON, M.D., Professor of Pathology and Morbid Anatomy, University of Pennsylvania. With Colored Plates and Wood Engravings. Fourth Edition. 12mo, cloth, $1.50

HEATH'S MINOR SURGERY. A Manual of Minor Surgery and Bandaging. By CHRISTOPHER HEATH, M.D., Surgeon to University College Hospital, London. 6th Edition. 115 Ill. 12mo, cloth, $2.00

REESE. A MANUAL OF MEDICAL JURISPRUDENCE and Toxicology, for Students and Physicians. Small 8vo, 606 pp. Cl. $4.00; Lea. 5.00

VIRCHOW'S POST-MORTEMS. Post-Mortem Examinations. A Description and Explanation of the Methods of Performing them. By PROF. RUDOLPH VIRCHOW, of Berlin. Translated by DR. T. B. SMITH. 2d Ed. 4 Lithographic Plates. 12mo, cloth, $1.25

DULLES' ACCIDENTS AND EMERGENCIES. What To Do First in Accidents and Emergencies. A Manual Explaining the Treatment of Surgical and other Accidents, Poisoning, etc. By CHARLES W. DULLES, M.D., Surgeon Out-door Department, Presbyterian Hospital, Philadelphia. Colored Plate and other Illustrations. 32mo, cloth, .75

BEALE, ON SLIGHT AILMENTS. Their Nature and Treatment. By LIONEL S. BEALE, M.D., F.R.S. Second Edition. Revised, Enlarged and Illustrated. 283 pages. 8vo.
Paper covers, 75 cents; cloth, $1.25

ALLINGHAM, ON THE RECTUM. Fistulæ, Hemorrhoids, Painful Ulcer, Stricture, Prolapsus, and other Diseases of the Rectum; Their Diagnosis and Treatment. By WM. ALLINGHAM, M.D. Fourth Revised and Enlarged Edition. Illustrated. 8vo.
Paper covers, 75 cents; cloth, $1.25

THOMPSON, ON THE URINARY ORGANS. On Diseases of the Urinary Organs. By SIR HENRY THOMPSON, M.D., F.R.C.S. Seventh Edition. 84 Illustrations. 8vo. Paper covers, 75 cents; cloth, $1.25

STUDENTS' MANUALS.

MARSHALL AND SMITH, ON THE URINE. The Chemical Analysis of the Urine. By JOHN MARSHALL, M.D., Chemical Laboratory, University of Pennsylvania, and PROF. E. F. SMITH. Illus. Cloth, $1.00

MEARS' PRACTICAL SURGERY. Surgical Dressings, Bandaging, Ligation, Amputation, etc. By J. EWING MEARS, M.D., Demonstrator of Surgery in Jefferson Med. College. 227 Illus. 2d Ed. *In Press.*

HOLDEN'S ANATOMY. A Manual of the Dissection of the Human Body. Fifth Edition, Revised and Enlarged, with over 190 Illustrations. *In Press.*

BLOXAM'S LABORATORY TEACHINGS. Progressive Exercises in Practical Chemistry. By PROF. C. L. BLOXAM. 89 Illustrations. 12mo, cloth, $1.75

TYSON, ON THE CELL DOCTRINE; its History and Present State. By PROF. JAMES TYSON, M.D. Second Edition. Illustrated. 12mo, cloth, $2.00

MEADOWS' MIDWIFERY. A Manual for Students. By ALFRED MEADOWS, M.D. From Fourth London Edition. 145 Illustrations. 8vo, cloth, $2.00

WYTHE'S DOSE AND SYMPTOM BOOK. Containing the Doses and Uses of all the principal Articles of the Materia Medica, etc. Eleventh Edition. 32mo, cloth, $1.00; pocket-book style, $1.25

PHYSICIAN'S PRESCRIPTION BOOK. Containing Lists of Terms, Phrases, Contractions and Abbreviations used in Prescriptions, Explanatory Notes, Grammatical Construction of Prescriptions, etc., etc. By PROF. JONATHAN PEREIRA, M.D. Sixteenth Edition. 32mo, cloth, $1.00; pocket-book style, $1.25

POCKET LEXICONS.

CLEAVELAND'S POCKET MEDICAL LEXICON. A Medical Lexicon, containing correct Pronunciation and Definition of Terms used in Medicine and the Collateral Sciences. Thirtieth Edition. Very small pocket size. Red Edges.
Cloth, 75 cents; pocket-book style, $1.00

LONGLEY'S POCKET DICTIONARY. The Student's Medical Lexicon, giving Definition and Pronunciation of all Terms used in Medicine, with an Appendix giving Poisons and Their Antidotes, Abbreviations used in Prescriptions, Metric Scale of Doses, etc. 24mo, cloth, $1.00; pocket-book style, $1.25

ROBERTS' PRACTICE.
FIFTH EDITION.

Recommended as a Text-book at University of Pennsylvania, Long Island College Hospital, Yale and Harvard Colleges, Bishop's College, Montreal, University of Michigan, and over twenty other Medical Schools.

A HANDBOOK OF THE THEORY AND PRACTICE OF MEDICINE. By FREDERICK T. ROBERTS, M.D., M.R.C.P., Professor of Clinical Medicine and Therapeutics in University College Hospital, London. Fifth Edition. Octavo.

CLOTH, $5.00; LEATHER, $6.00.

⁎⁎ This new edition has been subjected to a careful revision. Many chapters have been rewritten. Important alterations and additions have been made throughout, and new illustrations introduced.

"A clear, yet concise, scientific and practical work. It is a capital compendium of the classified knowledge of the subject."—*Prof. J. Adams Allen, Rush Medical College, Chicago.*

"I have become thoroughly convinced of its great value, and have cordially recommended it to my class in *Yale College.*"—*Prof. David P. Smith.*

"I have examined it with some care, and think it a good book, and shall take pleasure in mentioning it among the works which may properly be put in the hands of students."—*A. B. Palmer, Prof. of the Practice of Medicine, University of Michigan.*

"It is unsurpassed by any work that has fallen into our hands, as a compendium for students preparing for examination. It is thoroughly practical, and fully up to the times."—*The Clinic.*

"Our opinion of it is one of almost unqualified praise. The style is clear, and the amount of useful and, indeed, indispensable information which it contains is marvelous."—*Boston Medical and Surgical Journal.*

BIDDLE'S MATERIA MEDICA.
NINTH REVISED EDITION.

Recommended as a Text-book at Yale College, University of Michigan, College of Physicians and Surgeons, Baltimore, Baltimore Medical College, Louisville Medical College, and a number of other Colleges throughout the U. S.

BIDDLE'S MATERIA MEDICA. For the Use of Students and Physicians. By the late PROF. JOHN B. BIDDLE, M.D., Professor of Materia Medica in Jefferson Medical College, Philadelphia. The Ninth Edition, thoroughly revised, and in many parts rewritten, by his son, CLEMENT BIDDLE, M.D., Past Assistant Surgeon, U. S. Navy, assisted by HENRY MORRIS, M.D.

CLOTH, $4.00; LEATHER, $4.75.

"I shall unhesitatingly recommend it (the 9th Edition) to my students at the BELLEVUE HOSPITAL MEDICAL COLLEGE.—*Prof. A. A. Smith, New York, June, 1883.*

"The standard 'Materia Medica' with a large number of medical students is Biddle's."—*Buffalo Medical and Surgical Journal.*

"The larger works usually recommended as text-books in our medical schools are too voluminous for convenient use. This work will be found to contain in a condensed form all that is most valuable, and will supply students with a reliable guide."—*Chicago Med. Jl.*

⁎⁎ This Ninth Edition contains all the additions and changes in the U. S. Pharmacopœia, Sixth Revision.

Just Published, September, 1884.

VAN HARLINGEN ON SKIN DISEASES.

A Handbook of the Diseases of the Skin, their Diagnosis and Treatment. By Arthur Van Harlingen, M.D., Professor of Diseases of the Skin in the Philadelphia Polyclinic, Consulting Physician to the Dispensary for Skin Diseases, etc. Illustrated by two colored lithographic plates.

12MO. 284 PAGES. CLOTH. PRICE, $1.75.

*₊*This is a complete epitome of skin disease, arranged in alphabetical order, giving the diagnosis and treatment in a concise, practical way. Many prescriptions are given that have never been published in any text-book, and an article incorporated on Diet. The plates do not represent one or two cases, but are composed of a number of figures, accurately colored, showing the appearance of various lesions, and will be found to give great aid in diagnosing.

BYFORD, DISEASES OF WOMEN.
NEW REVISED EDITION.

The Practice of Medicine and Surgery, as applied to the Diseases of Women. By W. H. BYFORD, A.M., M.D., Professor of Gynæcology in Rush Medical College; of Obstetrics in the Woman's Medical College; Surgeon to the Woman's Hospital; President of the American Gynæcological Society, etc. Third Edition. Revised and Enlarged; much of it Rewritten; with over 160 Illustrations. Octavo.

PRICE, CLOTH, $5.00; LEATHER, $6.00.

"The treatise is as complete a one as the present state of our science will admit of being written. We commend it to the diligent study of every practitioner and student, as a work calculated to inculcate sound principles and lead to enlightened practice."—*New York Medical Record.*

"The author is an experienced writer, an able teacher in his department, and has embodied in the present work the results of a wide field of practical observation. We have not had time to read its pages critically, but freely commend it to all our readers, as one of the most valuable practical works issued from the American press."—*Chicago Medical Examiner.*

MACKENZIE, THE THROAT AND NOSE.

By MORELL MACKENZIE, M.D., Senior Physician to the Hospital for Diseases of the Chest and Throat; Lecturer on Diseases of the Throat at the London Hospital, etc.
VOL. I. Including the PHARYNX, LARYNX, TRACHEA, etc. 112 Illustrations. Cloth, $4.00; Leather, $5.00
VOL. II. DISEASES OF THE ŒSOPHAGUS, NASAL CAVITIES AND NECK. Cloth, $3.00; Leather, $4.00
The two volumes at one time. Cloth, $6.00; Leather, $7.50

☞ An Encyclopædia of Medical Knowledge. ☜

INDEX OF DISEASES;
WITH TREATMENT AND FORMULÆ.

By THOS. HAWKES TANNER, M.D.

REVISED AND ENLARGED BY DR. BROADBENT.

Octavo, Cloth. Price $3.00.

** The worth of a work of this kind, by so eminent a professor as Dr. Tanner, cannot be over-estimated. As an aid to physicians and druggists, both in the country and city, it must be invaluable. It contains a full list of all diseases, arranged in alphabetical order, with list of formulæ, and appendix giving points of interest regarding health resorts, mineral waters, and information about cooking and preparing food, etc., for the invalid and convalescent. The page headings are so indexed that the reader is enabled to find at once the disease wanted; its synonyms, classification, varieties, description, etc., with the course of treatment recommended by the best authorities, and is referred, by number, to the several prescriptions that have proved most efficacious. These prescriptions are also arranged so that they can be easily referred to, with directions how to use them, when to use them, and what diseases they are generally used in treating. The directions for cooking foods and preparing poultices, lotions, etc., are very full. The work will be found specially useful to students and young physicians.

RICHTER'S CHEMISTRY,
A TEXT-BOOK of INORGANIC CHEMISTRY for STUDENTS.

By PROF. VICTOR von RICHTER,

University of Breslau,

AUTHORIZED TRANSLATION FROM THE THIRD GERMAN EDITION,

By EDGAR F. SMITH, M.A., Ph.D.,

Professor of Chemistry in Wittenberg College, Springfield, Ohio; formerly in the Laboratories of the University of Pennsylvania; Member of the Chemical Society of Berlin.

12mo. 89 Wood-cuts and Col. Lithographic Plate of Spectra. $2.00

In the chemical text-books of the present day, one of the striking features and difficulties we have to contend with is the separate presentation of the theories and facts of the science. These are usually taught apart, as if entirely independent of each other, and those experienced in teaching the subject know only too well the trouble encountered in attempting to get the student properly interested in the science and in bringing him to a clear comprehension of the same. In this work of PROF. VON RICHTER, which has been received abroad with such hearty welcome, two editions having been rapidly disposed of, theory and fact are brought close together, and their intimate relation clearly shown. From careful observation of experiments and their results, the student is led to a correct understanding of the interesting principles of chemistry. The descriptions of the various inorganic substances are full, and embody the results of the latest discoveries.

In preparation, "ORGANIC CHEMISTRY,' By the same author. Translated.

YEO'S PHYSIOLOGY.
A MANUAL FOR STUDENTS. JUST READY.
300 CAREFULLY PRINTED ILLUSTRATIONS.
FULL GLOSSARY AND INDEX.

By GERALD F. YEO, M.D., F.R.C.S., Professor of Physiology in King's College, London. Small Octavo. 750 pages. Over 300 carefully printed Illustrations.

PRICE, CLOTH, $4.00; LEATHER, $5.00.

"By his excellent manual, Prof. Yeo has supplied a want which must have been felt by every teacher of physiology. * * * * In conclusion, we heartily congratulate Prof. Yeo on his work, which we can recommend to all those who wish to find within a moderate compass a reliable and pleasantly written exposition of all the essential facts of physiology as the science now stands."— *The Dublin Journal of Med. Science.*

"The work will take a high rank among the smaller text-books of Physiology."—*Prof. H. P. Bowditch, Harvard Med. School, Boston.*

"The brief examination I have given it was so favorable that I placed it in the list of text-books recommended in the circular of the University Medical College."—*Prof. Lewis A. Stimpson, M. D., 37 East 33d Street, New York.*

"For students' use it is one of the very best text-books in Physiology."—*Prof. L. B. How, Dartmouth Med. College, Hanover, N. H.*

RINDFLEISCH.
THE ELEMENTS OF PATHOLOGY.
TRANSLATED BY WM. H. MERCUR, M.D.
REVISED AND EDITED BY PROF. JAS. TYSON,
Of the University of Pennsylvania.
380 PAGES.   CLOTH.   PRICE $2.00.

⁎⁎* It is the object of Prof. Rindfleisch to present in this volume of moderate size the fundamental principles of Pathology A large number of the general processes which underlie disease, a knowledge of which is essential to the practical physician, are plainly presented. They include, among others, inflammation, tumor formation, fever, derangements of nutrition, including atrophy, derangements of the movement of the blood, of blood formation and blood purification, hyperæsthesia, anæsthesia, convulsions, paralysis, etc.   The well-known reputation of the author, his thorough familiarity with, and his method of treating the subject, make this most recent work peculiarly useful to the student, as well as to the practicing physician who wishes to brush up his pathology.

STANDARD TEXT-BOOKS.

BLOXAM'S CHEMISTRY. Inorganic and Organic, with Experiments. Fifth Edition. Revised and Illustrated.
8vo, cloth, $3.75; leather, $4.75.
CARPENTER ON THE MICROSCOPE and Its Revelations. Sixth Edition, Enlarged. With 500 Illustrations and Colored Plates, handsomely printed. Demi 8vo, cloth, $5.50
DRUITT'S SURGERY. A Manual of Modern Surgery. Eleventh London Edition. 369 Illustrations. Demi 8vo, cloth, $5.00
FLOWER, DIAGRAMS OF THE NERVES of the Human Body, Origin, Divisions, Connections, etc. 4to. Cloth, $3.50
GALLABIN'S MIDWIFERY. A Manual for Students. Illustrated. *In Preparation.*
GLISAN'S MODERN MIDWIFERY. A Text-book. 129 Illustrations. 8vo, cloth, $4.00; leather, $5.00
HOLDEN'S ANATOMY and Manual of Dissections of the Human Body. Fourth Edition. Illus. New Ed. *In Press.*
HOLDEN'S OSTEOLOGY. A Description of the Bones, with Colored Delineations of the Attachments of the Muscles. Sixth Edition. 61 Lithographic Plates and many Wood Engravings.
Royal 8vo, cloth, $6.00
HEATH'S PRACTICAL ANATOMY and Manual of Dissections. Fifth Edition. 24 Colored Plates and nearly 300 other Illustrations. Demi 8vo, cloth, $5.00
HEADLAND, THE ACTION OF MEDICINE in the System. Ninth American Edition. 8vo, cloth, $3.00
KIRKE'S PHYSIOLOGY. A Handbook for Students. Eleventh Edition, 1884. 420 Illustrations. Demi 8vo, cloth, $5.00
MANN'S PSYCHOLOGICAL MEDICINE and Allied Nervous Diseases; including the Medico-Legal Aspects of Insanity. With Illustrations. 8vo. cloth, $5.00; leather, $6.00.
MACNAMARA ON THE EYE. A Manual for Students and Physicians. Illustrated. Demi 8vo, cloth, $4.00
MEIGS AND PEPPER ON CHILDREN. A Practical Treatise on Diseases of Children. Seventh Edition, Revised.
8vo, cloth, $6.00; leather, $7.00
PARKES' PRACTICAL HYGIENE. Sixth Revised and Enlarged Edition. Illustrated. 8vo, cloth, $3.00
RIGBY'S OBSTETRIC MEMORANDA. 32mo, cloth, .50
SANDERSON & FOSTER'S PHYSIOLOGICAL LABORATORY. A Handbook for the Laboratory. Over 350 Illustrations. 8vo, cloth, $5.00; leather, $6.00
WILSON'S HUMAN ANATOMY. General and Special. Tenth Edition. 26 Colored Plates and 424 Illustrations. $6.00
WYTHE'S MICROSCOPIST. A Manual of Microscopy and Compend of the Microscopic Sciences. Fourth Edition. 252 Illustrations. 8vo, cloth, $3.00; leather, $4.00
AITKEN, THE SCIENCE AND PRACTICE OF MEDICINE. A New (Seventh) Edition. 2 Vols.
8vo, cloth, $12.00; leather, $14.00
ACTON, ON THE REPRODUCTIVE ORGANS. Their Functions, Disorders and Treatment. 6th Edition. Cloth, $2.00
FENNER, ON VISION. Its Optical Defects and the Adaptation of Spectacles. 2d Edition, Enlarged. Illus. 8vo., cloth, $3.50
FOTHERGILL, ON THE HEART. Its Diseases and their Treatment Second Edition. 8vo, cloth, $3.50
HARLEY ON THE LIVER. Diagnosis and Treatment. Colored Plates and other Illustrations. 8vo, cloth, $5.00; sheep, $9.00

www.ingramcontent.com/pod-product-compliance
Lightning Source LLC
Chambersburg PA
CBHW031935230426
43672CB00010B/1932